THE
SYMPHONY
OF
PROFOUND
KNOWLEDGE

THE
SYMPHONY
OF
PROFOUND
KNOWLEDGE

———————— ~ ————————

W. Edwards Deming's Score for Leading,
Performing, and Living in Concert

EDWARD MARTIN BAKER

OPEN BOOK
EDITIONS
A Berrett-Koehler Partner

THE SYMPHONY OF PROFOUND KNOWLEDGE:
W. EDWARDS DEMING'S SCORE FOR LEADING,
PERFORMING, AND LIVING IN CONCERT

iUniverse books may be ordered through booksellers or by contacting:

iUniverse
1663 Liberty Drive
Bloomington, IN 47403
www.iuniverse.com
1-800-Authors (1-800-288-4677)

Because of the dynamic nature of the Internet, any web addresses or links contained in
this book may have changed since publication and may no longer be valid. The views
expressed in this work are solely those of the author and do not necessarily reflect the
views of the publisher, and the publisher hereby disclaims any responsibility for them.

Any people depicted in stock imagery provided by Thinkstock are models,
and such images are being used for illustrative purposes only.
Certain stock imagery © Thinkstock.

ISBN: 978-1-5320-0239-7 (sc)
ISBN: 978-1-5320-0240-3 (hc)
ISBN: 978-1-5320-0241-0 (e)

Library of Congress Control Number: 2016913184

Print information available on the last page.

iUniverse rev. date: 11/30/2016

To Shige and Evan
In loving memory of W. Edwards Deming

CONTENTS

ABOUT THE AUTHOR

Ed Baker was with the Ford Motor Company for twenty years. During the years that he served as corporate director, Quality Strategy and Operations Support, his responsibilities included the orchestration of Dr. Deming's interaction with the company, as well as the development and application of standards and methods to improve quality and strengthen competitive position. He assisted Dr. Deming in more than seventy public and private seminars, including those at Ford.

Ed has served as a trustee of the W. Edwards Deming Institute and has been an Aspen Institute senior fellow. He is a fellow of the American Society for Quality, which honored him with the Deming Medal and the Ishikawa Medal.

Ed has consulted to a variety of organizations in business and government to help them develop their capability to shape a better future through application of Deming's theories, principles, and methods.

He received his BA degree from the City College of the City University of New York, an MBA from the Baruch College of Business Administration of the City University of New York, and a PhD in industrial and organization psychology from Bowling Green State University, Ohio.

FOREWORD

We were very excited to hear that Ed Baker had finished this book, and we were honored that he asked us to write this foreword. Ed's journey in the writing of this book began in the late 1980s after Ed already had worked closely with Dr. Deming for many years. Dr. Deming believed in the importance of a book that examined and explained the Deming philosophy in words other than his own. He believed Ed could provide that invaluable alterative insight into the Deming System of Profound Knowledge® and had him promise to do so. Over the years as Ed collected notes and ideas to form the book, Dr. Deming never gave up on the idea. In fact he teased and constantly reminded Ed of his promise to write the book. Now that it is written and published, we feel that it fulfills the commitment to Dr. Deming while providing an exciting and illuminating alternative perspective of Dr. Deming's teachings and philosophy.

Some people may wonder why Dr. Deming was so insistent that Ed provide an alternative view. Did Dr. Deming feel that his books were incomplete or lacked full explanation? The answer is simple and is based on the principle that everyone learns and absorbs a theory, concept, or explanation differently. Dr. Deming knew that Ed had a deep understanding of the Deming philosophy, and when combined with Ed's unique perspective, experiences, and knowledge that formed his individual "map," his way of seeing and interpreting would provide an alternative yet accurate depiction of the philosophy. Ed examines and applies mental maps to help the reader understand the Deming ideals and concepts. Ed knew Dr. Deming realized that "a map of theory" was a powerful mechanism that the brain uses to interpret reality to understand a concept and to explain an outcome. The fact that the Deming theory was complete and thorough but would be explained from a different person with a different map would help explain concepts because they would be viewed through a slightly different lens and therefore explained as such. The unique viewpoints, examples, and analogies used by Ed will expand the reach of the philosophy to new readers. Existing devotees will also gain from this new perspective; their knowledge, too, will become deeper and broader.

The organization of the book into movements, as in a symphony, is particularly symbolic. Not only did our father and grandfather love music, but the underlying symbolism of a musical score where the whole is greater than the sum of the parts is a foundational theory of the "systems" view that is the basis for much of the management theory. While this book provides some modern viewpoints to help explain the Deming System of Profound Knowledge, variation, and systems thinking, it also reaches back into time and quotes ancient philosophers. It is interesting to observe that many of the social issues faced by the ancients are not only relevant but of significant concern in the modern world, and it is remarkable that the application of the Deming philosophy is truly just as pertinent today as it was in the past. The philosophy is timeless because it has a basis in systems thinking, which is natural.

Ed explores the mechanics of modern ranking, rating, organizational structures, and management philosophies and how they are based on the law of mechanics, which applies well to mechanical implements but not human beings. While people accept the principle of mechanics and the application to humanity as reasonable, it is only because they haven't been introduced to systems thinking. Regardless of our positions in life, at some point everyone has fallen victim to the artificial laws of mechanics when they are applied toward humans. While applying pressure to a piece of metal might lead to a predictable outcome, applying the same pressure to a human will not. Ed points out that it is such an obvious observation we must only wonder how anyone ever accepted a different logic. Parents don't treat their children exactly the same to obtain a desired outcome, because each child reacts differently to different pressures. Even a child knows which parent is best to approach and which tactic to use to achieve a desired outcome. If a child understands that mechanics don't apply to humans, why is it that today's so-called successful management in industry, education, and government do not grasp the same understanding? Ed explains the reasons in the book through an explanation of mental maps, systems thinking, and the laws of mechanics.

As we each read this book, it is interesting to note that while we are all in different phases of life, with different interests and immediate concerns, the teachings and philosophy apply evenly and very powerfully. The numerous explanations and examples provide a comprehensive and deep understanding, enabling this book to resonate equally with students, parents, workers, leaders, and anyone with an interest in learning. The problems Dr. Deming sought to address are most commonly attributed to business but in reality apply to life and all human interaction. Anyone who reads the book will be able to quickly relate the myriad of examples and quotes to a personal experience or state and use the philosophy to better understand or help improve the circumstance.

We are very grateful to Ed for writing this book and hope that you will enjoy reading this book as much as we have. We hope that the theoretical discussion will provide a new lens with which to view the world and that the applications and solutions described will provide a way to improve your life experience, to bring you more joy and fulfillment.

—Diana Deming Cahill, Linda Deming Ratcliff, Kevin Edwards Cahill, and John Vincent Cahill, founding trustees, the W. Edwards Deming Institute

NOTE FROM AILERON
BY CLAY MATHILE

———— ∾ ————

Humility is a characteristic common to the great leaders from whom I have learned and been privileged to know. This humility is, I think, a way of acknowledging that we all build on the knowledge and wisdom we gain from others. We share knowledge to empower and enlighten one another so that we fulfill the greatest contribution of leadership, to pass along what we have learned to develop future generations.

It is in this forward thinking and philanthropic spirit that Aileron feels passionate and privileged to partner with Ed Baker in the publication of this book. Aileron is a nonprofit organization that began as my commitment to pay forward the invaluable learning and mentoring I received from others when I was growing Iams, a dog- and cat-food company. While at Iams, I studied Dr. Deming's teachings, and it contributed to the company's success.

At Aileron, we have developed a system influenced by Dr. W. Edwards Deming and other great thought leaders. Dr. Deming's timeless teachings have been, and will continue to be, a driving influence because we've seen his philosophies work. From viewing our working life as part of our whole life, to feeling that we are valued collaborators not competitors, and that we can experience fun, joy, and pride while working ... Dr. Deming's teachings are as relevant and practical today as they were during his lifetime in the twentieth century.

We need more than models and philosophies. We need great teachers, mentors, and interpreters to guide us. Ed's book will help Aileron carry

Dr. Deming's teachings to any willing learner and to the business owners we serve.

As Dr. Deming and Ed have taught us, every leader's responsibility is to give people the knowledge that they need to work within a system and to succeed in it. In effect, Aileron is fulfilling that responsibility. We are being responsible leaders ... stewards of this valuable, timeless knowledge ... by capturing and sharing Dr. Deming's philosophy through Ed Baker's lens.

PRELUDE

〜

An example of a system, well optimized, is a good orchestra.
The players are not there to play solos as prima donnas, each one
trying to catch the ear of the listener. They are there to support
each other. Individually they need not be the best players in
the country ... An orchestra is judged by listeners, not so much
by illustrious players, but by the way they work together.

—W. Edwards Deming[1]

Leaders Can Make Music

W. Edwards Deming was a moral philosopher, prophet, virtuoso, and sage with profound insights into the management of organizations and the art of leadership and living. He also was a composer of liturgical music, a singer, and a musician. He saw significant relationships between the world of music and synergy in orchestras and the world of organizational management and the synergy in sustainable organizations. Often he used music and orchestral analogies, such as the one that opens this prelude, to express his views about the benefits of managing an organization as a whole-system and not as a collection of separate parts. Appreciation for a system is a key component of the composition and orchestration of music. It also is a key component of Deming's System of Profound Knowledge. Other components are knowledge of variation, knowledge of psychology, and theory of knowledge. Deming believed that these areas of knowledge are necessary to lead organizations as whole-systems and for each of us to have greater control and influence in our individual lives. It is knowledge that can improve the quality of human relationships.

We will learn more about Deming and his insights in the coming pages. As we reflect on how we might embody them in the leadership of organizations and of our lives, it will be valuable to keep in mind these simple definitions that derive from the world of music:

- Symphony: something that is harmonious in its complexity or variety, as a symphony of ideas.
- Orchestrate: to combine in a harmonious way.

Max DePree, former chairman of Herman Miller, Inc. and author of *Leadership Jazz*, understood that his leadership role was to orchestrate human expression. He described it this way: the job of a leader is to enable collaboration and the harmony that comes from the quality relationships among unique individuals.[2] The musician Joshua Redman said, "Music isn't just the notes that you play. Music is a set of relationships."[3] Deming applied this principle when he observed that if you listen to Beethoven's Symphony No. 5 played by the Royal Philharmonic Orchestra of London and the same piece played by an amateur orchestra, there is a difference, even if the amateur orchestra does not make a mistake. Deming's point was that even if the producer meets specifications, it doesn't guarantee a quality experience for the customer. The professional orchestra and the amateur orchestra each meet specifications, but the performance and the listener's experience of that performance will be different.

W. Edwards Deming's System of Profound Knowledge can be thought of as analogous to a musical score for a symphony. The score is a map that guides the orchestration of the musicians into a harmonious whole—a *whole-in-one*—to produce a quality performance. The musicians may be members of a large orchestra that is led by a conductor, or a chamber group or a jazz quartet who self-manage their interactions with each other in ways that enable them to play in concert. A whole-in-one means a healthy, coherent system or organization of people fitting and working together as one.

You will find analogies like these throughout this book. I use them to offer you an appreciation for Deming's teaching and practice and to connect them to ideas and experiences that may be more familiar to you. We can think of an analogy as the mapping of the visible world that is sensed to the invisible world where the sensations are translated into words, images, and symbols to give them meaning. Things that are analogous share characteristics, similarities, which allow them to be compared.

Deming's System of Profound Knowledge, viewed as a mental map, is a conceptual representation of the world outside of ourselves. This external world is, for each of us, the territory that we all must navigate as we live our lives and *play* our various roles. A physical map can be seen and touched. A mental map is invisible, yet it influences our behavior, as can a physical map. We will build on these important ideas throughout this book. They are essential in widening our vision and thinking in terms of systems. A system itself is a conceptual representation on a person's mental map.

A Baker's Dozen: My Years with W. Edwards Deming

In June 1980, NBC News aired the documentary *If Japan Can, Why Can't We?*, which is credited with accelerating the quality revolution in America and with introducing W. Edwards Deming to American management. After seeing this television program, Ford executives invited Dr. Deming to speak at their headquarters in Dearborn, Michigan. He did not agree right away, explaining that he didn't know if Ford was serious about transformation. He had good reason for skepticism. During World War II, American manufacturers had attended seminars conducted by Deming and others to help them improve the quality of products they were supplying for the war effort. After the war, a hungry consumer society was in a buying mood. American manufacturers no longer felt the need to apply their learning since quality seemed not to offer a competitive advantage. The Japanese, however, began to apply the lessons they learned from seminars on quality, productivity, and consumer research conducted by Deming, beginning in 1950, and by others such as Joseph M. Juran, Kaoru Ishikawa, and Genichi Taguchi. Within five years, their product quality was good enough for export. This did not surprise Deming since he knew that they had a culture that would support the cooperation and constancy of purpose needed to apply their knowledge to improve product quality, which in turn would reduce costs, improve productivity, increase exports, and grow the economy. By the time Western management was alerted in June 1980 to Deming and his role in Japan's economic recovery, the Japanese had made significant incursions into the North American markets, especially in car sales.

A visit by Ford executives in October 1980 to his office in Washington, DC, convinced Deming that Ford was serious about doing what was needed to improve quality, reduce costs, and help it emerge from its financial crisis. This opened the door to his work with the company. However, having not yet studied Deming's work, management could not possibly imagine the extent of the transformation—organizational and personal—that Deming would ask of them. Some executives, including Ford's CEO, Don Petersen, gave Deming their full support. Others were skeptical. Some managers shied away from personal contact with Deming. Others engaged with Deming because they could see that traditional techniques, such as management by financial objectives and by employee performance goals, were not producing the results that they thought the company was capable of achieving. They believed that they could learn and benefit from Deming's wisdom and help to improve Ford's competitive position.

Dr. Deming first visited Ford's headquarters in January 1981, when he met with the chairman, CEO, and other company officers. He impressed the Ford executives with his confident, direct style. He was eighty years old yet full of vitality, and that meeting began his thirteen-year relationship with Ford.[4] After that first visit, he was there every month to meet with executives and others. He conducted many of his four-day seminars, which were open to Ford employees, suppliers, and others in the extended community who wanted to attend, especially educators, administrators, and teachers from public and private high schools and colleges. The seminars covered the four interrelated components of profound knowledge, although Deming did not begin to refer to them as a system of profound knowledge until the late 1980s.

I first met Dr. Deming during his second visit to Ford in March 1981. He walked into a conference room filled with a group of Ford executives. His presence communicated tremendous strength, confidence, and energy. Despite his age, there was nothing frail about him. He appeared larger than life, certainly as large as he appeared in TV interviews where he filled the screen with his six-foot-plus frame, crew-cut white hair, baritone voice, and crisp speech, which was shaped by his youth in Wyoming in the early twentieth century. His suit jacket was a mobile office in which he carried pens, a small flashlight, business cards people gave him, and anything else he needed to conduct his work. Deming made some brief remarks to the group and then took questions. I realized that this was his way of assessing our depth of understanding and what needed to be done.

When the meeting ended, we had a short conversation, and I told him about some papers I had written. It turned out that he was very interested in these topics, especially the ones on the evaluation of individual and organizational performance.[5] After that conversation, we pretty much hit it off. I knew that I wanted to work with this man. I was drawn to his knowledge, wisdom, and integrity, as well as his sense of humor. He appeared to enjoy his work and was dedicated to helping others—individuals and organizations—to enjoy theirs.

I think it was more than chance that soon after that meeting I moved to the Corporate Quality Office, one of the central staff organizations reporting to Jim Bakken, the Ford vice president and corporate officer who had become Deming's primary senior executive contact at Ford. Jim accurately characterized Deming's role as mentor, catalyst, conscience, and burr under the saddle. Deming insisted that he meet frequently with Ford's top management, so he was there every month, meeting often with Don Petersen when he was president and later when he became chairman. Deming also met with Harold "Red" Poling, who became chairman when Petersen retired. While consulting to Ford, Deming also was consulting to General Motors during some of the same time period. He saw no conflict in this. His primary interest was in the national economy, as well as the success of his clients. He believed that working with automotive manufacturers could accelerate the changes he envisioned because of the large base of their suppliers and subsuppliers who would adopt his management philosophy and teaching.

Deming thought it was important to bring in someone outside of Ford's culture to manage the corporate staff support activities related to his consulting. He wanted this person to report directly to the CEO, but he agreed with Jim Bakken's plan to create the Statistical Methods Office with its director reporting directly to Jim. In 1982, Bill Scherkenbach, who had been an MBA student of Deming's at the NYU Stern School of Business, filled this position. I moved across the hall from the Corporate Quality Office and became an associate of this group. I also held a joint assignment reporting to Lynn Halstead, vice president of Latin American Operations. Lynn told me that he wanted me to assist him in promoting the Deming philosophy throughout the Ford businesses that reported to him.[6] These assignments enabled me to meet with and influence individuals throughout the company, from top management to the shop floor.

When Bill left Ford in 1987 to help General Motors implement the Deming philosophy, I headed up a new group that incorporated functions of the Statistical Methods Office and the Corporate Quality Office. Our job was to develop strategy to continually improve quality and to support the operations with internal consulting. I now had the responsibility to manage Deming's monthly visits to Ford and to schedule his meetings and seminars at Ford headquarters and other company locations, including one in Sao Paulo, Brazil.

Deming's first four-day seminar for Ford was conducted in the auditorium of World Headquarters in April 1981. The auditorium was a theater with a raised stage and with seats for five hundred people. I was surprised to discover that part of my new job with the Corporate Quality Office was to be seated discreetly in a corner of the stage during the seminar. Deming was quite animated during his seminars, and one of my jobs was to run interference in case he was getting too close to the edge of the stage, in the manner of a Secret Service agent taking a bullet for the president. In addition to acting as Dr. Deming's protector, I took questions from the room full of management attendees, most of whom were reluctant to stand up and speak. Instead they wrote their questions on cards, and I read them aloud. I was the messenger, Deming's foil, whom he could criticize for the question in order to make a point. It was all in jest, and some of the audience understood that, but some, insecure in their lack of knowledge, avoided engaging with Dr. Deming after that seminar. Those who were less intimidated and did interact with him learned much during seminars and during private meetings. They developed new understandings of how the interaction of the many parts of the company's systems could work at cross-purposes to the performance of the various organizations and to the company as a whole. They also could see the gains in quality and reduction of cost from applying Deming's theory of variation to the numbers produced by Ford's processes, especially in the operations.

I was privileged and fortunate to work with Dr. Deming during the thirteen years from 1981 until his passing in December 1993—my baker's dozen. Working closely with him influenced me deeply. I was changed not only by his words but by his actions. He was a generous, caring, and ethical man. He demonstrated a deep sense of personal responsibility to teach and help others who wanted to learn. He was an historical figure, a concerned American citizen whose family traces back to the early settlers of America, a great human being, and a contributor to world society.

The primary and fundamental lesson Dr. Deming taught me was that each individual, who is capable and intrinsically motivated to do so, must take responsibility for their own learning and development. I understood this to mean that I needed to be open, to question what I believed and thought I knew. When I attended that first four-day seminar at Ford in 1981, I was shocked. Much of what Deming was saying contradicted what I had learned throughout my professional education and what I had seen in the management of organizations, including schools. I had to reevaluate not just what I saw as fact but the possibility that what we think and believe is factual may not be so for others. People see things in very different ways, some of which are not rational or consistent. Deming, who was concerned about language, its limitations and our ability to use it well to think and to communicate, taught me to be more aware of the critical role of language in human interactions.

Deming was not afraid to challenge authority and the status quo, especially in education. He occasionally met with school administrators as well as with statistics professors and their department heads in university statistics departments. They were reluctant to take on the changes in curriculum that Dr. Deming recommended. Even when his ideas were not thoughtfully considered, Deming continued to encourage people to question assumptions and challenge accepted fact in order to learn and expand awareness of new possibilities.

When I left Ford in October 1992 to promote Deming's philosophy to other organizations, I especially wanted to consult to small, privately held businesses since change could occur within the organization more quickly than in large, publically owned firms. I continued to participate with Dr. Deming in some of his seminars throughout 1993. He was ill and yet always found the strength for four days to conduct his seminar. I was not at his final seminar, which he completed on December 10, 1993. He told the people helping him, "We have done it," which I interpreted as meaning that he met his obligation to the attendees at that seminar and his commitments for the year. He died ten days later.

Dr. Deming founded the nonprofit W. Edwards Deming Institute[7] in November 1993, a month before his passing. While he lived, Dr. Deming had no interest in creating any kind of formal organization since he wanted to spend his time teaching and writing. Until they learned that his staff consisted only of his secretary Cecilia (Ceil) Kilian, many people thought that Dr. Deming had a large organization. In a sense, Dr. Deming's organization was a worldwide network that developed long before the technology of social media. Deming was a leader because he inspired and mobilized people around the world to work for the aims he stated in his 14 Points for Management of Organizations (see appendix) and his System of Profound Knowledge.[8] They are intended to help managers become leaders in their organizations and individuals to become leaders in their own lives. These are discussed in later chapters.

Deming Reprised as a Symphony of Knowledge

I have a note that I made after a conversation with Dr. Deming in February 1988. He said, "Ed, you have to write that book." I told him that I would simply be repeating what is in his books and what I learned from him. He disagreed, insisting and telling me that the book would reflect my perspective, which would be different from his and therefore a new contribution. Therefore, in that spirit, and with a belief that he would have approved, this book reprises W. Edwards Deming's System of Profound Knowledge as a symphony. The music and lyrics are based on Deming's composition, with some variations on his theme and with some additional lyrics composed by other profound thinkers.

I have included comments and quips that Dr. Deming made in his seminars and during other times I was with him. He had observations about organizations and life that were humorous but really were statements about the folly that resulted from what he sarcastically called "great ideas."

Many of these comments did not get into his own books, and I think they expand our understanding of the man.

Other analogies and metaphors are used to add context to his ideas, especially as a map to navigate the territory of management and of life. There is no one way to apply the map. It is not doctrine, not a formula or a to-do list. It is a way of thinking about enterprise, about all organizations of human beings, and about one's own life. It is a basis on which to undertake management as a profession, to be a leader of people, to orchestrate the interactions between the players in the system.

A quote from Dr. Russell Ackoff, a longtime friend and colleague of Dr. Deming and a man from whom I also was privileged to learn, sums up my philosophy: "I have no desire to think *for* managers, but I do enjoy thinking *with* and *about* them, particularly with and about those who think for themselves."[9]

This book is intended to be a companion to Deming's two books on knowledge necessary for leadership: *The New Economics* and *Out of the Crisis*. Readers will vary in their knowledge of Deming's teaching, but I intend for everyone who wants to study Deming's work to benefit, regardless of their knowledge. A primary aim is to open a door to thinking that is not common sense. If it were common, our economy would be in much better shape, managers would be leaders of people, and people would be better leaders of their own lives.

Many others have written about Dr. Deming. Some books have been written based on second- or third-hand accounts by people who did not know Deming or interact with him. In many cases, these books misrepresent him and his teachings. He has been referred to as the father of Total Quality Management (TQM). Deming knew that people tended to associate him with TQM, but he also saw that just about all the so-called quality-improvement programs that had the label TQM—Six Sigma or other popular programs at the time—violated his teaching. The narrow focus of these writers prevented them from seeing the broad transformation Deming was trying to achieve. Most of all, many writers do not see him as a moral philosopher. His teaching provided lessons of ethics, service, generosity, and responsibility. My aim is to offer my perspective, as Deming encouraged, and for his teaching to reach the hearts and minds of a wide audience in a world that needs it more than ever.

The book presents a whole-system of thought. Many years ago, Dr. Deming wrote, "the value of a book is not just the sum of the values of the chapters separately; each chapter, even each paragraph, has a meaning that is conditioned by all the others." He went on to say that the subject of a book is not fully expressed by any single idea, and the first chapter must be interpreted in the light of the last.[10] Rosamund and Benjamin Zander described their book, *The Art of Possibility*, as like a piece of music where each chapter is a variation upon the theme of leadership and relationship. This description also applies to this book.[11]

OVERTURE

Chapter 1

The Multifaceted W. Edwards Deming

> The great moral teachers of humanity were, in a
> way, artistic geniuses in the art of living.
> —Albert Einstein[12]

The foundation of W. Edwards Deming's teaching and practice is his System of Profound Knowledge. His teaching cannot be separated from Deming the person—his genius, knowledge, values, and experiences over a long life. "I was there," he often said about how his stories and examples got into his books and teaching. Detailed discussion of his system begins in chapter 4. The first three chapters in this overture are intended to give a greater appreciation for the man and his concerns and visions for the leadership of organizations and for individuals living their lives and interacting with the various institutions of society. His teaching is relevant to all of us, in all of our roles in society.

Deming never labeled himself except for on his business card, which identified him as "Consultant in Statistical Studies." This self-description doesn't capture the breadth and depth of the man and his contributions. They were many and diverse. He was a multifaceted person who wove his many areas of expertise, experience, and knowledge into the fabric of his life. In order to know Deming and his work, the impact that it had, and its relevance to leadership in organizations and in living, I think it is worthwhile to take a look at these facets and to understand him by way of the analogies that follow.

A Doctor Fighting Deadly Diseases

Deming's aim was to diagnose and cure organizations of what he called "deadly diseases."[13] This included bringing organizations to economic health and individuals to spiritual and psychological health by attaining dignity and joy in work. The following quote by Henri Amiel, the Swiss philosopher, poet, and critic, seems to apply to Deming: "To me the ideal doctor would be a man endowed with profound knowledge of life and of the soul, intuitively divining any suffering or disorder of whatever kind, and restoring peace by his mere presence."[14]

This is a description that I am sure Deming would have liked to have seen applied to managers as professionals, with the diagnostic skill of a physician. The physician understands the body as a system where the health of the whole body depends on the healthy functioning of the parts and their relationships. Likewise, the health and proper functioning of the organization as a whole, especially as a social system, depends on the functioning of individuals and the quality of their interactions with each other.

In his book *Out of the Crisis*, Deming diagnosed the deadly diseases and the interrelated management practices that afflict most businesses, as well as other organizations in the Western world.[15] He began that particular chapter by quoting Hosea 4:6: "My people are destroyed for lack of knowledge." In summary, he explains that our ills are due primarily to the following:

1. Lack of constancy of purpose, knowing what business you are in.
2. Emphasis on the short term, the immediate, rather than thinking long-term to keep the organization viable. Short-term thinking, such as focusing on maximizing this quarter's sales and profits, is promoted by the pressures produced by management by objectives (MBO), also known as management by results (MBR).
3. Management solely by use of visible figures, ignoring figures that are unknown or unknowable, also called management by numbers (MBN).
4. The annual performance review, with its reliance on rating, ranking, and grading is short-term thinking that requires visible

figures and fosters internal competition for the few top ratings at the cost of cooperation and teamwork.

5. Mobility of management and other employees.

These practices create internal conditions that present obstacles to the organization's potential for success. They produce competition between individuals and units that interfere with the cooperation and sharing necessary for an organization to perform as a unified whole. They cause loss by degrading the organization's ability to optimize its resources. It was management practices such as these that caused him to say that management is living in an age of destructive mythology.

A Moral Philosopher

Deming did not label his teaching as moral philosophy, yet he followed the tradition of economists such as Adam Smith, whom Robert Heilbroner named one of the "worldly philosophers."[16] The Adam Smith Award was given in 1990 to both Dr. Deming and Malcolm S. Forbes Jr. It is the highest honor given by the Association of Private Enterprise Education to recognize an individual who has made a sustained and lasting contribution to the perpetuation of the ideals of a free market economy as first laid out in Adam Smith's *The Wealth of Nations*. The recipient of this award is one who through their writing, speaking, and professional life has acquired an international reputation as an eloquent scholar and advocate of free enterprise and the system of entrepreneurship that underlies it.

The following description by John Maynard Keynes, a British economist, applies to economists regardless of theoretical orientation. It surely seems to apply to Deming.

> The master-economist must possess a rare combination of gifts. He must be mathematician, historian, statesman, philosopher—in some degree. He must understand symbols and speak in words. He must contemplate the particular in terms of the general, and touch abstract and concrete in the same flight of thought. He must study the present in light of the past for the purposes of the

future. No part of man's nature or his institutions must lie entirely outside his regard.[17]

His contributions and his stature are so valued in Japan that the Union of Japanese Scientists and Engineers (JUSE) in 1951 instituted the Deming Prize. It has been suggested that Deming should have been nominated for the Nobel Prize in Economics since his theory of variation and its application to the reduction of cost and waste are essential to sound manufacturing economics.[18]

Deming's association with economists goes back many years. In 1937, he organized a series of lectures by his colleague, the statistician Walter Shewhart. In her book about Deming, *The Man Who Discovered Quality*,[19] Andrea Gabor reported that W. Allen Wallis, who would become assistant secretary of state in the Reagan administration, told her that he [Wallis] and the economist Milton Friedman both attended Shewhart's lectures.[20] Deming sometimes humorously remarked, "Milton Friedman once attended a class of mine. Neither he nor I knew why he was there." While Deming believed in free enterprise, I think his comment implied in a friendly way that he did not share Friedman's strict conservative view. Friedman is said to have greatly respected Deming. I think Friedman's attendance at his lecture further validates Deming's credibility with some economists.

A Sage, Prophet, Master

A *sage* is defined as a profoundly wise person. To be sagacious is to have keen perception, discernment, penetrating intelligence, sound judgment, and foresight. Deming's life and work are in the tradition of sages and spiritual leaders who for millennia have addressed the perennial problems that have characterized human living. "The Way of the sage is to act but not to compete," according to Lao-tzu. "Lao" means venerable or old. "Zi" or "tzu" means master. Deming was *Lao-tzu* in that he saw no advantage to destructive adversarial competition, no need to have losers in order to have winners, whether in business, education, or life. Rather than obsession with increased market share, he thought that management should focus on expanding the market with innovative and high-quality products and services. Competition, said Deming, should be against the past, to improve, not to destroy. He worried about America's balance of trade and its competitive position in the world. He warned, "Problems of the future command first and foremost constancy of purpose and dedication to improvement of competitive position to keep the company alive and to provide jobs for their employees."[21]

The word "guru" often is an abused and misplaced label. In Sanskrit, the syllable "gu" means shadows or darkness, and "ru" means to dispel. I think that the label applies to Deming since he tried through his teaching to dispel the darkness of ignorance and enlighten the minds of others.

Dr. Deming went to Japan after WWII to assist in the design of a census. While working with the Economic and Scientific Staff of General MacArthur's Headquarters, he saw much suffering. His daughter, Linda Deming Ratcliff, told me she thinks that this reminded him of the hardships of his own youth. He had survived and prospered and believed that if he passed on the knowledge he had acquired and developed over half a century, he could help the Japanese do the same. In 1950, he began teaching his theories and methods to engineers, scientists, and top management that helped to put Japan on the road to success in exporting. Although unknown to most businesses in America, Deming was viewed in Japan as a master and a visionary for accurately predicting their success in manufacturing and export from the lessons he taught. Much as in the myth of the hero, Deming was seen as an authority figure and sage by the Japanese scientists and engineers who knew him.

Daniel Boorstin, Librarian of Congress Emeritus and Pulitzer Prize–winning historian, wrote in *U.S. News & World Report* that Deming was "one of nine turning points in history," a recognition he deserved for his early work in Japan and later for "America's belated embrace of a prophet." Boorstin also wrote that Deming was tough on American business managers since they were "several decades late to class."[22]

Fifth Business

In his novel *Fifth Business*, Robertson Davies created the term "fifth business" to apply to the individual in a drama (novel, play, or opera) who is behind the scenes but who is necessary to get things done.[23] This person is necessary to make the plot work because he or she knows something that others do not know. That person is not a prima donna or self-centered; in fact, this person is humble despite his or her important role. Davies also provides this description of a person in the role of fifth business, which I think applies to Deming: "He was a genius—that is to say, a man who does superlatively and without obvious effort something that most people cannot do by the uttermost exertion of their abilities."[24]

Deming received many accolades and honors,[25] yet he was humble. He took great joy and satisfaction from helping others learn and in learning from others. This was much more important to him than the formal recognition that society bestowed upon him in great abundance over the years in the form of awards. On October 21, 1989, in Dearborn, Michigan, on the sixtieth anniversary of the Henry Ford Museum and Greenfield Village, Dr. Deming was presented with the Edison-Ford Medal "in recognition of his lifelong contribution to the spirit of American ingenuity, innovation and enterprise." Following remarks by Dr. Boorstin, whose praise of Deming appeared to embarrass him, the audience anticipated some words of wisdom from Dr. Deming, perhaps some new insights into the complexities of management. After receiving the medal, Dr. Deming told two stories. First, he said, "I appreciate this honor. I feel like the dog a woman entered every year in the Philadelphia dog show. The woman was asked why, year after year, she entered the dog in the show since the dog has no chance to win a prize. 'Well that's true,' said the woman, 'but it gives him a chance to associate with some good dogs.'" Then Deming added, "I know just how the dog felt." He then told this second story: "I also feel like the horse doctor. A little girl was late coming home from school. Her mother was very much worried. Finally the little girl showed up at home with the explanation. She was on her way home from school when a horse took sick, and she heard somebody say they had sent for the horse doctor. 'And, Mamma, I had never seen a horse doctor, and I wanted so much to see a horse doctor. And, Mamma, when he came, he was only a man, only a man.'"

This was typical of Deming's humorous way of showing his humility. In the video *The Deming of America*, there is a poignant scene in Dr. Deming's modest basement office of his home in Washington, DC. Priscilla Petty, the video's producer, asked Dr. Deming how he felt when he received the Second Order Medal of the Sacred Treasure from Emperor Hirohito. He replied, "I felt unworthy ... it was a matter of luck."

David Halberstam, in his book *The Reckoning*, described Deming this way:

> Among the many things the Japanese liked about Deming was that he lived so modestly. The productivity teams had visited many American cities, and they were often entertained at the rather grand homes of American businessmen. Yet here was, to them, the most important man in America living in an ordinary house. The furniture was simple and the rooms were rather poorly lit, with a certain mustiness to them. That impressed them all the more. Deming's passion was for making better products, or more accurately, for creating a system that could make better products. It was not for making money. He clearly had little interest in material things. He was the kind of American they had always heard about, a spiritual man, not a materialistic one. The Japanese who trekked to see him were aware that he could have profited immensely in those days, selling himself and his services to Japanese companies. The subject just never seemed to come up. There was another way in which he differed from the other Americans they were visiting. The others would lecture them, and the lectures were, however unconsciously, an exercise in power. Deming listened as much as he talked.[26]

Halberstam continued that Deming:

> ... was often brusque with his fellow countrymen and scornful of them. He hated waste, and felt that America had become a wasteful country, not only of its abundant natural resources but also of its human talents ... He had little tolerance for fools ... specially those who pretended to care about his principles but had no intention of changing their ways.[27]

During the 1980s, there were many authors and journalists who wanted to interview Deming for a book or article. It usually was not the case that the writers wanted to explore with Deming his ideas and their implications for society. Deming was willing to engage in conversation with those truly interested and somewhat aware of his views and theories. If they came to him unprepared, they were subject to what Deming's friend the late Professor David Chambers called "Deming's melt-down technique." I remember one time when an author who was writing a book about the Ford Motor Company had scheduled two hours with Deming. Shortly after the interview started, it was clear to Deming that this person knew nothing about Deming's ideas. For the next two hours, Deming taught this author by a method of interrogation. After the two hours, the interviewer, quite shaken up, said that the interview was over and he was leaving. Deming said not to leave since "now we are ready to talk." The interviewer left, and Deming said to me, "Perhaps I was a little too rough on him."

A Virtuoso in the Art of Living

Virtuoso has the same root in Latin, *virtus*: strength, as virtue—virtuous, morally excellent, decent, ethical, just, right-minded. A virtuoso is one skilled in the arts and sciences, or having a taste for the fine arts, a master, an authority, educated, with exceptional knowledge, accomplished and distinguished in any intellectual or artistic field of endeavor.

Dr. Deming was a religious and spiritual man who appreciated what human talents can contribute to living. He was a music theorist and composer who expressed his faith through his liturgical music. In his spare time, he rearranged "The Star-Spangled Banner" to make it easier to sing.[28] His daughter, Diana Deming Cahill, told me, "My father played our piano daily. He wrote eight compositions. One uses only the three notes that he and I heard the monks chant at a Tokyo temple."

Composing music and playing the piano weren't the only activities that allowed him to continually navigate between theory and action. "My father was a skilled carpenter. He taught us the proper way to use and handle tools," wrote Diana. Deming's System of Profound Knowledge, as with his music and carpentry, also is a continual movement between the invisible world of theory and its application to the visible world of living.

He saw wisdom for living in scripture and began some chapters of his books directed to management, *Out of the Crisis* and *The New Economics* (Second Edition), with a quote from the Bible that characterized the aim of his teaching. One can see his concern with language and communication from these examples:

"Understanding is a wellspring of life unto him that hath it; but the instruction of fools is folly." —Proverbs 16:22 (*Out of the Crisis,* chapter 8, "Some New Principles of Training and Leadership," p. 248)

"Who is it that darkeneth counsel by words without knowledge?" —Job 38:2. (*Out of the Crisis,* chapter 1, "Chain Reaction," p. 1)

"My people are destroyed for lack of knowledge." —Hosea 4:6 (*Out of the Crisis,* chapter 3, "Diseases and Obstacles," p. 97)

"A wise man will hold his tongue till he see opportunity: but a babbler and a fool will regard no time." —Ecclesiasticus 20, v. 7 (*The New Economics,* 2nd ed., chapter 8, "Shewhart and Control Charts," p. 172)

"Prefer a slip on the pavement over a slip of the tongue." —Ecclesiasticus 20, v. 18 (*The New Economics,* 2nd ed., chapter 10, "Some Lessons in Variation," p. 207)

"For whoso despiseth wisdom and nurture, he is miserable, and his hope is in vain, his labours unfruitful, and his works unprofitable." —The Wisdom of Solomon 3:11 (*Sample Design in Business Research,* p. 243)

Deming understood that the material, psychological, and spiritual well-being of people depend on a healthy economic system that fosters trade of goods and services.[29] He took joy in his work and in his life. He believed everyone should be able to do so. Diana wrote to me, "His laugh was a crescendo of mirth, his bass voice was magnificent, he spoke with depth and expression. On weekends, friends gathered for dinner, homemade wine, discussions, and music." He introduced his chapter "Introduction to a System"[30] with this quote from Ecclesiastes 2, verse 24: "There is nothing better for a man to do than to eat and drink and enjoy himself in return for his labours."

Ceil Kilian, Deming's secretary for nearly forty years, described his work ethic as "ageless in wisdom and young in spirit," a man in perpetual motion. "You'd need roller skates to keep up with him, no matter what your age."[31]

Deming taught how application of his principles could contribute to better living. Such knowledge would simplify life and reduce the cost of living. He did not hesitate to provide feedback to the management of organizations whose service quality disappointed him. Some examples follow:

Letter to a nursery: "Gentlemen, I made a regrettable mistake in asking (Name of Nursery) to put in my front lawn. Nothing came up but nurse grass, and now a bountiful crop of crab grass. We never had any crab grass before; we were always careful to eliminate any sign of it. Please do not come and reseed it. We have enough crab grass."

Letter to an airline: "Dear Sir, The beef that you people served on board today was the toughest yet. It was big enough, but inedible. I suggest that you pay a higher price for your beef, and cut the quantity, if you must cut costs."

Letter to a private club in Washington, DC: "I have dinner at the Club whenever possible, which is only some Saturday nights as I am away during the week. I eat most of my meals in hotels and restaurants and ought to have some basis for judgment. I should say that a restaurant, if it provided service like that at (Name of Club), would be out of business in two months ... Seated, one waits in wonder about what will happen. Have we a waitress? Finally, yes. Long periods go by with no attention. Will she return? The waitresses are a closed society. The prices are high enough for excellent food and good service."

Deming made many trips to Japan over the years. He documented his seventh trip to Japan with a booklet describing his observations and impressions and expressing his appreciation for Japanese art and culture.[32] He loved the food and described his meals, including a flow chart he drew for the manufacturer of _shirataki_, the transparent noodles he liked. He made a comment in the booklet on page 1 that is revealing: "Life would be more enjoyable if I didn't have to give a public lecture Friday ... I fear that there will be 1800 disappointed people if they all come. I'd rather sing for them."

Dr. Deming's daughter, Linda, described a situation in Washington, DC. A parkway was being built, which cut through a woods near their home. The turtles traveled each day, as they had for generations, from one area of the woods to another. Some likely would get crushed by traffic as they attempted to cross the new road. Linda and her father were horrified, so every day he would pack Linda into the car, and off they would go to save turtles. When they saw a turtle, he would stop the car, and Linda would jump out and move it across the street in the direction it was headed. Linda summed up her view of her father with these words: "Like most anyone else, he was complicated. He was a man who loved nature and people. Most of the time, he was a gentle man who enjoyed life and all it had to offer."[33]

Deming's Profound Knowledge Is Universal and Timeless

Many people, including some so-called consultants, still do not understand the universality and timelessness of what Deming offered to the world. When it was suggested to Dr. Deming that his philosophy transcended all cultures and religions, he agreed. Its relevance continues in today's global economy.

He left footprints, unlike many economic theorists who never came down to the ground from their conceptual perches. Some may consider Deming's ideas to be too idealistic to work, unattainable in this "real world." But the so-called real world was made by the actions of people thinking in a way that needs to be transformed. A different real world can be created.

Deming Spoke Truth to Power

Deming tolerated initial ignorance but abhorred an unwillingness to learn. He told people in authority what he knew they needed to hear, not what they wanted to hear. Some ran for cover. Some were angered. He had observed that the eighty Nobel Prize winners were answerable only to themselves.[34] They did not worry about ratings. Neither did Deming worry about evaluation of his teaching. He wrote to me in 1989 that evaluation of his teaching, of the teaching of any scholar, can be made only with the experience and understanding that comes with time.

Chapter 2

Deming in an Age of Management Mythology

Every man takes the limits of his own field of vision for the limits of the world. This is an error of the intellect as inevitable as that error of the eye which lets us fancy that on the horizon heaven and earth meet.
—Arthur Schopenhauer[35]

This chapter describes some of the mythology that formed the basis of Deming's condemnation of management systems and practices. Chapter 3 describes a vision for a better future that can come from a mythology derived from the light provided by Deming's System of Profound Knowledge, which is discussed in the rest of the book.

Deming could be harsh. He said that everything that needs to be done is against tradition.[36] He often began his seminars by saying that management is living in an age of mythology. He meant that management operates according to assumptions and myths that harm their organizations.[37] He felt so strongly about this that he said that we are living under the tyranny of the present style of management, which he described as a modern invention that has led us into decline. The losses it has caused and continues to cause cannot be measured. We continue to dig deeper the pit that we are in. Deming was referring to his "present day," which was most of the twentieth century. These myths continue to pervade our thinking. They suppress the wider possibilities inherent in living. Deming wrote that it is only through the illumination of knowledge outside of current thinking that will help us move out of the present system and into another. Industry, education, and government are in need of transformation.[38]

Myths and Meaning

Cultures have their myths. These are the stories passed down from generation to generation by which we live. Our myths can shape our views and actions, especially in the way we relate to others. They define our values by telling us how things should be. They tell us what is right and wrong, good and bad, what to believe and not to believe. We may not be aware of the myths that influence our thinking and actions.

Myths can be about ourselves or about other people, groups, nations, races, and cultures, and they may include verbal labels and categories, which lead to judging people positively or negatively, and so they can divide us from each other. If we are aware of how myths influence our values and behaviors, we may choose to act differently and not live by those myths. In so doing, we may have to accept ostracism, or worse, from others.

While myths can help us, they also can hurt us when they no longer bear any relationship to the world that existed when they first emerged. They are no longer relevant. An example is the term "labor," a remnant of the age of industrialization, when employees in production were managed as if they were parts of a mechanical system, to be pushed and pulled by the extrinsic forces of rewards and punishments and kept in line by fear. In this myth, employees were only hands, not minds. They worked in the system with little or no discretion or influence as to how the work was done. Even today, a time of so-called knowledge work and employee involvement in problem solving, the word *labor* persists in referring to human beings. Intentionally or unintentionally, the term carries the same meaning as that earlier period and implies a disregard of the person as a thinking, feeling, and spiritual human being.

Myths can help us to understand the world, to provide wisdom and insights for living. Deming saw many of the traditional myths of enterprise, discussed later in this chapter, not as a guiding wisdom but as perpetuating ignorance and erroneous thinking. He liked to cite the humorist Josh Billings who said that he would rather know a little less than to know so much that isn't so.[39]

Many of the myths Deming saw in management practice were based on false premises and beliefs. In his writings, Deming sometimes used the term "folklore" or "common sense" instead of myth. He wrote that common sense tells us to rank children, employees, students, and teams; to reward the "best" and punish the "worst"; to have quotas and numerical goals for individuals or groups; to assume that a problem always is caused by the people doing the work instead of the system in which they operate. He worked hard to help people to see the irrelevance, limitations, and the cost of these major myths entrenched in society. He wrote, "It is wrong to suppose that if you can't measure it, you can't manage it—a costly myth."[40]

These management practices usually are not questioned. The knowledge to question them does not exist in the minds of the practitioners—managers, administrators, teachers, even parents. The costs to individuals and to the nation produced by these practices are, as Deming called them, "unknown and unknowable."

The Myth of Best Practices

One myth prevalent in enterprise is "best practices." Programs that appear to work in other organizations may be copied, "benchmarked," without understanding the context that allowed them to work, if in fact they really did work. Practices and programs may be adopted because they have been recommended and promoted by so-called expert consultants without an understanding of the context that allowed them to work, if in fact they really did work. My colleague Heero Hacquebord used the Pieter Bruegel painting of the blind leading the blind to warn about unquestioned reliance on so-called experts and uncritical copying of programs, practices, and methods.

Myths that Fragment Wholeness

Russell Ackoff wrote that the mode of thought introduced to the Western world during the Renaissance subjected everything to analysis, including life itself. Life was decomposed into three distinct types of activity—work, play, and learning—with separate institutions devoted to each. Ackoff explained that we designed factories for work. We designed country clubs, arenas, and stadiums exclusively for fun. We designed schools only for learning. Thus the Industrial Revolution led to the creation of work and workplaces that excluded fun and learning, and therefore it also excluded the development of the worker.

Society viewed work as necessarily unpleasant, and worker dissatisfaction had to be accepted as a necessary part of it. Ackoff saw that the Protestant ethic carried this further and viewed work as an earthly purgatory in which sin is expiated and virtue is gradually accumulated. Work was thought of as a type of punishment, not as an opportunity for self-fulfillment and pleasure. Some even thought that the displeasure associated with work was good for the soul; the greater the displeasure, the more it cleansed the soul.[41]

Whole-system thinking is the appreciation that problems occur within a larger context, that life is lived within a larger context. Just as the weather outside your door is produced by a complex interaction of forces that occurred earlier and in other places, the same is the case for enterprise. Managers should be able to mentally trace the various system consequences of their plans and actions. *Tampering*, Deming's word for overadjustment and overcontrol, discussed in chapter 14, is an example of fragmented thinking that illustrates the hazards of not acting with the larger system in mind.

Deming provided many examples of how failure to think from a whole-system view leads to incomplete information and wrong conclusions. He gave an example of a situation he saw in a plant that manufactures tires.[42] The engineers studied only the defective tires to determine the causes of defects. They also should have studied the nondefective tires in order to understand the functioning of the system as a whole. Without the appropriate theory, in this case theory of variation and appreciation for a system, how could they know the source of the defective tires?

This type of thinking has broad application that we can apply every day in our lives. You might have this experience in a restaurant. You ask the server what the chef's special is. The server tells you, and you say that you don't like that kind of meal. Then you list other things that you don't like, including seasoning and methods of cooking. Of course the server still doesn't know what to do because he doesn't know what you like. If you give the server an idea of what you do like as well as what you don't (i.e., provide a sample from your whole-system of preferences), it will increase the chance that you will get what you want. This highlights a weakness of defining quality only as the absence of defects as well as the limitations of zero-defects programs that don't define what does satisfy the customer. Eliminating defects can't help customers if the product or service does not meet their requirements.

Consider, for example, the firm that advertises that customers love its products, or an investment adviser who claims to have made his clients wealthy. Wouldn't you like to know how many customers and clients were not happy?[43] Were only the good results reported?

An example of Deming's whole-system view was his interest and expertise in consumer research. He gave examples of poor design of consumer products and wondered whether the enterprise had ever done consumer research to understand how its products would be used, how they fit into the life of consumers. It is the producer's responsibility to design and produce products that the consumer can't foresee. It is difficult for consumers to say what new product or service they could use in the future. In general, consumers can only project what they will need or want from the technology and products they currently know. New products and new types of service are not developed by asking the consumer but by knowledge, imagination, innovation, risk, and trial and error by the producer. Deming said that he would not have thought of telling manufacturers that he would like to replace his pocket watch with a quartz watch.[44] If he were alive today, Deming would be citing examples of modern technology. However, he would remind us that the future is of interest, much more so than the past. It takes knowledge to predict and plan for the future, and this future thinking is best done with the larger system in mind.

The Myth of Management by Lists

There is a practice that I call "management by lists," where individual problems are prioritized in a to-do list and distributed to different employees or departments. This method results from the failure to see problems as part of a whole-system pattern of interacting problems that the systems theorist Dr. Russell Ackoff called a _mess_.[45] Patchwork solutions that result from managing by lists contribute to a larger mess. Messes have their origin in the myth that the whole is the sum of the parts taken separately. We tend to see living not as a unified whole but as the addition of the separate parts of living. Unless the systemic sources of problems are removed, there will be an unending supply of problems, and the list can never be discarded.

The Myth of the Deadwood

The rank ordering of employees from "best" to "worst" based on ratings by their supervisors is a management practice that could be called "the myth of the deadwood," or "removing the weeds." These words are used in some organizations to describe human beings. Rating methods are used in most organizations as part of the performance appraisal process. The word "appraisal" reveals the mind-set behind the method. The worth of human beings is judged in the same manner that material objects are evaluated. When management rates employees, they are rating themselves since they are responsible for hiring, placing, and training employees.

The Myth of Rising Cream

The practice of rating and ranking of employees' performance seems to be partly based on myths such as "rugged individualism" and "the cream will rise to the top." Such practices result from a profound lack of knowledge about systems and variation, to say nothing of the fear it puts into the hearts of employees and the lack of cooperation it fosters. Instead of sorting employees into performance categories based on rankings and thinking that the evaluation process is complete, or correct, management should know how the forces of the system interact with employees to produce performance. While there are individuals, outliers with outstanding and rare talents, as well as some who are unfit for their present job, knowledge of variation likely will confirm that the vast majority of employees perform within the enabling or constraining forces of the organization's systems.

Manager as Hero Myth

Managers believe that adopting the practices of admired executives, such as the ones Jack Welch, former CEO of General Electric, described in his book, *Winning*, will contribute to their own success.[46] Deming believed that much of the economic illnesses that afflict the United States and other countries are attributable to management in business and in government. A lot of these ills have roots in business schools, which teach how business is currently conducted with no consideration of what might be possible in the future. In so doing, schools perpetuate the present style of management. They have an obligation to change their curricula to serve the needs of students of management, administration, and accounting as they will be in ten or twenty years. Deming expressed his thinking in a memo to the dean of a business school. He recommended that business schools should look ahead and assess the future needs of business and government. No one can see the future, but we must try. He went on to explain that the school must differentiate between teaching knowledge and teaching information. Students should not graduate from schools of business without having studied the theory of knowledge. The limitations of knowledge are the most important ingredients of knowledge itself. Management needs to *know* how to improve; therefore students need to study statistical theory for detection of causes of trouble and for indication of the level of responsibility for improvement.[47]

The Myth of Extrinsic Incentives

Associated with the myth of rugged individualism and rising cream is what could be called the myth of extrinsic incentives. The assumption is that poorer performing employees are just not trying hard enough and that management can produce better performance by applying the right balance of reward and punishment. The belief is that just as physical objects can be moved by extrinsic force, by pushing or pulling, so can the employee be moved in the desired direction by the right balance of extrinsic incentives. This is a false premise and leads to the false promise of improved performance by manipulation and bribery of employees who have little control over the outcomes of their performance. It is no substitute for leadership.

Deming's principles apply especially to the critical profession of teaching, which is not immune to such practices. Grading and rank ordering of students based on test scores is at odds with the laws of variation, as we shall see in later chapters. It is harmful psychologically since children with poor grades often are labeled, by others and themselves, as "losers." It is harmful socially when it discourages student cooperation in learning by treating it as cheating and creates an individualistic, competitive mind-set that teaches students not to share what they know. Unfortunately, this prepares them for the same dysfunctional management styles they will see in their jobs. They will fit in, and, again unfortunately, it may help them move up the management ladder and engage in the same practices that shaped them.

The Myth of Management by the Numbers

Another myth is that management of performance, people, and processes must be by the numbers. A corollary is that if you can't measure it, you can't manage it. The ritual, the enactment of the myth in the evaluation of individuals, is rating and ranking in organizations and grading and ranking in schools. A manager, teacher, administrator, or parent participates in the myth by participating in or condoning the ritual. Grading was developed more than 150 years ago as a method for the teacher to have a private conversation with the student's parents. It has been replaced by what could be called the myth of defect detection. Rating and grading is analogous to inspection of parts in the factory. Inspection is after the fact, after the parts are produced. Therefore it does not improve the process that produced the parts; it does not prevent defects from occurring. Likewise, many administrative practices in schools do not help to improve the system of education, practices such as improvement goals without a method to achieve them and grading and comparing schools to provide pressures to be above average, as if more than half of any group ever could be above average in any measurement.

Deming reported the case of an elementary school student who received two successive test scores below average. The teacher took that as a diagnosis of the need for remedial training and informed the parents. Most people understand that you can flip a coin and get two or three, even four successive heads or tails just by chance. This happened to the daughter of a colleague of mine, a consultant to organizations to help them learn and apply Deming's System of Profound Knowledge, especially his theory of variation. When he was notified by the teacher of the "problem," he provided her with some unsolicited consultation.[48] Obviously, the teacher did not intend to hurt the child. She thought she was doing the right thing, but if she did send the child to a remedial class, it could have communicated to the child that she was not smart and begin a downward spiral of "Why bother to study since I can't learn?" In this case, the teacher and the administration could have used remedial education to gain some knowledge of variation.

Dr. Deming did not grade his students because he believed that would cause them to value the grade over learning and diminish both their learning and their joy in that learning. Some observers said that it encouraged students to get away without studying or writing papers. Deming gave an Incomplete to students who had not submitted required papers within one year, but more importantly, Deming wanted students to realize that they were cheating themselves.

Dr. Deming's daughter, Linda, a grade-school teacher, said about her father, "I remember he was amused when I told him that following his teachings, I refused to grade my first graders. I gave them all 'Outstanding' in their subjects and then wrote comments that explained how hard they worked to learn and where they were in the general curriculum of first grade. There was no reason to criticize a first grader for not reading when he is not developmentally ready."[49]

The evaluation of teachers by student ratings has become popular. Deming reported his own experience seeing a teacher hold 150 students spellbound. This teacher's students rated him as a great teacher, yet he was teaching "what is wrong." A teacher must have something to teach, be a leader of thought, and inspire students.[50] How can a student know at the time the class ends what he or she has learned? It can take years to see the value.

Ranking is not a measurement system. Ranking is ordering, not measuring. What do the differences between ranks mean? We can't say how much better the person ranked as first is than the person ranked as second. Doing arithmetic on ranks, such as adding, subtracting, multiplying, or dividing the numbers, reflects tremendous ignorance about the information contained in the numbers. The only information rankings give you are whether objects or people, with respect to a characteristic, are the same or different and greater or lesser, but not by how much. Besides, the most important things management must know can't be quantified. Yet numbers are used, inappropriately, to give credibility to evaluations and judgments.

Whether in business, industry, or education, quality doesn't come from inspection. Grading, whether of steel or meat or children, is inspection. The questions are: Do test scores improve a child's education? Do test scores capture the quality of a child's thinking? In a monthly meeting of the Detroit Deming Study Group, Dr. Ed Rothman, professor of statistics at the University of Michigan, observed that a grade measures the amount of information given to a student during classes that the student returns to the teacher on the test.

This phenomenon also occurs in the home. Have you ever heard a parent question a child, "Why can't you be as good as your sister?" thereby informing one of the children he or she is inferior to a sibling or to other children? The parent may want to display a bumper sticker proclaiming that their children are on the school honor roll. Certainly parents should be proud of their children, and all efforts should be made to help children cultivate their talents and fulfill their interests and potential. But what is the thinking of the school that feels it has to rank order and label children according to an honor roll or dean's list? Why isn't learning its own reward? Why do we rely on extrinsic rewards? One might say that this is the way it is, the so-called real world, but we made it that way. We have been conditioned and teach others to think the same way.

A little knowledge of variation would inform parents, teachers, and school administrators that in a system of grading, someone has to be at the head of the class and someone has to be at the bottom, and that for the most part, scores consistently in a middle range indicate nothing more than chance variation. A little knowledge of psychology would inform them that those not on the honor roll may be seen as losers, feel like losers, and be treated like losers, a vicious cycle that could allow the system to create losers. People should be proud of their own achievements and those of their children, spouse, and friends. Bumper stickers are visible. The harm and loss to children and to society from school evaluation processes cannot be seen.

Deming's two books on management, *Out of the Crisis* and *The New Economics*, are full of examples of faulty practices. They reflect the predominant thinking, perhaps more so today than when Deming made sound arguments against such thinking. Deming frequently stated, "There is no substitute for knowledge." Reasoning from the foundation of Deming's System of Profound Knowledge aligns with sound moral judgment, but unfortunately it doesn't always prevail.

Dr. Russell Ackoff, the eminent systems thinker and longtime friend of Dr. Deming, said that when he talks to managers, he usually starts with a quote from Einstein: "Without changing our pattern of thought, we will not be able to solve the problems we created with our current patterns of thought." Ackoff said that managers always agree with this, but when he asks them what their current pattern of thought is, they haven't the foggiest idea. Because of this, they cannot understand their failures. We need to understand the way we think and what we think about and change it to actively shape our future.[51]

Chapter 3

Deming's Vision for a New Mythology

*The material of myth is the material of our life, the material
of our body, and the material of our environment, and a
living, vital mythology deals with these in terms that are
appropriate to the nature of knowledge of the time.*
—Joseph Campbell[52]

Dr. Deming disagreed with the prevalent view of work and school as
something to be endured, no matter how punishing, and with the division
of our lives into separate parts. He began each seminar with the question,
"Why are we here?" He then answered his own question: "To learn and to
have fun," which he applied to himself as well as to the audience. Deming
viewed enjoyable and meaningful work as an integral part of life. People
should not be denied work that provides joy, pride, and opportunities to
learn and develop. Employees must know how the results of their work
will be used by others, how it contributes to the aim of the system, how it
fits into the bigger picture. Part of the role of leadership is to engage each
person by connecting their role and contribution in a meaningful way to
the work and learning of others, to a greater purpose and to the joy of the
collaborative effort. This was Deming's vision and what he tried to help
others to see.

Deming wrote that under most of the management systems that he
saw during the early to late twentieth century, joy in work and innovation
become secondary to a good rating. Extrinsic motivation in the extreme
crushes intrinsic motivation. No one, child or grown-up, can enjoy learning

if they must constantly be concerned about grading and gold stars for their performance. No one can enjoy their work if they will be ranked with others.[53] Dr. Deming asked why some people do not move to another organization when they are offered higher pay. They stay because they like it where they are. They have a chance to use their knowledge for the benefit of the whole-system. They take joy in their work.[54]

In the world of new possibilities that Dr. Deming envisioned, competition for high rating, high grades, and to be "first" or "number one" will be replaced by cooperation on problems of common interest between people, divisions, companies, competitors, governments, and countries. The result will be greater innovation, greater material reward for everyone, joy in work, and learning. Anyone who enjoys their work is a pleasure to work with. Everyone will win. There will be no losers.[55] Joy in learning comes not so much from what is learned but from learning. Joy on the job comes not so much from the result—the product—but from the contribution to optimization of the system in which everybody wins.[56]

Deming asked us to break down the barriers between people and departments in business organizations. He also implied that through the understanding and application of profound knowledge, we can dissolve the compartmentalization that fragments our lives. Dr. Deming himself was a unique blend of mathematician, physical scientist, psychologist, and humanitarian. He understood what it means to be a whole human being.

Transformation to a New Mythology

Transformation means change of shape, form, structure, appearance, function, inner nature, and character. In biology, transformation refers to the metamorphosis of a caterpillar to butterfly. In the physical world, transformation refers to a change of state, such as ice to water or water to steam. Transformation produces qualitative differences from the previous state. Relationships that exist in one phase do not exist in other phases. For example, the behavior of a solid can't be predicted from the behavior of a liquid. Therefore, knowledge of the behavior in one state cannot help to understand and predict behavior in another. A lesson for managers is that the knowledge, skills, and practices that worked in the past will not work as well, and may even be counterproductive, in a qualitatively different future state. Deming envisioned that his system of profound knowledge, discussed later, would provide the basis for a transformation to a new state of human behavior, relationships, and understanding.

Joseph Campbell, an authority on mythology, thought that the photo of earth from space could be the image for a new mythology for living. Unlike human-made geographical maps, there were no divisions based on political, cultural, economic, and military criteria. There were no lines dividing areas and people. The photo suggested to him a new myth, one of connection and wholeness that could replace myths that produce destructive relationships.[57]

According to Campbell, myths provide models for living, but the models must be appropriate to the present time. What once seemed appropriate may no longer be so. Previous models may not be right for today's world. The virtues of the past can be the vices of today.[58] Dr. Deming's System of Profound Knowledge can be viewed as a new map, a mythology for leadership and for living, one that breaks down barriers and divisions between people and organizations, one that helps individuals to understand that they are part of a larger system and that their well-being is tied into the well-being of that system in business, government, and everywhere in life.

The new mythology requires, in Deming's words, an "outside view," much like a view of earth from space. He said that his System of Profound Knowledge is an outside view.[59] The crisis that Deming addressed is essentially a crisis of mind. We may even call it a *crisis of consciousness*. It continues to our present day, and perhaps it is worse now than when he described it. He called for a way of thinking and being that is rational, sane, and spiritual. He envisioned a whole, healthy individual, not fragmented in thought and action, existing as part of undivided larger wholes, the organizations, families, communities, and nation in which the individuals participate.

Deming criticized the functioning of government. He believed that "the function of government should be to work with business, not to harass business."[60] He was adamant that government regulations can add cost and make America less competitive in the global economy. He said that it is wasteful and ridiculous that people in various industries are prevented by antitrust laws from working together on problems of common interest or that the Interstate Commerce Commission doesn't facilitate cooperation between the various components of the system of commercial transportation.[61] Firm leadership of the executive and legislative branches of government is needed to move into a new world in which industry, government, and education perform as a system.[62] I can imagine that Deming would have been dismayed to see the present failures of our elected officials to work together. Joseph Campbell questioned whether the United States would exist today if the thirteen separate colonies decided that they would be better off as separate and independent nations. Fortunately, they saw mutual benefit from becoming "indivisible" while at the same time respecting their individual interests.[63]

Deming was not political and understood that in order to bring about a transformation of government, he must have the ear of influential officials in government, regardless of political leanings. Newt Gingrich, history professor turned politician, was the only member of Congress willing to have conversations with Deming. These conversations took place during 1991 and 1992 and lasted many hours. Their purpose was to try to convey and understand the implications of Deming's System of Profound Knowledge for governance. Newt told Deming that he thought that Deming understood the twenty-first century better than anyone he had met and that America would not be competitive without an understanding of profound knowledge. When one looks at developments since Deming's passing in 1993, one is struck by the accuracy of Deming's warning that thinking and practices prevalent in business, education, and government were helping us to dig ourselves deeper into a pit.[64]

The new mythology is about creating a whole-in-one where people are able to play in concert in enterprise and in life. The term refers to healthy individuals functioning in an organization with leadership that orchestrates a flow of harmonious relationships to accomplish the aim of the organization. In the English language, the words "whole," "healthy," "healing," and "holy" derive from the same Old English root word *hal* and have closely related meanings.

Being whole and seeing whole is more than seeing the big picture, more than just seeing the forest for the trees. It is understanding the ecology of the forest, knowing the relationships and interactions of all the components and dynamics that give and maintain life to the system as a whole. A business, any organization, is a social ecology where viability requires that the parts be in harmony. That is the function of leadership, to orchestrate a concert of interactions between the players. Deming wrote: "The job of management is not supervision, but leadership. The required transformation of Western style of management requires that managers be leaders." Deming continued that management by numerical goals and other outcomes is not leadership.[65] "The leader has responsibility to improve the system, i.e., to make it possible, on a continuing basis, for everybody to do a better job with greater satisfaction."[66] He believed that understanding of profound knowledge will lead to a transformation of management.

Leaders in organizations, or life, can be prominent if need be, like the conductor of a symphony orchestra. However, leadership doesn't have to be a visible exercise of power. Its purpose is to enable others, to help others develop, as discussed by Robert Greenleaf in his book *Servant Leadership.*[67] It doesn't have to be obtrusive or exercised by an individual who formally is recognized as leader. The individual doesn't have to be in the spotlight to help others, as Robertson Davies wrote in *Fifth Business.*

Deming used the word "spiritual" as part of the wholeness of living, together with the economic-material aspects of living. He considered that both domains were necessary for well-being. The term "spirituality" is derived from the Latin *spiritualitas,* which means to be put in motion, to be spirited, full of life. Over the millennia, it has taken on many meanings, some consistent with wholeness—our connection and relationships, the inner aspects of life and psychological health.

The verb *to map* means to transform from the mental map in the mind of the cartographer to a geographical map. The geographical map enables more people than the cartographer to navigate the territory. Similarly, the score of a musical piece has been mapped from the composer's or arranger's mental map to something physical and visible, such as sheet music. The sheet music is like a geographical map to be navigated by the musicians so they can play in concert as a harmonious whole-in-one. The sheet music becomes, with practice, part of each musician's mental map.

Transformation Paradox

Managers in business, school administrators, and teachers may believe that they have to grade, rate, and rank, to manage by numbers and use other traditional methods because these are necessary to do their job. They may think that they must perpetuate these practices because it is the way it has always been done. They may not be able to envision another way. Therefore, to begin a study of Deming's System of Profound Knowledge requires both a leap of faith that it will have value and curiosity about it. This is a paradox of transformation. The individual starts out on a journey of transformation before even having the map for that journey. Studying the map and integrating it into thinking and acting is the journey.

Another aspect of the paradox is that senior executives and business owners who have the power to transform the management system most likely are in their current positions because of their success applying that system. It may be difficult for some of them to understand that there is any reason that they have to change the system or their methods of managing. After a presentation to senior management of a large company, I was asked why they should believe me, and therefore why believe Deming. They said that the previous week a consultant told them that managing the organization as separate parts, silos, chimneys, as they were now doing, is the right way to manage. In fact, everything he told them supported present practice and therefore contradicted Deming's ideas. Why should they believe me? That is a legitimate question. Why should they? Why should anyone be willing to entertain new possibilities, be willing to learn?

The answer may be prompted with a question: Do you want to continue to face day-to-day problems that are costly in time and resources, or do you want to face the process of change that will eventually dissolve many of the organization's problems and your own problems? Management—anyone—may not know they have a choice of whether to continue to face the continual supply of everyday problems or face the challenge of changing thinking to dissolve the source of problems before they occur rather than solve them after they occur. Deming's way of thinking about a system can help management understand how an organization can create many of its own problems and do a better job of preventing them from occurring. Jim (Mac) McIngvale, the owner of Gallery Furniture in Houston, Texas, accepted the challenge to dissolve the source of his problems and eventually quadrupled his sales volume. He made the change based not on numbers but on a leap of faith that Deming's teaching would help him to put an end to the wasted time and fatigue produced by the problems he continually was facing. This is discussed in chapter 12.

It is not likely to be productive to tell someone directly that they have to change their assumptions, that things will be better if they think and act differently. We human beings tend to become defensive when told that we have to change. We may think we are being told that something is wrong with us; or we may be very comfortable with the ways things are. Deming never told people that they had to accept his ideas. Deming often said that profound knowledge comes by invitation. He mirrored the insight of Plato, "Knowledge which is acquired under compulsion obtains no hold on the mind,"[68] also expressed as, "The teacher can't teach if the student is not ready to learn." A characteristic of a leader is the will and discipline to learn, to take the time to study, practice, and learn from the experience. This learning includes learning about oneself. Leadership requires self-knowledge.

Mythologies about Leaders

There is a myth that leaders are born, that there is a genetic factor that produces leaders. This myth asserts that people simply either have certain leadership qualities or they do not. The management theorist and business school professor Warren Bennis, who studied leadership for decades, believed that leaders are made rather than born.[69] Regardless how much truth there is to the myth that leaders are born, Dr. Deming believed that leadership requires profound knowledge and the values that flow from it. Profound knowledge opens up possibilities for managing our own lives, especially for managing our relationships. It has implications for how we evaluate people and things. We all are, or should be, leaders of our lives. We interact with other people and with the prescriptions and proscriptions of our organization and community cultures. Leadership requires an outside view, which is what Deming said his System of Profound Knowledge offers to us.

The Leadership Transformation: Campbell's Myth of the Hero

Joseph Campbell wrote about the myth of the hero, a story of transformation that appears in many world cultures.[70] The story is about the journey of a person who eventually is transformed into one with the potential for leadership, thus showing the greater possibilities of being human. This myth has formed the basis for many modern stories, notably the *Star Wars* films by George Lucas.

The stories usually are about a man—most of the older hero stories are culturally biased in favor of men—living an ordinary life. The story begins when the future hero is "called" to begin a journey. In some cases, the future hero refuses because of fear of the unknown and the uncertainty of what is to follow. In others, the future hero accepts the challenge for his own reasons and perhaps because of the encouragement of others. This person leaves a familiar and perhaps comfortable situation to face new challenges and difficulties. He learns and develops new capabilities from the wisdom of sages he meets along the way who are willing to teach him. The wisdom of the sage may not be obvious at first. It may even appear foolish. Eventually the future hero recognizes the power, wisdom, and authority of the sage.

The journey transforms the individual into a potential leader, and he must decide whether to take on the challenge of leading. He now has an outside view. He sees the world differently from the culture of the society and the organization. Different values flow from the new knowledge, including self-knowledge. In the myth, when the journey is completed, the individual may decide to reject what has been learned if he thinks he is not up to the role of leader or is too anxious to face an uncertain future.

The Business Owner as Entrepreneur, Leader, and Hero of the Free Market

The economist Dr. Cyril Morong has written about the relationship between economics and mythology. In his paper "The Calling of the Entrepreneur," he writes, "Entrepreneurs are heroes ... Heroes and entrepreneurs are called to and take part in the greatest and most universal adventure that life has to offer: the simultaneous journey of self-discovery, spiritual growth, and the personal creativity they make possible."[71] Morong compares the entrepreneur's adventure to the journey taken by the mythological hero described by Joseph Campbell. Both are about universal human desires and conflicts. The entrepreneur has been called, as the hero is called, to leave the ordinary, predictable, comfortable life. The entrepreneur and the hero are helped by mentors and are humble enough to learn from them.

Morong views the entrepreneur's journey as an adventure undertaken to fulfill some creative destiny, for example to discover a previously undreamt of technique or product that could benefit others. The entrepreneur, as hero, can create beneficial change in a manner suggested by Joseph Schumpeter's theory of entrepreneurship called "creative destruction." A successful entrepreneur simultaneously destroys and creates a new world or a new way of living. The entrepreneur has the vision to anticipate the changing needs of people, the changing market conditions, or the changing desires for products. Morong gives the example of Henry Ford, whose creation of the age of the automobile destroyed the horse-and-buggy age.

"Entrepreneurs," writes Morong, are "masters of two worlds, one of imagination and creativity and the other of material things and business." People become creative when, in the words of Joseph Campbell, they "follow their bliss," when they do what they love to do. The drive comes from within and not outside … from dictates of society. Morong's interpretation of the hero myth aligns with Deming's view that joy in work comes from intrinsic motivation, not from the compulsion of extrinsic forces, even if the individual does not have an entrepreneurial spirit.[72]

America Need Not Commit Suicide

Deming often said that survival is not mandatory for a business. He wrote that in order for a business to survive, management must approach the business with intelligence and perseverance, with constancy of purpose and offer products and services that have a market. The law of survival of the fittest, he wrote, holds in free enterprise.[73]

Deming offered profound knowledge, knowledge that wasn't common or common sense, to business, education, government, parents, to everyone who would listen, in order to get "out of the crisis." He was referring not only to problems that he observed but to a continual supply of problems that could be dissolved with a radical change in thinking. Unless we understand the systemic nature of problems we face—that they are interrelated—the solution to a problem is likely to produce other problems, a "mess," as Russell Ackoff called it. Hence, we need knowledge about what it means "to know" about the way systems behave, about the nature of variation, and about the psychology of human motivation and relationships. This is the substance of Deming's System of Profound Knowledge.

Deming once was asked how he would like to be remembered. "I probably won't even be remembered," he said. After a pause, he added, "Well, maybe … as someone who spent his life trying to keep America from committing suicide." He asked, "How rapidly will American management remove the obstacles that block the road to restoration of American leadership?" He went on to describe the deadly and destructive diseases that have been produced by American management. Only American management can eradicate them.[74] This was decades before the diseases contributed to the economic crises of the early twenty-first century.

Deming sought a transformation, a revolution of thinking, a "map of theory by which to understand the organizations that we work in."[75] The prevailing style of management has led us into decline, "a prison created by the way in which people interact. This interaction afflicts all aspects of our lives—government, industry, education, healthcare." He wrote, for example, "We have been taught by economists that competition will solve our problems. Actually, competition, as it is practiced, is destructive. It would be better if everyone would work together as a system, with the aim for everybody to win".[76] Rather than dog-eat-dog as the guiding principle of competition, he saw cooperation as a tool for competition. One could compete with rather than against. "Competitors are part of the system."[77] "In place of competition for high rating, high grades, to be Number One, there will be cooperation on problems of common interest between people, divisions, companies, competitors, governments, countries. The result will in time be greater innovation, applied science, technology, expansion of market, greater service, greater material reward for everyone."[78]

In the coming chapters, we will explore Deming's System of Profound Knowledge as a map for leading, performing, and living in concert.

Chapter 4

Deming's Masterwork: A Symphony of Profound Knowledge

> Music is a set of relationships. Music is communication.
> —Joshua Redman[79]

Deming advocated that managers and every person willing to learn can begin to exercise leadership in their organizations and in their lives with a map of theory that he called a System of Profound Knowledge.[80] This was the content of his seminars and the foundation of his thinking that guided his questions to managers, students, and others with whom he interacted. In the early 1980s, he did not use the term "System of Profound Knowledge," but the components were the foundation of his teaching. Deming said that his teaching is "based on knowledge of living, knowledge about a system."[81] Therefore, his System of Profound Knowledge is directed not only at the management of organizations but is a mental map to navigate the whole territory of living, which consists of the interrelated activities of work, play, school, and family.

His system consists of four interacting components of knowledge. These parts, when understood as a whole-system of thought, will help individuals gain the insights to provide leadership within organizations and in their lives. We begin to explore the System of Profound Knowledge in this chapter and more deeply in those that follow.

Why Did Deming Call His System of Knowledge "Profound"?

He did not refer to his System of Profound Knowledge in his book *Out of the Crisis*. It appeared later in *The New Economics*.[82] This was not the first time he characterized his knowledge as profound.[83] When asked why he called the content of his teaching "profound knowledge," he replied, "Because it is profound." While various secular, religious, spiritual, philosophical, and scientific writers have described their own work as profound, some writers and their texts have received that laudatory description from others. Religious scholars and wisdom teachers have used the adjective to characterize knowledge that reflects a way of being. Profound knowledge was viewed as a guide to daily living, to the thinking and values that are manifested in the daily conduct of one's life. The intent was to help individuals live a moral life. The term ranges in application and characterization from broad, total knowledge to deep, specialized knowledge. The term has been used to refer to wisdom and to morality. Here is a brief sampling:

Philosophy

"In proportion as the mind is more capable of understanding things by the profound kind of knowledge, it desires more to understand things by that kind."[84]

"Philosophy means the intimate knowledge of the causes and reasons of things, the profound knowledge of the universal order ... in the sense of having for its object the simplest and most general principles, by means of which all other objects of thought are, in the last resort, explained."[85]

Medicine

"... his medical writings show a profound knowledge of ancient Greek authors ..."[86]

Religious and Spiritual Teachings, Practice, and Literature

"… his deep humility, his profound knowledge of the Scriptures and the writings of the Fathers, coupled with his understanding of human nature and its needs, make him a wise and trustworthy counselor to all who seek to know and fulfill the true purpose of human life."[87]

Eastern Thought

"Mental freedom must come from the most profound knowledge of the 'what is what.'" [88]

"The Buddhist system of meditation is based on the most profound knowledge of psychology."[89]

"Impiety is beyond those of profound knowledge."[90]

Deming's System of Profound Knowledge

The four major components of Deming's System of Profound Knowledge are somewhat arbitrary classifications or labels. Four is not sacred. It is where he ended up in the late 1980s in structuring his ideas for teaching purposes. At one time, most of his teaching was conducted under the title "Theory of Variation," even though he touched on all of the components that now constitute his System of Profound Knowledge. A brief description of the components and their relationships is given below. Much more explanation is contained in subsequent chapters.

Theory of Knowledge

Theory of knowledge is the study of how what we think we know and claim to know actually is the way we say it is. The accuracy of prediction is an observable measure of knowledge. Prediction, which can take the form of a plan, a strategy, a decision, or any statement about the future, requires a theory. Accuracy of prediction depends on the extent to which a theory is aligned with the world to which the prediction refers.

Appreciation for a System

The processes of thinking, within business, education, and government organizations, family, and life in general, often are fragmented. Fragmented action derives from fragmented thinking. It is costly materially, psychologically, socially, and spiritually. We tend to separate the various areas of our life—work, play, education, family, spirituality, and so on. We work in organizations where specialists don't communicate with each other, or are unable to do so, because of their specialist languages, or because systems of reward and punishment inhibit communication. We separate individuals into departments, usually organized as command and control, top-down pyramid structures with departments in parallel that never meet. Individuals and departments often are pitted against each other for the appearance of successful performance in order to gain recognition and rewards. Such competition destroys the harmonious functioning of the parts. When this occurs, as it often does in organizations, the quality of products and services is degraded. This affects sales, increases costs, reduces profits, and causes loss of jobs. Organizations are mainly systems of human relationships where individuals should be, but likely are not, communicating and cooperating for the good of the organization and eventually for themselves.

Knowledge of Variation

Since processes vary, the product and service outcomes of those processes vary. Deming's approach to the study of variation provides powerful insights to answer his very important question, "What do the differences mean?" Deming helps us to distinguish systemic causes of problems from unique events. This can reduce costly mistakes and improve the bottom line of the organization and the psychological well-being of employees. Knowledge of variation enables us to understand the irrationality of practices of grading, rating, and ranking of employees in organizations, of students in schools, and of children at home. Deming has provided knowledge about variation that is not taught in typical statistics courses. It tells us, among other things, how to understand how numbers reflect the behavior of processes and how to interpret the numbers.

Knowledge of Psychology

Deming's main message in this part of his System of Profound Knowledge is that our systems of management in business organizations, schools, and family life must be evaluated to understand how they destroy human intrinsic motivation, creativity, imagination, and relationships. Models of human motivation used in business enterprise, schools, and family can no longer be based solely on the results of studies of animals in a cage, whose behavior is manipulated by extrinsic incentives. Individuals need, want, and deserve respect, dignity, and the freedom that goes along with that. People want to be proud of their work and to feel they are making a contribution beyond financial rewards. Intrinsic motivation, motivation from within, is more effective than forces of extrinsic motivation for the long-term health of an organization and its employees.

A Harmonious Whole-System of Knowledge

Although the four components are labeled separately, being a system, they can't be separated in thinking and practice, action, and application. The system, as a whole, is not the simple addition of the components. It is a system, which means that the four parts are inseparable and in a mutually reinforcing relationship, working together to provide knowledge and insight about whatever systems and performance are of interest. In application, the components function as a dynamic system of thought, interacting simultaneously, much like musicians playing in concert. Deming put it this way: "The various segments of the system of profound knowledge proposed here cannot be separated. They interact with each other. Thus, knowledge of psychology is incomplete without knowledge of variation."[91]

Deming did not characterize his System of Profound Knowledge as a symphony. However, I see it as analogous to a symphony with four movements. Each movement is embedded in the whole of the system. The movements are connected to each other. Understanding them as part of a whole makes them more meaningful. I think that this analogy is fitting given Deming's study of music theory, his composing of liturgical pieces, and his scoring of "The Star-Spangled Banner" to *optimize* it for a wider range of singers.[92] In fact, Deming was so accomplished as a musician that on April 3, 1993, an evening dedicated to his music was presented by the Washington Civic Symphony at Constitution Hall in Washington, DC. It was titled "W. Edwards Deming: The Man and His Music."

A symphony is a system. "Symphony" (*syn* means together, *phone* means sounding) conveys the idea of individuals playing in concert, whether in organizations or in life. The symphony score functions as a map of the process for the conductor and the musicians. *Symphony* expresses the movement, flow, fluidity, dynamic relationship of the parts, each of which fits into the composition as a whole. Unlike the traditional music symphony where the normal linear order of the movements does not change from one performance to the next, Deming's symphony when applied is a movement of the whole where all of the parts of knowledge are simultaneously in motion, working together, interacting seamlessly. The philosopher C. I. Lewis, who greatly influenced Deming's thinking about theory of knowledge through his book *Mind and the World Order*, wrote that a person does not hear a symphony in its opening passage, nor in the middle of the second movement, nor in the finale: one hears it and appreciates it as a progressive and cumulative whole.[93]

Deming's System of Profound Knowledge is a symphony of thought that can reach the heart as well as the intellect. Deming did just that in a four-day seminar he conducted for members of the United Auto Workers from Ford Motor Company facilities throughout the United States. Most participants were mesmerized by the words and stories that Deming spoke and the demonstrations he gave. There was a shock of recognition as he described their lives at work as well as a feeling of optimism that there is a better way to manage and be managed.

He was adept at showing empathy for their lives at work and at using humor for comic relief. He communicated optimism that things could be improved. His baritone voice as well as his artistry in the way he spoke and performed were invaluable talents that elevated his stage performances to theater ("theater" and "theory" having the same root) that were somewhat Shakespearian. He was a master of communication and did not hesitate to use metaphorical language if it helped make his points. His presentations were at times serious drama and at other times comedy.

The violinist Hilary Hahn has said that music represents a composer's artistic ideas that are reflections on everything that composers experience. A musical composition comes from the composer's own life story and reflects the things that the composer has been exposed to.[94] Deming's intellectual and spiritual symphony took him a lifetime to compose. He would never finish it because it always was a work in progress. He had developed various parts over the years, documented in a large body of work, including books and papers.[95] He continually elaborated his ideas until his passing. In this sense, Deming's work was unfinished like Schubert's Symphony No. 8 and the unfinished works of other composers and writers.

The Foundation of the 14 Points

Deming's insights about management became widely known in the West when his 14 Points for Management appeared in his book *Quality, Productivity, and Competitive Position*, published in 1982. He expanded on these a few years later in an updated edition of that book under the title *Out of the Crisis* (see appendix). Both books were based on his seminar lecture notes. In the late 1980s, he rarely referred to the "14 Points." He organized his lectures around his System of Profound Knowledge, elaborated in his book *The New Economics for Industry, Government, Education,* first published in 1993, and slightly revised in the second edition, published in 1994.

One may be tempted to draw a matrix relating each of the 14 Points to the separate components of his System of Profound Knowledge. This would violate the system aspects of his thinking. The 14 Points are not independent statements; rather they are interrelated ideas that form a whole-system of thought. In the coming chapters, we will examine the four movements (components) and their relationships to each other and to the symphony (system) as a whole.

FIRST MOVEMENT: THEORY OF KNOWLEDGE

Chapter 5

~

Management Is Prediction

Principles of the theory of knowledge are gravely serious
to those faced with the problems of industry.
—W. Edwards Deming[96]

Theory of knowledge, also known as epistemology, is from the
Greek *episteme*, meaning knowledge, and *logos*, meaning study of. The
philosopher C. I. Lewis presented his theory of knowledge in his book
Mind and the World Order. Deming translated Lewis's ideas into a more
easily understandable language and directed it primarily to management.
Lewis named his approach *conceptual pragmatism*, but Deming did not use
the term, even when referring to Lewis's philosophy. Pragmatism comes
from the Greek words meaning *practice, practical, action*, to *achieve*. The
function of knowledge is to *guide* action rather than to *describe* reality.
Concepts, theories, and hypotheses have value in terms of their usefulness
as means to achieve ends. Lewis wrote: "The practical value of knowledge
is its value as foresight."[97] Lewis described this kind of knowledge as
empirical. Empirical knowledge provides the ability to predict. It gives us
power because it enables us to act in ways to influence the quality of our
future experience, to make a transition from "the actual present to a future
which is desired and which the present is believed to signalize as possible."[98]

In Dr. Deming's view, management in any form is prediction.
Prediction is *inference* about future events since they can't be observed
when the prediction is made. Knowledge makes prediction possible.[99]
Knowledge *gives* power to management to bring about the future it wants

for the organization. It can help each of us to produce the future that we want and prevent or avoid what we don't want.

Deming made a distinction between information and knowledge. Information is not sufficient for making predictions. Knowledge enables prediction, and it requires theory. A dictionary provides information. One must have a theory to apply to the information, to the data. A dictionary will not write an essay. Theory makes it possible to use information. Knowledge comes from theory. Without theory, there is no way to use the information that comes to you. Without interpretation enabled by theory, there is no learning, no knowledge. There is no experience. Experience has no meaning. Theory makes experience possible. Without theory, one doesn't know what questions to ask or how to interpret the answers. Without theory, you have nothing to revise, nothing to learn.[100] There is no learning, no progress without theory. Deming gave the example of the kind of grade school exam he preferred. Rather than a test that asked a student to name the major cities of various states, his test would ask why they came to be major cities. Minneapolis, for example, became head of navigation because of its position on the Mississippi River. In addition, geography would be taught in the context of a system of knowledge, which included economics, history, sociology, and anthropology.[101]

Empirical Knowledge

The word "knowledge" in the writing of Lewis and Deming means "empirical knowledge." Knowing the world is not simply a matter of passively sensing it. The mind of each person actively participates in creating what that person knows. It depends on what is sensed and then is interpreted by a person's active mind using a priori concepts, such as theories and models. These a priori concepts are so called because they precede a sense experience (i.e., the individual brings them to the experience). Thus mind and experience are inseparable and influence each other. Theory makes possible interpretation of experience, and experience either strengthens or weakens degree of belief in the theory.[102]

Walter Shewhart observed that formal mathematical a priori concepts, such as limits and continuity, exist in the mind and can't be proven to exist in the physical world, yet they work.[103] Deming once was asked why the normal curve (distribution), a pure concept, works. He said, "That's a good question," and left it there. His answer may have been his way of saying that is the nature of formal a priori concepts, as Shewhart observed about mathematical concepts.

Management Is Prediction

Deming's criterion of knowledge is whether it helps us to predict and not whether we discover truth, because there is no such thing in the domain of empirical knowledge. In the empirical world, statements are only probable rather than true and absolute. If we can *predict*, then we have *knowledge*. We could have a beautifully constructed theory that has little or no relevance to the real problems that people face. Euclidean geometry, Plato's forms, the normal curve, and other examples of abstract reasoning are true in their own world of mind, regardless of whether they apply to the empirical world. A theory that is internally consistent (i.e., true in its own world) has construct validity but may not have predictive validity. We learn about the ability of a theory to help us in predicting by structuring our predictions to be testable by empirical investigation. A theory is evaluated by future experience, whether in science, in management, or in everyday living. Theories can be revised as learning occurs, and as evidence accrues, we increase or decrease our degree of belief in their ability to help us predict.

Humans have the ability to apply knowledge to anticipate the future, not just to react to the present. To be able to say one *knows* means that one is able to predict, with some degree of certainty, the consequences of one's own actions or that of others. Knowledge makes it possible to go beyond specific data and observations and make predictions that apply over a greater spread of time and place. Knowledge grows through systematic revision and extension of theory based on how things turn out. If a theory is shown to be inadequate, if it's limited in its ability to help us predict, it should be revised or replaced. If a theory is taken to be truth, it can't change, so there is no learning.[104]

Any rational plan is a prediction of future performance and outcomes. Deming was amused by the cartoon "Diary of a Cat," which he saw in the *New Yorker* magazine.[105] Each day is the same as the day before. Wake up and there is the food; finish eating and there is the ball of yarn.

Play with the yarn. There is no need for theory if you don't have to plan for tomorrow. Without theory, humans can't interpret experience, can't make meaningful changes. We need knowledge. Knowledge has temporal spread. Knowledge comes from theory.

When a theory predicts without fail for a range of phenomena, it is said to be a law. Deming used the example of gravity. He was very sure that anywhere he dropped a pencil it would fall downward. He demonstrated. The result was always the same, he said. However, the laws of nature don't exist out there—outside our mind; they exist in our minds. The descriptions and names we give to things are creations of the human mind, not the things to which they refer. "Gravity" is a word that represents a complex physical phenomenon that is not well understood, except perhaps by Einstein.[106]

Walter Shewhart described three essential components of knowledge: (1) the data of experience in which the process of knowing begins, (2) the prediction of data that one would expect to get in the future, and (3) the degree of belief in the prediction based on evidence. This corresponds to the statement by C. I. Lewis that knowledge begins in the original data or observation and ends in the predicted data or observation. If the prediction is verified, the degree of belief in the theory is strengthened. Shewhart wrote that this is not as abstract as it appears. It applies to everyday experience, such as predicting the weather.[107]

Deming was concerned about the absence of theory of knowledge in textbooks and in the teaching of management and administration. He asked, how can you do business or understand performance specifications for products, medicines, and human effort without such knowledge?

"Practice is more exacting than pure science," said Walter Shewhart. Deming explained this: The standards of knowledge and workmanship required in industry and public service are more severe than those of pure science. If the applied scientist were to act upon the meager evidence sometimes available to the pure scientist, he would make the same mistakes in estimates of accuracy and precision and know that because of those mistakes someone may lose a lot of money, suffer physical injury, or both. In addition, in industry, the specifications of quality may become the basis of contractual agreement, and indefiniteness in the meaning of terms used in a specification may lead to misunderstanding and even to legal action.[108]

Benchmarking, the copying of processes and methods of other companies, can do more harm than good. Deming wrote, "To copy an example of success, without understanding it with the aid of theory, may lead to disaster."[109] If you copy, do you understand _if and why_ it worked in that enterprise? The business being copied may appear healthy, but behind the apparent success, it could be in decline. The reported numbers may look good, but do you know how the company achieved high sales figures? Perhaps they were shipping empty boxes in order to record a sale. In the 1980s, managers of American firms who were losing market share to Japanese firms made numerous trips to Japan to learn about their methods to improve quality and productivity. What they got was information about methods—Kanban, Just-in-Time, statistical process control—not knowledge or understanding of why they worked. When the managers returned home, they copied what they saw, such as limited parts inventory in the plant. They failed to see other parts of the system that made Kanban feasible, such as the support of capable suppliers and the plant's own capability to produce nondefective parts so as to ensure they would not have parts shortages.

Deming had a similar criticism of the use of case studies used in business schools without an integrating theory to understand the underlying theory and principles of a system. The student needs to see the _whole_ picture. Dr. Jay Forrester, founder of the field of system dynamics and mentor to many contemporary system and learning organization teachers and consultants, had similar concerns about management education. Courses are taught by functional area in the same way that interactions between separate areas of the business are not obvious. Understanding and managing a business as an integrated system is not taught.[110]

Theory is necessary for all of us in our work lives and in daily living. Theory helps us to order experience. Deming explained it this way: "Experience alone, without theory, teaches management nothing about what to do to improve quality and competitive position, nor how to do it. If experience alone would be a teacher, then one may well ask why are we in this predicament?"[111] "In fact, experience cannot even be recorded unless there is some theory, however crude, that leads to a hypothesis and a system by which to catalog observations. Sometimes only a hunch, right or wrong, is sufficient theory to lead to useful observation."[112]

"Without a theory, any prediction, and any decision based thereon, is risky. The day has past when 'theoretical' means impractical."[113]

Dr. Deming asked a manager in a large company how he would know if problems were due to the system or due to specific, local, identifiable causes. When the manager answered that they rely on their experience, Deming knew that the man had incriminated himself. "How could he know?" This was a favorite Deming expression. Without appropriate theory of variation, he could not know what questions to ask or interpret the answers.[114] He did not know and apply appropriate knowledge to make sense of his experience and act constructively.

Conversely, theory without experience in application also has little practical value. The philosopher Epictetus said that theories should be treated as sheep eat grass. They don't throw up the grass before it is digested. Rather, after it is digested, they produce wool and milk. Theories should be digested inwardly and then be manifested in action.[115]

A theory can be internally consistent in its own world of thought, but it may not apply to the visible world, or if it does, its usefulness for application may be limited. The invisible world of Newton's theories helped engineers design and build the visible world in which we live, but it can't predict the behavior of particles in the subatomic world. The theories of Neils Bohr, Werner Heisenberg, and others in the field of quantum physics better address the properties of the subatomic world. Objects that we experience every day as solid are viewed from theories of quantum physics as particles in motion with lots of space in between them. However, theories of quantum physics should not replace Newton's laws in our daily lives, which are better for predicting the outcomes of ignoring traffic lights when walking or driving. It is safer for us to think of ourselves and vehicles as solid rather than as particles separated by a lot of space.

When we hear the word "theory," we may think of formal scientific theories, such as those in physics or medicine. Yet we all live by our own theories that come from prior learning and social conditioning. Deming said that even a simple hunch can function as a theory. We may not be conscious of holding and living by a theory, but when we cross a street when the electronic sign shows "walk," we are acting according to a theory that predicts that vehicles will stop. If they don't, we have to revise our theory, if we are able.

Deming's favorite illustration of the usefulness of a theory, even if it is logical in its own world of thought, is the application to a curved surface of Euclidean plane geometry, the geometry of a flat, two-dimensional surface.[116] It applies beautifully to a flat surface where the angles of a triangle add to 180 degrees but not to a curved surface where that is not the case. For example, the curvature of the earth must be considered when building structures such as highways and bridges that span substantial distances. If the length and force of the cables that span the bridge towers are calculated based on the straight-line distance at their base, there can be a problem when they are attached at the top of the towers. The tops of the towers may lean slightly away from each other, and the cables may be too short or more taut than originally calculated. The structure of thinking provided by spherical geometry aligns better with a curved earth. However, Deming did mention that when flying over the farmland of the US Midwest, a person might conclude that the earth really is flat.

This misapplication of theory, or the wrong theory, made me question something I learned in my graduate studies in industrial and organization psychology about the rating methods that management uses to evaluate employees. The measurement theory behind the methods is logical, well thought out, and useful for the evaluation of the characteristics and performance of materials and other nonhuman objects. I later learned from Deming how rating and ranking and grading of people as applied in business organizations, schools—everywhere—is based on the wrong application of measurement methods because the underlying theory doesn't provide a sound basis for prediction. It is like applying Euclidean geometry to a curved surface when spherical geometry is needed.

Just as plane geometry has limits of application, so does theory of variation, which will be discussed in later chapters. Theory of variation, also called statistical theory, is an aid to management. It is not a substitute for knowledge and theory in engineering, psychology, economics, and so on. It will not in itself determine the right question or right answer, the correct definition of age or occupation, the criteria for pass and fail or good and bad. It does help to measure differences in performance in order to isolate and manage sources of variation.[117]

Deming's Plan, Do, Study, Act Cycle

Deming's Plan, Do, Study, Act (PDSA) cycle is a process to gain empirical knowledge by applying and evaluating theories, formal or informal, in order to learn, to improve, and maybe by serendipity to innovate. Innovation can occur during the cycle, but as Deming often said, we can't plan to make a discovery. Two components work together in the cycle: the invisible world of theory and observation of the visible world.

Dr. Deming brought the cycle, which he called the Shewhart Cycle, and others call the Deming Cycle, into the general theory of management. When we are aware of our theory and can see how well it helps to predict, we can either strengthen our belief in it or revise or discard it. We are continually predicting in the form of anticipating future events. Whether or not we are consciously aware, we bring prior knowledge to the process of observation. We see particular events and take them to confirm or disconfirm our theory. Even when informally planning our lives, we probably follow a process where we make a prediction based on a hunch or speculation or educated guess and based on the outcomes revise our hunch or strengthen or weaken our degree of belief in our theory.

Shewhart's Method for Statistical Control of Quality in Mass Production Processes	Scientific Method
Specification	Hypothesis
Production	Experiment
Inspection	Test of Hypothesis (Comparison of Results with Prediction)

Table 5-1. Dynamic processes of acquiring knowledge

Table 5-1 presents Deming's summary of the concepts behind Shewhart's cycle.[118] Shewhart said that it may be helpful to think of the steps shown on the left side of table 5-1 as corresponding to the steps in the scientific method shown on the right side of table 5-1. Shewhart described his cycle as a "dynamic scientific process of acquiring knowledge."[119] Deming emphasized that Shewhart's cycle aligned with the scientific method as it applied to the statistical control of mass production processes.

The scientific method provides a means to visualize the act of control as a scientific one.

Deming extended and modified Shewhart's three-step cycle. He did not say that *his* PDSA cycle *was* scientific method, although others have characterized it that way. As Deming developed his cycle over the years, it evolved to encompass a broader, general application in consumer research, product design, process design, agriculture, and any areas of business, education, government, and living. He called it a "flow diagram for learning, and for improvement of a product or of a process."[120]

The Four Stages of the Deming Cycle[121]

Plan: Planning is prediction, and strategically it can have two kinds of aims—passive and active. In *passive planning*, the future is forecasted by an organization or individual in order to *adapt* to a future that someone else has planned. This is the strategy of fast followers who study the advances in product, service, and technology developed and marketed by others and then copy and sell them, supposedly legally. *Active planning* is aimed at *shaping* a future to an organization's or individual's own vision, as does an innovative company that others try to copy.

"A system includes the future," said Deming.[122] Planning is guided by long-term purpose in order to create a desired future, actively or passively. The design of a new product or service is a prediction. Personnel practices such as selection, assignment, and promotion are predictions. Planning is the responsibility of management and may be delegated to a team with substantive knowledge in specific areas, such as chemistry, engineering, economics, marketing, medicine, and especially knowledgeable statisticians.[123] In addition to their special expertise, the individuals doing the planning, as a group, should have sufficient knowledge of the organization as a system so that they can predict the effects of the plan—within the organization and its environment—when it is carried out in the next stage.[124]

Evaluating the morality and ethics of plans is a matter of predicting the consequences of action. C. I. Lewis warned that much of human behavior, for which we must be responsible, is rarely a result of explicit foresight and assignment of values, and that much of people's actions, for which they are held legally accountable, could not be regarded as taken with prevision and evaluation of consequences. Behavior, rather than being thoughtful, results from automatic responses or habits without assessment of consequences.[125]

Problems of management in general are similar, although the specifics depend on the processes, products, services, and the costs of errors and poor quality. The further out in time you look, the less relevant are the figures you have, and the more theory you need. Deming observed that when machines are turning out piece parts by the thousands or even millions monthly, it does not take long to see predictions tested out. In agriculture, years are often required. A crop must be sowed and harvested again and again until the evidence is definitely for or against the prediction that one treatment is actually better than another, and by the time the question is settled, the prediction may be forgotten.[126]

Do: Planning involves a lot of thinking and communicating. We may think that doing is visible. Yet thinking is doing but is invisible. When people are sitting and thinking, individually or together, they may appear not to be doing. When pressure is on, there may be a tendency to rush through the planning process in order to get to the visible doing. Pressure, in the form of "don't sit there, do something," always threatens to disrupt the smooth unfolding of any process.

Poor planning can have expensive consequences. If the plan is viewed also as part of a process of organization learning, it may be a good idea to carry it out on a small scale and see if results suggest that it be implemented on a large scale. In the case of production, for example, offline production can be done in parallel to regular production. Consumer research is doing, carrying out the planned study.

Study: Evaluate the results. A study is undertaken to improve the future performance of a product or service by action on a system of processes. What was learned? Which of various methods, materials, equipment, training, or other process variables and environmental conditions were better than the others? How good were our predictions, our expectations? Should we modify our theories? If we didn't have the outcomes we expected, can we view the process as one of learning, not of failure?

Act: Unfortunately, fear and political considerations may hide results and block or delay application of the knowledge gained. A senior executive told me the story of when he was a young engineering manager working on the development of an industrial engine. In order to be commercially viable, the engine had to run for two thousand hours without failure before it needed maintenance. Testing showed that the engine would run only an average of five hundred hours before failure. In a review with senior executives, the manager explained the challenges, even though his immediate management did not want to reveal the problems, hoping they could overcome them. Senior management appreciated his candid assessment of the likely future of the engine and canceled the program. The executive, who later became one of the top five officers of the firm, told me that he thought he might be fired but knew that it was in the best interests of the firm to cancel the program. Obviously, his decision didn't hurt his career but rather it made clear to top management his leadership qualities.

Use of the PDSA cycle in a given context should not be a one-time effort. Empirical knowledge is never complete. The world keeps changing, the observer keeps changing, and a theory reaches its limits of application. As resources, priorities, and needs allow, the cycle should be repeated in a continuing process to learn and improve. In this sense, the PDSA cycle has a purpose similar to the scientific method. Verification of predictions increases confidence in a theory. If the theory improves prediction over some other theory, one's confidence in the theory increases, and knowledge and learning increase.

Knowledge is communicated by statements and by action. A statement conveys knowledge when it predicts the future with some degree of accuracy and it fits observations of the past. The more often our predictions are confirmed, the stronger is our degree of belief that the theory is valid and useful. Yet, no matter how strong our degree of belief is, we should keep in mind that empirical knowledge is probable and never completely verified. Empirical knowledge is in the form of judgments made at some particular present moment. Just as a flowing stream is ever changing as it passes a point, no one can have the same empirical knowledge twice because new and pertinent experience is always flowing into one's perception.[127] In this complex, continually changing world, there is no end to knowledge, no end to obtaining a richer view of the world. Therefore degree of belief can't be quantified as 90 percent or 95 percent certain or with other levels of confidence, as we often see in research papers and statistics books.

Chapter 6

Map and Territory of the Observer

Everything that we see in life is something of a shadow
cast by that which we do not see. Plato was right:
"The visible is a shadow cast by the invisible."
—Martin Luther King Jr.[128]

The allegory of the cave in Plato's *Republic* tells of human beings who lived since childhood in a dark cave, shackled so they couldn't move their bodies, not even their heads. They faced a wall. Above and behind them was a fire that cast the shadows of themselves and the people and objects behind them moving in front of the fire. The visible shadows were their reality. The source of what they were seeing was invisible to them. They did not have the knowledge to understand that the world they could not see contributed to the world they could see.[129]

Dr. Deming used a metaphor similar to Plato's cave that expressed his concern about the effects of management's lack of the knowledge necessary to be competitive in a global economy. He wrote: "It is only by illumination of outside knowledge that we may observe that we are in a pit."[130]

E. F. Schumacher, economist, thought leader, and statistician, wrote about this theme in *A Guide for the Perplexed*:

> We do not understand that life, before all other definitions
> of it, is a drama of the visible and the invisible. There is
> the external world, in which things are visible, i.e., directly
> accessible to our senses; and there is "inner space" where

things are not directly accessible to us … we live in visible humanity, a humanity of appearances. All our thoughts, emotions, feelings, imaginations, reveries, dreams, fantasies, are invisible. All that belongs to our scheming, planning, secret ambitions, all our hopes, fears, doubts, perplexities, all our affections, speculations, ponderings, vacuities, uncertainties, all our desires, longings, appetites, sensations, our likes, dislikes, aversions, loves and hates— all are themselves invisible. They constitute oneself.[131]

The invisible world can be thought of as an internal map of the visible world, the external territory to which the map refers. However, in the discussions that follow, we will see that they are woven together and often hard to separate.

Map and Territory

Many years ago, Alfred Korzybski, in his book *Science and Sanity*, introduced the metaphor *map and territory* to distinguish the invisible mental maps that we have in our heads from the visible territory to which the maps refer. This is the foundation of a discipline, originated by Korzybski, called *general semantics*, which is about our processes of thinking, our views and interpretation of objects and events, and how they affect our relationships.[132]

When I first read Korzybski's book and considered the idea of map and territory, it was for me a key to unlocking the meaning in the writings of philosophers, which usually I found obtuse. Most of us may find philosophy texts hard to navigate since, as a philosophy professor once told me, philosophers write for other philosophers, not for the general public. That is unfortunate because philosophy can be very useful for thinking about the problems we face in management and in life in general. Dr. Deming was a master at translating the complex (to me, unnecessarily complex) conceptual maps from philosophy, mathematics, physics, and statistics into maps that could be more easily understood and productively applied. In the terminology of Alfred Korzybski's discipline of general semantics, the objects and events in the territory, which Lewis calls "given," are abstracted by the sensory system and then further abstracted conceptually by our mental map.

Dr. Deming frequently referred to the influence of the book *Mind and the World Order* by the philosopher C. I. Lewis on his own approach to theory of knowledge. Korzybski quoted Lewis a number of times in his book. Lewis, like Deming, did not use the term "map and territory" but succinctly expressed the concept: "There are, in our cognitive experience, two elements; the immediate data, such as those of sense, which are presented or given to the mind, and a form, construction, or interpretation, which represents the activity of thought."[133] *Territory* refers to the world of energy outside of our bodies that provides the given that is sensed and then converted or abstracted to the language, images, and symbols of our mental maps. The mental map interprets sensory information and gives it meaning. As with a geographical map, a mental map is an abstraction of the territory. All we can know about the territory is in our map, and much of the detail in the territory does not get on the map.

Mental map is used here to refer to a dynamic *system* of interacting mental processes, patterns of thinking that include an individual's knowledge, theories, models of cause-and-effect relationships, values, beliefs, assumptions, stories and myths, images, biases, prejudices, categories, labels, and other abstractions.

The philosopher and scientist Michael Polanyi regarded theory as a "kind of map extended over space and time."[134] This is a definition consistent with Deming's views of knowledge, influenced by Lewis, that theory is a map and that knowledge has temporal spread. It also aligns with Korzybski's view that knowledge is time binding, meaning that knowledge in communities and cultures advance from the gains of each preceding generation, which is another way to say that we stand on the shoulders of those who came before us.

In Walter Shewhart's book *Statistical Method from the Viewpoint of Quality Control*, which Deming edited, Shewhart discussed the idea of map and territory without using those terms. He wrote that there are at least three important aspects to every symbol: (1) the relation of the symbol to the objective thing symbolized, (2) the relation of the symbol to the individual or group interpreting the symbol, and (3) the relation of a symbol to other symbols.[135]

Thinking, Thought, and Consciousness

Mentally mapping the sensed external world to the internal world of mind is a dynamic process that we call by various names, such as thinking, reasoning, inferring, imagining, judging, reacting, evaluating, feeling, and believing.

The word *think* comes from Old English and means "to conceive, form, imagine, and have in the mind." Thinking is a process of movement. Thinking is present tense. It occurs in the present moment, as in "I am thinking," or "I think." Thinking is an active state of being conscious of something that we are observing in the moment or that we have previously observed or thought about and have recalled from memory. Consciousness, also called sentience and subjectivity, is our awareness of what we are thinking and observing in the present moment.

Thoughts are the results of previous thinking and observations stored in memory. Thoughts are coded in various ways—as symbols, words, images, formulas. Thinking often is called a thought process, but a thought has already been produced by the process of thinking, as when we say, "I have a thought," or, if referring to previous thinking, "I thought." When thinking, we recall thoughts from memory as if we were looking at a previously drawn map, an abstract representation of a territory. The physicist David Bohm, who also theorized about consciousness, said that memory also is movement in the brain. It is more than just something stored up.[136]

The origin of "map" is *mappa mundi*, Latin for "sheet of the world." A geographical map is an abstraction of the physical territory, a representation of the parts and their relationships that the mapmaker considers important in light of the purpose of the map and how it should be used. A geographical map divides the territory—land or sea or sky—according to the purpose and mental map of the maker of the physical map. The physical map can overlay on the territory political boundaries, such as counties, states, or provinces, or administrative boundaries, such as sales regions and school districts. Thus the map will enable or cause individuals to perceive the territory differently, depending on their purposes and needs as well as their biases.

The cartographer J. B. Harley described geographical maps of the physical world as "unique systems of signs, whose codes may be at once iconic, linguistic, numerical, and temporal, and as a spatial form of knowledge."[137] Our own mental maps also represent the territory symbolically.

C. I. Lewis said that when we speak, we are abstracting.[138] Language doesn't enable us to describe to others the complexity and detail of the world we sense. It should seem obvious that our words are not the actual objects and events to which they refer. Reading the menu or the recipe is not the same experience as eating the meal. To say "apple" doesn't communicate to others our individual experience of seeing or tasting an apple, even when we qualify our experience with adjectives such as sweet or bitter. Yet words about an object, event, or person can produce emotions similar to actually seeing them.

Since we are unable to sense everything in the territory and cannot describe completely what we do sense, we have to rely on our maps—geographical and mental—to navigate. A map is not a complete representation of the territory. A map is not in a one-to-one relationship with the territory. If all the detail of the entire territory were on the map, besides being unwieldy, the map would not be needed. The cartographer David Turnbull highlighted this relationship between a geographical map and the physical territory:

> If the map were identical with the territory it would literally be the territory. It would have a scale of an inch to the inch and, apart from anything else, it would be unworkable as a map since you would have to be standing on it or in it. Lewis Carroll described such a map in Sylvie and Bruno Concluded. In this fantasy, a Professor explains how his country's cartographers experimented with ever larger maps until they finally made one with a scale of a mile to a mile. "It has never been spread out, yet," he says. "The farmers objected: they said it would cover the whole country, and shut out the sunlight! So now we use the country itself, as its own map, and I assure you it does nearly as well."[139]

Our mental map is in a reciprocal relationship, a continual loop, with the world since the observer's map interprets what is observed, and what is observed shapes and produces the observer's actions on the environment. David Bohm recalled an experience when he was about twelve years old, exploring in the Pennsylvania mountains with other boys, and they had to cross a stream. There were lots of rocks. He was afraid until he realized that even though he couldn't simply step across because the rocks were small and far apart, if he jumped from one to another, kept moving, pivoting from one rock to the next, he could get across. Bohm's point was that consciousness is like that movement ... awareness moment by moment.[140]

Our mental maps help us to navigate the territory of living. They represent what's *out there*, from the route to return home from work, the meaning of traffic signals that we observe, to more complex maps that represent our thinking about politics, economics, work, family, other people, and things. Mental maps can contain scientific theories, religious theologies, mental models, and the theories, hunches, beliefs, and biases of everyday thinking. To say that a person's mental map is not *the* territory means that our individual perceptions of reality are unique to each of us. Our individual map is the territory for each of us. The territory that we know is *our* territory. Every person's experience is subjective. We each have our own maps, our own representations, our own versions of reality, and our own needs. Being aware of this and having insight into our own map can help managers and coworkers, teachers and students and parents get beyond disagreements about who is "right" and "wrong," appreciate that others see the world differently than we do, and work together to dissolve problems. It can greatly facilitate communication, reduce conflict, and facilitate cooperative and constructive human relationships. This is essential for the productive conduct of business and all of the other social interactions of people.

It would help to be conscious of the *what is* that we perceive—that what we are aware of is on our map and *is not* the territory. Our sensory system has abstracted only some of the energy impinging on it, and then our minds have translated the sensations to words and images, which we use to think about that experience. The map *is not* the territory; our image of the meal we will have at the restaurant is not the meal, nor is the menu. Other people *are not* what we think and say about them. Our categories and descriptions of other people, especially our use of the words *is* and *are*, refer to our thoughts about them and not to them. When we use *is* and *are*, we attribute a characteristic to something outside of us. When we say that something *has* value or *is* valuable, we imply that the value exists in the object or activity, that its value is inherent in the thing being evaluated. However, since not everyone finds the same things valuable, value can't be an inherent characteristic of things in the territory. Value, to use a cliché, *is* in the eye of the beholder, in their map. Most of us probably have thought or said at one time something to the effect that one person's trash is another person's gold. Some attribute aesthetic value to art, some see economic value, some value the artist's technique. You can't assume that other people share your values and knowledge. Russell Ackoff often said that it is not rational to tell someone, "If I were you, I wouldn't do that," because if you were that person, you would do that.

The invisible world of mental maps does not have the physical properties that we associate with the visible world. Geographical maps are physical expressions of the mapmaker's mental map.

Mental maps cannot be represented by replicas or scale models or literal pictures. They have no physical properties. There is no unit of measure that we can apply. They can't be weighed, although we do speak of things weighing heavily on our mind. But they produce things that are visible. Units of measure in the physical world, such as units of weight, length, and movement, came from concepts in mental maps. They have been devised to help humans advance their knowledge of the visible world. We also make our maps visible through speaking and writing and performances such as acting, dancing ... and managing.

Boundaries of Mental Maps

Cartographers have defined geographical maps as "graphic representations that facilitate a spatial understanding of things, concepts, conditions, processes, or events in the human world."[141] This also characterizes the boundaries of a mental map. C. I. Lewis wrote that experience is a process that extends over time and space. Past and future exist in our maps. The past is brought into the present through memory. The *possible* experience of the future is brought into the present through prediction.[142] Only the immediate moment exists, and once we think about that moment, it has passed. The "now" is a continual actuality. "Someday" exists only in thought, on the map. Only a plan followed by action can make someday happen. Thus our maps, with their accumulated knowledge, enable us to transcend by interpretation what is given to the senses in the immediate moment.[143]

When a geographical map is constructed, conceptual boundaries are overlaid, imposed on the territory for political, social, economic, business, and other purposes. Each of us is like a cartographer of our own mind, mapping the territory of life, creating boundaries, drawing lines on our mental maps. Thought can do just two things, according to C. I. Lewis. It can separate by analysis entities that are not separated in time or space, and it can join together by synthesis entities that exist separately.[144] In other words, our mental processes of abstraction can create differences where there are none and can bring together into a whole objects and events that are separated in time and place. This idea is critical to managing wholes rather than individual parts and for evaluation, especially of people. We use the abstractions of language, such as labels and categories, to divide and separate things and people.

We draw boundary lines in our mental maps with words, and these boundaries appear to exist in the territory. Although the distinctions are in our mind, they are not seen as abstractions produced by thinking but as things in themselves. Some of the differences are based on concrete differences that are observed like physical-geographical boundaries of land, mountains, rivers, and oceans when viewing earth from space. Political and other human-made boundaries can't be seen when standing back and viewing earth as a natural, whole-system.

Our mental maps, with their theories, models, and values, define the boundaries that separate the parts or join them into a system. Any *system* is defined by the boundaries we establish, where we draw the lines. We see lines, and then we reify them, treat them as concrete. For example, we may imagine that people are *inputs* to the process along with materials, electricity, and other factors that produce outputs. Maps can be qualitatively changed with new knowledge and new understandings. We can redraw boundaries to view people not as inputs but as managers of the process.

A geographical map can help us navigate accurately or can lead us astray. A map, geographical or mental, is useful to the extent that its structure aligns with the territory, something that can be known as a result of prediction. If a geographical map depicts a structure different from the territory, such as placing the cities in the wrong order and in the wrong spatial relationships, then the map is less than useless. We discover this when we end up in the wrong place or take the long way to reach our destination, especially when time is a critical factor.

The mental map, as a whole-system of thought, contains past, present, and future, yet all of the whole is not in awareness at the same time. When I first joined Ford and visited the assembly plants, I marveled at the complete vehicles being driven off the end of the line. I naively wondered, *Is there anyone who understands the whole Ford Motor Company system of design and engineering, finance, purchasing, manufacturing, and all of the other systems that contributed to production of the final product?* I soon realized that there was no single individual who could have a map with such detail and complexity so that they could "see" the business as a whole-system, not even Henry Ford II when he was chairman of the board. Perhaps his grandfather, Henry Ford, did have a whole-system map when he started the company. I was amused when Ford Vice President Jim Bakken told me that in the early days the company was totally integrated because Henry Ford held the board of directors meetings in his head. I suppose this is still possible with small, privately held businesses, but the top executive, who may be the owner, does need the feedback to know if his or her map is aligned with the territory. We have to keep in mind that employees, suppliers, and customers are separated in time and place but connected by the contributions of their functions and actions to the whole.

Appearance and Reality

"Reality is not an exhibit for man's inspection, labeled, 'Do not touch.' There are no appearances to be photographed, no experiences to be copied, in which we do not take part."
—J. Bronowski[145]

Our maps are for each of us our reality. What we call *reality* is an interaction, a joint product of the observer and the observed. This idea was illuminated many years ago by the philosopher Immanuel Kant. He said that we can't know the thing in itself; we can't separate the object—the thing known—from the subject, the knower. We can only know things as they appear to us, only as we perceive them. We cannot know with certainty what the world is like in itself, but we can know what it is like for ourselves. It must be known through the mind. Kant discussed this concept in his various books, including *Prolegomena*,[146] which I once saw open on Deming's desk.

Theory is not only a way to look at things, but it also *shapes the appearance* of those things. Seen with a different theory, objects have a different appearance. What is invisible from one theory, especially one particular theory of management, may be visible, illuminated, by another theory. Theory is seeing with the *eye of mind*. It seems to me that the greater power to influence the future lies in the invisible world of theory. Theories are a means to learn and improve and to bring about a revolution in management practice. Of course, it depends on the theory that is applied. Usefulness, not truth, is the appropriate criterion to evaluate a theory.

A theory is a component of a person's mental map. The word *theory* has the same root as the word *theater*.[147] It comes from the Greek *theoria*, which has a number of meanings, including viewing, looking at, and being aware of the abstract thinking involved in contemplating and speculating what is behind the appearance of what has been viewed. David Bohm characterized theory as a theater of the mind that gives insight into what is seen. He explained it with the following example where he uses the terms "appearance" and "essence," which I think have meanings similar to "map" and "territory." Let's say we are looking at a solid, circular object. Depending on where we stand, it may appear to us as an ellipse. The ellipse is the appearance; the circle is the essence. On another level, the circle is the appearance, and atoms moving around in mostly open space are the essence. But from another perspective, atoms become the appearance, and electrons become the essence. This suggested to Bohm that even our thoughts are how things appear to the mind. The "what is" depends on one's perspective.[148]

Our maps give us different points of view, different interpretations, and different recommendations for action. Russell Ackoff has used the metaphor of orange slices to illustrate how individuals, looking at the same objects or events, interpret them differently. The cross-sectional view of an orange sliced vertically is different from the view one gets when it is sliced horizontally, yet both are views of the same thing.[149] Ackoff explained this with an example. When asked, "What is a hospital?" three people answered from their own slice of the orange. The physician viewed it as a place to practice medicine. The patient saw it as a place to be cured, to get well. A member of hospital administration saw it as a place to care for sick patients or to prevent illness. This raises the question: Is there such a thing as "the hospital" or is it "my hospital"? Harry Weinberg, in his book *Levels of Knowing and Existence*, made the point that since the territory exists in the map of each individual, when I leave the office, so does the image or idea of the desk. When I think about that thing I saw in the office, it is not *the desk*, it is *my desk* since it is in my thoughts. A map is unique to each individual.[150]

Deming did not use the metaphor of map and territory; however, he did describe his System of Profound Knowledge as a *map of theory* by which to understand the organizations in which we work. In the same paragraph, he also used "lens" to describe his system of profound knowledge.[151] "Lens" refers to seeing with the eye, as if Deming's System of Profound Knowledge were new eyeglasses. Deming also described "theory" as "a window into the world."[152] Deming's map of theory refers to seeing with the eye of mind, which enables us to see with better illumination beyond what the eye can see.

I once participated in a discussion about theory with Dr. Deming and a few other people. One person said that he thought that before one has a theory one first observes and then by inductive reasoning develops a theory to account for the observation. Deming replied that people have known for years that there is no observation without theory. Without theory, data are meaningless. Observation requires a priori knowledge. The premise that we can observe without theory, without a priori knowledge, represents the theory of knowledge of seventeenth- and eighteenth-century empiricists. They argued that we observe only through the senses and that ideas come to the mind after sensory experience. It seems to be that this view, itself being a theory, refutes its own premise since the philosopher-experimenter observes the observer with the a priori theory of not having a theory. He draws his conclusions with a theory biased against the role of mind.

The philosophy of conceptual pragmatism and the thinking of Kant, Korzybski, and scientists such as Werner Heisenberg and David Bohm were aimed at directly refuting empiricism. They and Lewis, Shewhart, and Deming made the mind of the observer an explicit component of theory of knowledge.

Alan Greenspan explained his revised views of the economic disasters of the early twentieth century in his book *The Map and the Territory*. In an interview with *Time* magazine, he explained the title: "The map is supposed to be the conceptual framework of the world. The territory is the real world, and they don't always square. I'm trying to figure out what has been going on which I didn't understand."[153] Greenspan's statement could be taken to mean that there is a "real world" that exists independent of his mental map. Yet there is no *real world* that can be known independently, separately from the individual's mental map. The observer is not separate from the observed, and the territory is not separate from the map.

Some of the energy *given* to us, impinging on us from the external environment, is selected, abstracted by our sensory system. The meaning of that information is constructed in our mental maps. It is all within us even though it appears to be "out there." The term "objective" is usually used to refer to something that is real, true, exists out there. However, it is all subjective. Sensory impressions and interpretations of it occur within us. Gregory Bateson reminded us that when we think of coconuts or pigs, there are no coconuts or pigs in the brain.[154] Our experience of external objects is subjective, not objective. In this sense, the map can't be separated from the territory. We construct what we perceive. There is no color without eyes to see it, no sound in the forest without ears to hear it. A falling tree will produce vibrations in the air, but there is sound only when an ear hears it. The energy becomes an object, a thing, when we give it meaning. We look at the night sky and see the Big Dipper. This name of the configuration of stars is in our map, not out there. There is no Big Dipper out there. When I see and recognize an event or object, I am seeing the result of sensory processing followed by mental processing.

A related Korzybski principle underlies map and territory: "Whatever you might say the object 'is,' well, it is not."[155] The idea that the map is not the territory means that words, images, and symbols are not the objects and events they represent. There is a story of a stranger who asked Picasso why he did not paint things as they *really are*. Picasso said he did not quite understand what the man meant. The stranger took from his wallet a photograph of his wife. "I mean, like that," he said. "That's how she is." Picasso coughed hesitantly and said, "She is rather small, isn't she? And somewhat flat?"[156] The principle is stated in various ways: the menu is not the meal; the description is not the described. The external world is never known separately from the observer's mind. There is no experience that is objective. All experience is subjective.

When we say something "is," we should qualify the statement to "it appears to me" or "in my opinion." A spinning top appears to be standing still. A rapidly rotating color chart appears white. Our neurochemical-psychological systems produce the appearances of things. So, what does it mean to say what we see and know is real? That we know "what is"? In fact, we might say that we create or bring forth the world.[157]

Bill Clinton understood how the use of *is* can mislead and obfuscate. When asked by a grand jury about why he was lying about his relationship with Monica Lewinsky, President Clinton replied that he wasn't lying when he told his top aides, "There *is* nothing going on between us." He told the grand jury, "It depends on what the meaning of the word 'is' is." He claimed that his use of *is* referred to the present time when the question was asked, as when he told Jim Lehrer of PBS right after the Lewinsky story broke, "There is no improper relationship." He said that his statement that "there's nothing going on between us" had been truthful because he had no ongoing relationship with Lewinsky at the time he was questioned.

Our mental maps are influenced by the various forces of society, such as family, work, politics, religion, and education. C. I. Lewis wrote: "It is an error common to rationalism and to pure empiricism that both attempt an impossible separation of something called the mind from something called experience. Likewise both treat a knowledge as if it were a relation of the individual mind to external object in such wise [ways] that the existence of other minds is irrelevant; they do not sufficiently recognize the sense in which our truth is social."[158]

Lewis used the term *a priori knowledge,* as did Immanuel Kant before him, to refer to mental concepts that interpret the given sensory data as an experience. Lewis wrote that experience does not categorize itself but depends on preexisting concepts to interpret that experience. The choice of which conceptual systems to use is a pragmatic one. Experience itself, he wrote, does not itself determine what is good or bad, or the nature of goodness, nor does it determine what is valid or invalid, or the nature of logical validity. It does not determine what is real or unreal, or the nature of reality.[159]

According to the physicist Werner Heisenberg, Kant's idea of the a priori emphasizes that our knowledge is not simply derived from information obtained from the outer world through the senses and changed into data in the content of our brain. Instead, experience is only possible when we already have some concepts, which are the precondition of experience. Without these concepts, we would not even be able to speak about experience.[160]

Heisenberg introduced the idea of the a priori into quantum theory. He concluded from his research in subatomic physics that what we observe is not nature itself but nature exposed to our method of questioning. The answer you get depends on the question you ask. Ask a particle question, you get a particle answer. Ask a wave question, you get a wave answer. The observer cannot be separated from the phenomenon to be observed.[161] According to Heisenberg, science doesn't simply describe and explain nature; rather our understandings are produced by an interplay between nature and ourselves.[162] The economist Milton Friedman explained that natural science is as subjective as the social science of economics, since in both there is no way to avoid interaction between the observer and the observed.[163]

The profound question of what it means to perceive something as it *really is* was addressed by Deming regarding empirical knowledge: "There is no true value of any characteristic, state, or condition that is defined in terms of measurement or observation. Change of procedure for measurement (change in operational definition) or observation produces a new number."[164]

Deming liked to use differences in the measured speed of light to illustrate this point. Deming provides a number of values of the speed of light from measurements made by different methods at different times.[165]

Related to this understanding, Deming offers another insight: "There is no such thing as a fact concerning an empirical observation. Any two people may have different ideas about what is important to know about any event. Get the facts! Is there any meaning to this exhortation?"[166] In the world of empirical observation, there is no truth to reveal, no fact, no knowledge, independent of the theories and methods selected. Whatever is presented to us as a fact can't be evaluated without knowing the method used to obtain or establish the so-called fact.

David Turnbull summarized this notion for geographical maps: "... to ask for the facts and nothing but the facts, is to demand the impossible, like asking for a map to be drawn to no particular projection and having no particular scale."[167]

C. I. Lewis explained that the word *real* is ambiguous and can have a single meaning only in a special sense. The content of particular experience can be considered "real" only when qualified as material reality, psychological reality, mathematical reality. Whatever is real in one sense will be unreal in others. A mirage, for example, is real in one sense and not in others. Although not real trees and water, it is a real state of atmosphere and light. It is a genuine item of the objective world. A dream is illusory because the dreamer takes its images for physical things. The psychologist interested in the scientific study of the mental will consider these experienced images as constituting a reality that is in the realm of fact. The content of every experience is real when it is correctly understood. The problem of distinguishing real from unreal is always a problem of referring the given experience to its proper category.[168]

According to the physicist Stephen Hawking, the only reality we can know depends on our mental concepts, our models. We have created the models or maps that we use to interpret sensory input from the outside world. We have in our heads concepts of our home, trees, other people, electricity, atoms, molecules. These mental concepts constitute reality for the map holder. There is no test of reality independent of our model, our theory, our pictures. The test of a map, a theory, is how well it predicts— that is, how well it agrees with our observations.[169]

Michael Polanyi, scientist and philosopher, held that the reading of scientific instruments is a skill. They do not read themselves. The results of such readings are meaningful only in terms of the particular theories and general notions about the nature of things in the minds of the scientists who use these results. Polanyi related that Heisenberg told Einstein that in shaping his quantum theory he would go back to quantities that really could be observed. Heisenberg related that Einstein replied that the truth lay the other way around and that "whether you can observe a thing or not depends on the theory which you use. It is the theory which decides what can be observed." Polanyi also related that Max Planck, theoretical physicist, also rejected the claim that one can deal with the merely observable and that there exists absolutely no physical magnitude that can be measured in itself.[170]

Fritjof Capra wrote in *The Tao of Physics* that the consciousness of the human observer is an integral part of the observation, a participant in the observation. In atomic physics, for example, the human observer is not only necessary to observe the properties of an object but also to *define* these properties.[171] Properties of an object are meaningful only in the context of the object's interaction with the observer. Capra illustrates this with the issue of whether to measure the position or velocity/momentum of particles.

We express our experiences, our thoughts, our intentions mainly by words, yet the words we produce only represent the things to which they refer. Similarly, the words we hear from others are themselves not the things to which they refer. What does the speaker mean? What does the listener hear? How were words interpreted? The meanings of statements must be made explicit enough so they can be shared. How can we ensure that others understand the meaning to which our words refer? The next chapter discusses operational definitions, a method to make visible and share the invisible world of individual mental maps.

Chapter 7

Communicating Meaning with Operational Definitions

> Aye, just as you might a statue or a monument. You saw me! and
> that is all. But a man who meets a man is one who learns the
> other's mind, and lets him see his in turn. Learn my mind—
> show me yours; and then go and say that you met me.
> —Epictetus[172]

Deming was concerned that accurate communication was a significant problem, especially in business, which is why he quoted insights into the subject when he found them. For example, from Chaucer, he quoted, "My two ears ache from all your worthless speech" and "He that preaches to those who have ears but hear not makes of himself a nuisance."[173] And from Shakespeare, "I speak no more than everyone doth know."[174]

We have said that the map is not the territory—that words and images refer to things but are not those things. Whatever anyone says and thinks about something is more and different than that thing. The map can't have all the detail and complexity of the territory. Reading the menu or looking at a picture of the meal is not the same experience as eating the meal. Reading the score of a musical composition is not the same experience as listening to the musicians.

In order to *conduct* business or law or science, operational definitions are needed to convert the words that come from a mental map to concrete experience that people can share. The failure to share the meaning of the words we use, spoken or written, especially in contracts, can be costly. Deming often made the point, as he did with the various measurements of the speed of light, that there is no such thing as a fact concerning an empirical observation. He said, for example, that the adjective *red* has no meaning for business purposes unless it is defined operationally in terms of test and criterion.[175] Sellers and buyers can have the same understanding of the language of a contract or a product specification only when the statements refer to what can be observed. Language has to be made operational in order to do business. An operational definition specifies what to do to share or to communicate the experience. A concept has to be translated to something that can be experienced such as a measurement.

Alfred Korzybski divided the abstractions of our mental maps into two classes: (1) the language abstractions from the physical world of daily living and (2) abstractions in the language of mathematics. For example, a pure circle is defined as the locus of all points in a plane at equal distance from a point called the center. This definition completely specifies the circle, but a pure circle does not exist in the physical world; it does not refer to an actual physical object. A circle drawn on a sheet of paper is not a mathematical circle but a ring.[176]

Given the variation in life, this definition could never be met. Nothing is perfectly round, except in thought. "Roundness" is a concept. Deming made this point by giving a similar, conceptual definition of "round": "Every part of the surface or circumference in Euclidean two-dimensional space (a plane, a flat surface) is equidistant from a point called the center."[177] Deming wrote that if a statement cannot be put to a test, it has no value in practice.[178] The definition must move from conceptual to practical. He explained, "An operational definition translates a concept (round, random, safe, conforming, good) into a test and a criterion ... the test-method and the criterion to have meaning for business or legal purposes can only be stated in statistical terms: likewise a standard for safety, reliability, or performance."[179] The adjective *clean* has no communicable meaning unless defined in terms of test and criterion. The operations that define "clean" will depend on where the term applies (e.g., tables in a restaurant or the operating room in a hospital).[180] Operational definitions can help to make common and verifiable the meaning of statements used by people who must communicate with each other.

Experience Is Ineffable

C. I. Lewis gave an example, which may seem obvious. If you call for a taxi to meet you in one hour, the word "hour" may have a different meaning for the taxi driver and the caller. If hour is based on the personal experience of both parties, the taxi may be late if the driver has a different meaning of the word than the caller. Or the taxi may come in one hour but seem late to the caller who was impatient.[181] I recall a situation where some people had been complaining about the long wait times for the elevator in an office building. When management installed video monitors by the elevator to broadcast the news, the wait time was perceived to be much shorter, and complaints stopped.

There are times when we experience an emotional event, see a work of art, or hear music, and we can't find the words to express our feelings. In *Mind and the World Order*, C. I. Lewis spoke of the ways things appear to us. Lewis used the word "qualia" to refer to a person's sensory experiences of what is "given" in the territory. "Red rose," for example, refers to a different experience than does "yellow rose." A musical note produced by a piano is a different experience than the same note produced by a trumpet. The concept of qualia has been broadened by others to refer to the different properties of mental states produced by emotional experiences, such as envy, fear, and anger.

C. I. Lewis wrote that there is a gap "between words and what they signify," and that "more words will not build a bridge across it." A simple quality, like the redness of a red rose, is ineffable, unanalyzable, and indefinable. It has no parts or distinct ingredients to which we can refer to convey what the words intend. We can't "locate it map-wise through its external relationships."[182] The events in the external world are neither cold nor warm, green nor red, sweet nor bitter. These characteristics are produced by an interaction of the observer with the observed. "Warm" or "red" or "sweet" are not characteristics of the external world. One person may feel warm when the temperature is 75°F; another may feel cool. Some people, including a US president, reported that they intensely dislike the "bitter taste" of broccoli, while others said they like the way it tastes.[183]

Ineffable experience is a person's direct, firsthand experience that can't be adequately communicated to others by words. A person who sees the redness of a sunset cannot fully communicate the experience to a person who has never had that experience. Describing the experience in terms of the physical properties of the given, such as the wavelength of the light, won't communicate the subjective experience. What needs to be communicated is the content of the perceiver's consciousness. How to do that? How do you publicly communicate the private experience described by adjectives such as good, tired, safe, bitter, sweet, or concepts and feelings such as love, hate, and freedom? Words mean different things to different people. The word "justice" does not have the same meaning to each Supreme Court justice, for if it did, the nine justices would always agree, and we would need only one justice. Following Ackoff's analogy, they don't all view the same cross-sections of the orange or even the same orange.

An Operational Definition Puts Communicable Meaning into a Concept

Experience is coded in our mental maps in the form of words, symbols, and images. If they are to be communicated, they have to be expressed in a way that others can understand so they can be acted upon. An operational definition makes possible the sharing of meaning of an idea, concept, symbol, or term because it is stated in terms of operations (i.e., of sampling, test, and criterion). An operational definition of an ineffable experience allows it to be communicated. Deming began a discussion of operational definitions with the observation that "some of the explanations are more remarkable than the phenomenon itself." He then described the problem of sharing the private meanings of words and concepts: Meaning starts with the concept, which is in somebody's mind, and only there it is ineffable. The only communicable meaning of any word, prescription, instruction, specification, measure, attribute, regulation, law, system, or edict is the record of what happens on application of a specified operation or test.[184] An operational definition puts communicable meaning into a concept.[185]

The word "length," for example, refers to a concept that can be defined, operationally, with various instruments. The length of a desk can be measured with more and more precise instruments. However, when a concept or a characteristic can't be defined operationally, the concept has no meaning. If an instrument is used that can measure the movement of subatomic particles rather than a solid table, length has no meaning because it can't be defined in terms of operations.

Deming warned management that misunderstandings and conflicts between people who do business together often are rooted in their failure to state in advance and in operational language how they will know when a commitment of one to the other has been fulfilled. "Communication and negotiation (as between customer and supplier, between management and union, between countries) require for optimization operational definitions. An operational definition is a procedure agreed upon for translation of a concept into measurement of some kind."[186]

Operational definitions are needed because the way we ask questions or the way we observe or measure influences the answers that we get. A concept has meaning in terms of its operational definition. To ask which of the reported speeds of light is correct implies there is one true value. The result you get depends on the process used to measure the speed of light. When having dinner in a restaurant and ordering a "beef filet medium rare," the customer can get an operational definition of "medium rare" by asking the server how much pink will show in a slice of the steak. Medium rare is the outcome of a process of cooking the beef, which includes variables such as time and temperature. When I set the GPS on my car for a trip, the computer operationally defines trip length. Mileage depends on the route I prefer. The fastest may be the one with the most miles. The one that takes the most time may be the shortest.

A business that is thinking of relocating to Dayton, Ohio, may want to know how many people live in Dayton. Dr. Gipsie Ranney, professor of statistics, consultant, and longtime associate of Dr. Deming, explains that there is no single answer to that question.[187] Do we mean how many people reside inside the city limits or do we include suburbs? What date or dates will the answer apply to? If we come up with a plan to obtain a number that will take several days or weeks to execute, do we count the people who move in or out of Dayton during that time? Do we count people who are temporary residents; for example, people who have work to do in Dayton for several weeks who find temporary lodging in hotels or apartments or private homes? All of these questions call for an operational definition of the term "live." Once we decide upon what we mean by the term "live," we must come up with a method to arrive at a number. We could attempt a census, or we could come up with a plan to count only a subset or sample of areas and use that count to estimate the number of residents in the city. If we count only a subset, what methods and calculations will we use to arrive at a figure for total number of residents? Are there possibilities for errors in either a census or a subset or sample? How will we avoid those errors or compensate for their impact on the results? A manager who is aware of these issues could interpret the results only in terms of the methods used to obtain the numbers.

Deming cited a government regulation that states that a bicycle must be safe when assembled by a man of average intelligence. He asked what those words mean. What do "safe" and "unsafe" mean? What does "a man of average intelligence" mean—and what kind of intelligence? Maybe someone of lesser intelligence, however that is defined, could do better. How would you know if these vague requirements have been met? How could everyone interpret it in the same way? Deming concluded that the regulation had no meaning.[188]

Offering another example, Deming asked us to consider a specification for a blanket that states "must contain 50 percent wool." There are many ways that this specification for a blanket can be met in practice. How can a buyer and seller know if specifications have been met? Does the label "50 percent wool" mean that the top half is wool and the bottom half is some other material, or that the blanket is a blend of 50 percent wool and other materials? Defining the term "50 percent wool" operationally allows the words to have common meaning so that producers and consumers, sellers and buyers, will be able to agree that the specification has or has not been met. Operational definitions make it possible to share meanings of adjectives, such as good, reliable, round, uniform, tired, safe, unsafe, due care, and unemployed.[189]

Deming told a story about the statistics teacher who gave the class an appreciation for operational definitions. She emptied boxes of animal crackers on to a table in the classroom and asked the students to count the number of cows, horses, and pigs. The students soon asked questions and made observations. "Is this a cow? One leg is missing." The correct answer depends on the rule.[190]

Deming gave other examples of the need to operationally define terms.[191] How would you define the density of steel wool? How would you define a quart of oysters? How much liquid is allowed and how would you measure it? During his seminars, Deming asked the audience, "How many people are in this room?" The point is, who is to be counted? Only the seminar attendees, or also the hotel staff in the room and the audio-visual people? It depends on the purpose of counting. Two hotel employees asked to "count the number of people in the auditorium" will likely come up with different counts unless they know the purpose of counting. The purpose of counting will determine the method to be used. Is it to know how many people will have lunch? Is it to meet fire department regulations? There is no true value for the number of people in the auditorium.[192] Similarly, there is no such thing as a fact about an empirical observation separate from the process used to get the "facts."

The quality of the experience of a customer who purchased an automobile depends not only on the quality of the product but also on the quality of the dealer's administrative processes and other related services. One of the responsibilities of the Order Processing Center (OPC) of an automotive manufacturer was to respond to dealer claims for incorrect or damaged product. When receiving a claim, a claims analyst had to decide how the claim should be categorized, such as "not built as ordered" or "loss or damage in transit." The process began with the dealer's identification of a concern and submission of a claim to the OPC. Then the analyst had to allocate the claim to a category and approve or deny the claim. Analysts were not always clear about which category to use to allocate the claim. The problem was a lack of clarity about the meaning of the category labels. A process, which included the views of all stakeholders in the claims process, was conducted to develop operational definitions of the categories. This added consistency to the process, from the dealer to the claims analyst, and resulted in a 50 percent reduction in the number of dealer claims submitted to the OPC in less than one year.[193]

You might expect a teacher's perspective to be different from a student's. I spoke with a mother whose child's elementary school teacher gave the class the assignment to draw a picture of a cookie as it appears on a table. Her son was told he did not complete the task since he drew something that didn't look like a cookie. In the teacher's mind, the correct answer was to show the top view of the table so the whole cookie could be seen. The student, being short, drew the cookie the way he saw it, a side view of the cookie resting on top of the table. The child was devastated. His mother went to the teacher and expanded the teacher's mental map. The mother of a student in another school told me her daughter was criticized by the teacher because when asked to draw a blue person, she drew a sad person instead of coloring the person blue. Sensitivity to the mental maps of others how others see the world—and a better definition of terms would have helped in both of these cases.

There is the report of a class in a school near Baton Rouge, Louisiana, where the young students had read a lesson on birds that was in one of the standard textbooks. The teacher asked, "When do the robins come?" Jimmie answered, "In the fall." The teacher asked Jimmie to carefully reread the lesson, after which she again asked him, "When do the robins come?" He again answered, "In the fall." After reading the lesson a third time, the teacher again asked him the same question. He was almost in tears when he answered, "They come in the spring," which they do in Boston, where the book was written. However, the boy knew that to avoid the northern winter, they come to Louisiana in the fall.[194] These examples demonstrate the importance of awareness of individual differences in mental maps and the personal meaning of words. If something like this occurred in a business, would there be a discussion between the employee and supervisor to understand each other's viewpoint, or would the supervisor think the employee was a troublemaker and lower the performance evaluation?

In *Levels of Knowing and Existence*, author Harry Weinberg explained the lower and higher levels of abstraction.[195] I see an object that I have sensed. It is commonly called a pen. It has characteristics that enable me to talk about it: its length, the color of the ink, that it has a ball point. These are characteristics I abstract from the object as a whole. The scratches on the barrel and the taste of the ink and the plastic are not included in my meaning of the word "pen" at the present moment. However, to another person, say the manufacturer of the pen, the smell of the plastic and the tightness of the fit of the parts are important and would form his meaning of "pen." What one person abstracts from the object is different from what others abstract. The word or label "pen" has different meanings and doesn't include all that can be said about the pen. Previous experience with similar objects, purposes of the moment, context in which the word is used, and many other conscious and unconscious factors help determine which characteristics of an object will be abstracted at any given moment to form the verbal meaning of the name.

When we think and speak at higher levels of abstraction, we leave out more and more characteristics. The label "pen" refers to a specific object. The category or class "pens" or "pens in general," does not refer to anything specific that exists, anything you could point to. You could not show me "pens." You might show me various specific pens, individual objects that differ from each other, but not "pens." Similarly, while individual trees have specific characteristics, a "forest" is a higher level of abstraction. "Forest" is a word that refers to something that doesn't itself exist. What exists on the concrete level that can be sensed are different individual trees. The class term "forest" ignores most of the differences between individual trees. What exists on the object level are individual trees, all different from each other. Another example is the word "triangle." There are individual triangles of various shapes. A higher-order abstraction refers to "triangularity," a characteristic of triangles in general. It is not a quality or characteristic of any individual triangle. Rather it is a mental construct that emerges when comparing individual triangles.

Levels of Abstraction

If you stub your toe, there is immediate awareness of the sensation. It is not mediated by a mental map. It is a nonverbal experience. Soon after the incident, you may begin to think about the sensation and describe it as "painful," and you may judge yourself "stupid" for not being more careful. The initial sensation is pure, no theory, no thinking, no interpreting, no evaluating, no judging. It is in the moment, without time and place, without memory of the past or anticipation of the future. Direct observation also can occur with an aesthetic response, such as to the sunset. At the moment of awareness, there are no words that come to mind to describe that ineffable experience, no evaluation of good or bad. Memory doesn't intrude, nor does the desire to have that moment occur again and again. Then the map may come into play with thoughts such as, *How beautiful. I wish I could have stayed in that moment.* Or, *That sunset reminds me of a painting I once saw.* Some people in Phoenix think that Arizona has the most beautiful sunsets. Some residents of Michigan think that the view of the sun setting over Lake Michigan can't be beat. Same orange, different slices.

When we observe through our mental map, through the eye of our mind, we are not in direct contact with what we observe. Memory intrudes. We look, and at the same time we may judge and evaluate. When we try not to think about what we are sensing, our mental map has already intervened since we are talking to ourselves. Direct observation is unmediated by verbal abstractions. It occurs when thought stops and the map is not active.

Mental maps are active when we interact and communicate with others. Our thoughts are structured by language. Language makes it possible to build a hierarchy of generalizations, a Ladder of Abstraction[196] or a Ladder of Inference[197] that we apply to people and things. Our mental maps are active when we are on the ladder. On the lowest rung, there are words that name specific individual objects and events that can be pointed to; for example, "that apple," "that orange," and "that fastball pitch." These words refer directly to our sensations, to what we have seen, touched, or tasted. They are verbal abstractions in our map on the bottom rung of the ladder.

They verbally point to concrete objects and events, which may or may not be physically present. As we ascend to the higher-level abstractions, words do not refer to individual objects that can be pointed to and distinguished from each other but rather to categories or classes such as the more general "fruit," which includes apples and oranges, or the even more general "food." Higher-order abstractions, concepts such as "triangularity" or "laws of nature," enable us to infer or to generalize to a larger whole, from the similarities we do see to what we can see only with our eye of mind. Irving Lee, author of *Language Habits in Human Affairs*, points out that if researchers did nothing but describe what they found, there would be no science. Theories, which often are at conceptually higher levels of abstraction, can be verified with testable hypotheses stated at more concrete levels in operational language.[198]

High levels of abstraction and imagination also have their place in poetry, novels, and other forms of art. Lee also warns of the dangers of high-level abstractions as when demagogues and dictators speak at high levels of abstraction with conclusions and inferences.[199] Such declarations may be accepted as empirical knowledge even though they have not or cannot be verified and may be intended to deceive or mislead.

There is a sign at the entrance to my local library: "No deadly weapons allowed." Yet the books and the electronic media are full of words that can stimulate deadly actions and in some cases are specifically intended to raise emotions of all kinds. Some people resort to violence in response to the names they are called and to terrorism by the words they hear and read. Of course, words also can stir the heart to act in ways that benefit society. Epictetus wrote: "If a person gave your body to any stranger he met on his way, you would certainly be angry. And do you feel no shame in handing over your own mind to be confused and mystified by anyone who happens to verbally attack you?"[200]

Classes or categories of anything are constructed by human minds and do not exist in the same sense that objects we name actually do exist in the territory. Deming often joked with some of the audience members in his seminars who joined him on the stage to participate in a demonstration of variation. He named one of them as the "average man." The joke may not have been apparent to everyone in the audience. We can calculate an average from measurements made on individual people, but we can't see the average person. That is purely an abstract concept, although the operations to calculate an "average," such as an arithmetic average, a median, or a mode, can be defined. When a higher level of abstraction is reified, it is treated as something concrete that can be seen, heard, touched, and so on. It is a problem when higher levels of verbal abstractions, symbols, are treated as if they exist, as if they are concrete, can be seen and touched. This is called *reification* or *misplaced concreteness*. Who has an average family? Is it the parents with 2.3 children?

Even though higher levels of abstraction have no existence outside of the thoughts in a mental map, we may expect, even require, people to conform to verbal abstractions, those words without an actual referent in the territory, words such as "typical worker," "lazy student," "ideal candidate," "best practices," "those people." You may recognize the abstract terms "universe" and "population" if you took a course in inferential statistics. Any group as a whole, any universal, as opposed to a particular thing, does not exist "out there." If we say that the odds of getting heads or tails in coin flips are fifty-fifty, that statement does not refer to any particular coin but to the concept of an infinite number of coin flips. How will you know when you have flipped a coin an infinite number of times?

The language of business or law, of regulations and contracts, must be clear, and those who write them and those who have to conform to them must be able to agree when they are or are not met. The categories we use such as "laws of nature" or "ecosystem" are all constructed by humans. They exist in our heads, not out there. Their value is in anticipating, in predicting the future. We have to be aware when we reify our thoughts that they may be convenient and useful ways to think about a complex world and not to treat the words as if they actually exist as objects.

Chapter 8

~

Knowledge, Values, and Action

There are the basic value-judgments in the management of a business
enterprise, and the perception of the social, political, and economic
problems that a business encounters in the achievement of those aims.
—W. Edwards Deming[201]

The cartographer J. B. Harley wrote that geographical maps "are never
value-free images; they are not in themselves either true or false. Both in the
selectivity of their content and in their signs and styles of representation,
maps are a way of conceiving, articulating and structuring the human
world which is biased towards, promoted by, and exerts influence upon sets
of social relations."[202] Harley's comment raises questions about the values
in our mental maps, such as how a person's values are shaped by social
conditioning and how they are oriented to benefit that person, benefit
other people, and contribute to the more general and vague "greater good"
of the organization and society.

Values and Mental Maps of Causality

Thomas Sowell, economist and social theorist, maintained that our
understanding of how the world works, our mental representation of cause
and effect, precedes the development of our values. If these understandings
are changed, values will change accordingly. He noted that Copernicus
and Galileo were targets of the religious authorities because they presented
alternative models of causation and thus a different interpretation of

"facts." If their models were accepted, a change of values would have to follow, even though they were not promoting alternative values. Similarly, Sowell writes that the conversions to Marxism in the 1930s and from Marxism after the Nazi-Soviet pact of 1939 resulted from new visions of causation, new understandings of the different consequences of capitalism and communism. The understandings of cause-effect changed first. Reordering of values followed.[203]

There are two models that can describe the way people are valued and managed in organizations. One is the centuries-old model associated with Isaac Newton where the physical world is thought of as a machine. This model also was adopted by biology and physiology as well as the social sciences of psychology, sociology, economics, and politics. The other is a whole-system, ecological model, consistent with the mutual dependence and natural variation of living systems.

The management style that Deming criticized comes from the model of the organization as a machine. It has dominated management thinking for decades, although the managers who apply this model probably do not consciously recognize it as the basis for much of their thinking, values, and practices. Rather, they have been following the teaching of business schools, management consultants, business books, the management traditions of their own organizations, and the practices of CEOs that the media have anointed as leaders to emulate, as well as fads, fashions, and narrowly focused programs.

Following the principles of Newtonian mechanics, an organization is viewed as a complex mechanical system, like a clock. To understand how a clock works, it must be taken apart and *reduced* to its component parts. The parts are studied and then reassembled into a whole working mechanism. Russell Ackoff explained that it is a process of *analysis* by which the whole is understood by taking it apart, conceptually or physically.[204] It can be seen when children, trying to understand how something works, such as a new toy or something they haven't seen before, take it apart in order to understand the behavior of the separate parts and how they fit together. They then add together these separate understandings into an understanding of how the whole works.

Inherent in the model is the concept of causal determinism. The motion of visible objects is determined by a system of forces acting independently and sequentially. Machines behave by action and reaction. All motion is determined by the laws of linear cause and effect. Objects do not act until moved by energy from an external source. Every event is seen as the result of prior causes and the cause of subsequent events in a linear chain that follows the laws of motion. Explanation is complete when the causes that are sufficient to explain the behavior of objects are identified. In this model, perfect prediction conceptually is possible like dominos lined up behind each other. When a force causes the first one to fall, then in succession fall the second and third and all the rest. Theoretically, this behavior can be precisely predicted because action and reaction occurs in a vacuum (i.e., without the effect of external environmental influences). However, mechanical systems are not perfectly predictable outside of theory. The environment does have an effect.

The principles of Newton's mechanics were a foundation of the Industrial Revolution and made possible the engineered and built world in which we live and has enabled some of us to travel to the moon. It is an appealing model to extend beyond its original conceptualization of the physical world because it reduces a complex organization to one that is easier to understand and manage. It enables management to think in terms of the visible aspects of the physical world. Inherent in the model is a simple view of causality: do this and get that. People are valued as *inputs* to the organization machine. They are seen as "labor" and pushed and pulled by rewards for "good" performance and punishments for "poor" performance. Incentives, rewards, and punishments are applied as energy from a source outside of employees to push and pull them in order to move them to meet management's performance objectives. People are evaluated as if they have complete control over their performance once they are put into motion in a system where unwanted variation is viewed as someone's error rather than due to the system itself. In addition, the enterprise is viewed as a collection of independent parts where performance of the whole is conceptualized and calculated as the sum of the performances of the separate parts. If there is a problem or failure or defect, some person or persons get blamed.

Values are reflected in the language heard in these organizations, such as well-oiled machine, shift gears, rev up growth, and pump up sales. What do these metaphors reveal about the assumptions underlying management systems? What expectations do they create? What actions and performance do they produce? If, for example, you believe in a well-oiled machine, it is more likely that you value tight, top-down, extrinsic control of employees rather than employee intrinsic self-control and freedom and discretion to solve local problems, improve, and innovate. A machinelike system, managed by extrinsic values, discourages cooperative relationships between people and units and encourages adversarial competition to "bring out the best."

The machine model of management is reductive. Human beings are viewed as the sum of their biological components. Consider this description of the biological reductionism of a human life, which illustrates the fallacy of applying the model to living systems: "If it were to be taken literally, man could be ultimately defined as consisting of nothing but 90 per cent water and 10 per cent minerals—a statement which is no doubt true, but not very helpful."[205]

The philosopher and scientist Michael Polanyi maintained that we will never be able to reduce living things to the processes of physics and chemistry. Yet we try to do it anyway, for example by thinking that the discovery of DNA is completing our understanding of living things by reducing them to physical and chemical processes. Underlying this reductive model is the assumption that organisms are mechanisms, and since mechanisms work according to the laws of physics and chemistry, organisms must work according to the same laws. There is so much that a reductive model can't explain. Humans are sentient. They have individuality, and language, and social principles, and the ability to create. A reductive mental model does not respect the uniqueness of being human.[206]

Russell Ackoff tells us that no part of a human being is human; only the whole is.[207] It is a whole human being that comes to work. People have many aspects to their lives. Work is a person's contribution to the enterprise, and it also should contribute to the meaning of the person's life as a whole. The mechanistic-reductive model doesn't allow for human characteristics such as purpose and creativity. It promotes the extrinsic manipulation of people. People are viewed as parts of the machine and as economic entities rather than whole human beings. I recall one time when Dr. Deming heard that an employee was moving to another position and would be "replaced." Deming did not like that word. In his mind, human beings are unique individuals and are not replaceable like machine parts.

Organizations have their purposes, said Deming, but so do people. "How could there be life without aims and hopes? Everyone has aims, hopes, plans."[208] According to Russell Ackoff, in order for an organization to function as a whole-system, the purposes of whole must include purposes of parts.[209] Therefore, employees are valued not as inert parts of a machine that have to be pushed and pulled but as human beings who have their own aims, interests, and a life outside of the organization. Human motivation comes primarily from the internal energy of purpose, not from the external forces of positive and negative incentives. A different model of an organization is needed, one where management views the organization primarily as a social system, as an ecology of human relationships.

Dr. Deming and I visited a facility where a manager proudly showed us how they were applying statistical process control on the production line. Deming listened for about fifteen minutes; he was unusually patient! He then said that he was hearing a lot about mechanical processes but nothing about people. The manager did not understand the broader implications of statistical process control and the theory of variation for the management of people. He viewed the method as a tool to improve the operation of the production line to reduce defects and cost. Nothing wrong with that, of course, but when Dr. Deming asked him about assigning blame to individual employees for poor quality or about rank-ordering employees based on performance of the system, he was puzzled. He didn't see people as more than inputs to a mechanical process.

Dr. Deming was disappointed when organizations that claimed to be following his teaching were focused only on applications of statistical process control to production processes. He continually stressed that this was important, but a business could have big gains by transforming its strategy, planning, and company-wide management systems.[210]

Whole-System Ecological Model

Russell Ackoff saw how machine-age models and values dominate management thinking. This can be seen in the structure of all kinds of organization. Corporations and schools, for example, are taken apart and divided into departments and disciplines, which then are managed as separate units.[211] Dr. Ackoff said this was analogous to disassembling an automobile and laying the parts side by side. You no longer have an automobile, only a collection of parts that does not have the properties of an automobile. Analyzing the separate parts reveals the *structure* of the system and enables you to *describe how* it works but not to *explain why* it works. To explain why requires knowing its function—what it contributes to the larger system, the larger environment in which it is contained. Knowing the structure of an automobile, such as where the steering wheel is located, won't explain why it is on the right- or left-hand side. You would have to know something about the containing supra system, the environment in which the automobile functions. Similarly, to know why the transmission works, its function must be understood as a subsystem of the automobile. The explanation of *why* is not in the system that you want to explain. It is outside of it, in the containing system in which it functions.

Whole-system thinking makes explanation possible because it guides you to get an outside view, to go outside of the system you are trying to explain to the supra system in which the system of interest has a role or function. Whole-system thinking doesn't mean that managers have to understand all the details of the functioning of the system. Rather, it means that management appreciates that the system is embedded in a larger system and that it contains subsystems and processes that interact to produce performance. Relationships make the whole. Problems in front of us likely started elsewhere, and local solutions may have negative effects elsewhere. Appreciation for a system tells us what questions to ask and how to interpret the answers.

System, like *synthesis*, comes from the Greek word for uniting, unifying, putting together into a whole, standing together, whereas *analysis* means separating a whole into component parts. Table 8-1 summarizes Ackoff's comparison of the thinking processes of the machine-age and systems models.[212] Processes of analysis and synthesis are both used but in different ways.

Mechanistic-Reduction Thinking	Ecological-Expansion Thinking
The thing to be explained is treated as a whole to be taken apart. Focus is on the component parts and how they are organized in order to *describe how* the system works.	The thing to be explained is treated as a part of a containing whole. Focus is on the function the part serves in the larger system in order to *explain why* the system works as it does.
Analysis 1. Take apart the thing (the whole). 2. Describe the behavior or properties of the parts taken separately. **Synthesis** 3. Assemble, combine the separate descriptions of the parts into a description of the whole.	**Synthesis** 1. View the thing you want to explain as part of a larger whole in which it is contained. 2. Explain the behavior or properties of the containing whole. **Analysis** 3. Explain the behavior or properties of the thing to be explained in terms of its roles or functions in support of the purpose and goals of the containing whole.

Table 8-1. Ackoff's summary of models to understand the whole

Whereas the model of organization as machine reduces wholes to parts, the whole-system model expands a whole to consider its role and function, its value in a larger whole. Ackoff recommended that the concept of cause and effect in the Newtonian model be replaced with the model of producer-product in the whole-system model.[213] To establish one thing as the cause of another, it must be shown that it is both necessary and sufficient for the other. However, a simple cause-and-effect relationship may not be the case. An acorn is not the cause of oak. An acorn is necessary but not sufficient to produce an oak. Other things are necessary, such as the right soil conditions, moisture, and temperature. These other necessary conditions constitute the environment.

Rather than looking for a simple relationship between a result and its cause, an ecological model of producer-product is a better way to think about the dynamics of a system, with its many interactions internally and with the containing supra system. A producer-product model takes into account the dynamic behavior of a system over time and place. A problem that shows up in marketing should not be thought of as a marketing problem; it is the same for finance, engineering, purchasing, and the other areas of the organization. Dr. Gipsie Ranney made the related points that costs should not be viewed as causes—they are caused—and that management should not confuse coincidence with cause and effect.[214]

Conflict and a Balance of Values

I recall years ago when the chairman of Ford Motor Company was about to retire and the board was in the process of selecting the next chairman, a group of us were discussing who we would like. Somebody said, "Wouldn't it be nice if we all could vote to select the next chairman?" Dr. Deming reminded him that when it came to electing the top officer, Ford did not have a two-party system. Everyone laughed. Dr. Deming laughed the loudest at his observation.

Employees may prefer to work in a more democratic organization with more personal discretion and less management control. However, if an employee moves into management, they may tend to behave in the ways that they used to criticize. Have their values changed as they gained power, control, and perks? Whether values change as people move up is a difficult question. Perhaps the values did not change but were there all along. The employee's criticisms may have been based on a lack of power and perks or in an inability to understand the perspective and pressures on managers, ones that they may face in their new managerial role.

Popular vote is valued as a process for a free society, but Deming wondered if, even though it "acts as a ballast over a dictator," it always provides the right answer. Similarly, he said that enlargement of a committee doesn't necessarily improve results.[215] Without profound knowledge, democratic processes do not necessarily yield decisions in long-run interests of an organization and the people in it.

Jacob Bronowski, in his book *Science and Human Values*, discussed the inherent conflict between the individual's desire to be free and the need to live and work in a larger social system. A conflict of values occurs when the individual wants, or has to, do both. If an anarchist wants only freedom, whatever the cost, they will prefer the jungle of man at war with man, and if a tyrant wants only social order, they will create the totalitarian state. They will single out those who question or dissent. Bronowski observed that the concepts of value are profound and difficult, exactly because they do two things at once: they join individuals into societies and yet they preserve for them a freedom, which makes them single individuals. A philosophy that does not acknowledge both needs cannot allow or evolve values.[216]

The words that refer to values (e.g., fairness, excellence, integrity, quality, diversity, courage, honesty, responsibility) in an organization's statements and documents need to be defined so that they have the same meaning to management and to nonmanagement employees. It has become common practice for organizations to develop statements of mission, values, and guiding principles, which may be written by a group appointed for that purpose. The question is whether the people writing these statements reflect the deeply held values of the individuals in the organization, and whether the members of the organization act in ways consistent with the statements. Employees are expected to subscribe to these values, even if they conflict with their own values. If individuals don't agree with the organization's stated values. they may act in ways that are at odds with the statement in relationships within the organization and with customers, suppliers, and even with competitors. This could be partially due to the failure of management to operationally define the stated values and explain why management deems them necessary for the organization.

Deming devoted an entire chapter of *Out of the Crisis* (chapter 10) to voluntary industrial standards and government regulation. A statement of values expressed in a business standard or a government regulation must have operational meaning to be enforced. Conformance can be judged only in terms of one or more tests and criteria. Standards reflect values such as quality, safety, and concern for the environment. These values all could be classified under quality. In addition, there is a moral aspect to having a safe work environment and producing products and services that satisfy customers' needs and wants.[217]

The challenge for management is how to balance its values. What is the cost of unhappy customers who take their business elsewhere and tell others about that "lousy airline"? Consider the method of supervision by a group of airline reservation agents.[218] Management installed devices on the equipment to monitor the number of calls made, how long agents spent on the phone, and so on so that they could use reward and punishment to improve efficiency. Management believed that they improved the system. Some people might say, "Well, that's really a great system, because I believe people cannot be trusted; you really need to drive them from the outside." If you share the assumptions that employees cannot be trusted and need to be watched and threatened with punishment to keep them in line, you will think this is a great method. Others with a different mental model would not value such methods. They would see them as destructive to people and the ability of management to optimize the system.

The organization's values may conflict with its practices. Statements about an organization's quality orientation may be at odds with its finance and human resources management systems. Management actions rather than statements, laminated cards, and posters may better represent an organization's actual values. An individual's deeply held values may conflict with the organization's values-in-action. If pay is a means to a more valued end, one may endure the discomfort of the conflict between one's own values and those of management. If the discomfort becomes too great, they may leave the organization. For example, police officers who value maintaining public safety as their highest priority may find that they no longer can work under a system that diverts them from that obligation by requiring them to issue a quota of traffic tickets per month. Mavericks, so called because they do not conform to the expectations of the organization's culture and because they have the courage to act according to their deeply held values, may be fired or leave voluntarily. However, sometimes they are promoted because they are seen as leaders.

What appears to be a conflict in aims may actually be a conflict of values. Sharman Apt Russell in *Kill the Cowboy* wrote that cattle ranchers and ecologists both want to preserve the grasslands; however, they have different understandings of the effect of cattle grazing on the range. Ranchers see an instrumental value in the land, a means to feed cattle. Since the land must continually be used for grazing, in the rancher's causal model, cattle do no long-lasting damage since they aerate the soil by tromping on it. Ecologists value the land for its intrinsic worth, as an end in itself, and from a whole-system view, they also see it as instrumental, as a means to maintain the health of the larger ecology. They believe that grazing is destroying the grasses and the larger ecology. Both groups have the same aim, to keep the grasslands viable, but their different values put them at odds with each other.[219]

Attempts to balance more immediate organization needs with longer-term needs also may involve a conflict of values when implementing the Deming Cycle. Long-term basic research, where future value can't be quantified, can compete for funding with advances in product technology that can be developed more quickly to meet sales and profit goals. Looking at the United States as a whole, and the whole includes the future, an emphasis on immediate results while other countries are increasing private and public spending on basic scientific research puts the long-term competitive position of the United States at risk.[220]

James O'Toole, in his book *The Executive's Compass*, discusses a tool he developed—a compass card—to help executives make visible to themselves and to others their own invisible economic, political, social, and environmental values. Just as a navigational compass shows directions or points relative to four main directions or poles, values are represented as points on a compass. The four poles of the values compass are defined by different concepts. The values at opposite poles are defined so that they conflict. For example, to facilitate a discussion of democracy and the "good society," Liberty (north) was placed opposite Equality (south), and Efficiency (east) was placed opposite Community (west). The four poles divide the card into quadrants in which individuals place themselves once they understand the meaning of each pole. In another exercise, the poles were labeled Meritocracy (Merit and Freedom) versus Egalitarianism (Security and Equality), and Behaviorism (Efficiency and Order) versus Humanism (Quality of Work Life).[221]

When he was chairman and CEO of Atlantic Richfield Company, Lodwrick Cook wrote the foreword to O'Toole's book. He described the compass as a practical device to help business leaders understand the philosophical and ethical sources of differences of opinion on matters such as affirmative action, environmental regulations, and compensation. It has helped people to better understand why there are disagreements. Cook wrote that executives can't avoid disagreements that stem from differences in values. Efficiency often brings unemployment. Investment creates jobs but also pollution.

A desired outcome of such an exercise is to help individuals see where they fit on the quadrant, to understand that others have different values, which may conflict with their own, and to see where a balance may be both necessary and helpful to achieve aims. In addition, to see that in a democratic society, a diversity of values and points of view are part of a whole where progress in relationships requires a balance.

Everyone Can Win

"Win" and "lose" are words used in games and professional sports where numerical scores determine the outcome. They are structured to produce winners and losers. Traditional economic models teach that business and living is a zero-sum game, that in order to have winners, there must be losers, that competition has to be adversarial, pitting one party against the other rather than working together to achieve goals that they could see as common. People may not think they are competing against each other for rewards, but the result is the same when they fail to help each other for fear that those they help will come out ahead of them. Adversarial competition may not necessarily be the way to better material living, to a rising standard of living.[222] In an organization managed as a whole-system ecology, people do not participate in a zero-sum game. With cooperation, everyone can gain. Deming gave the example of two service stations across the street from each other, each with one truck. By loaning a truck to the other when their own truck was not needed, each had the equivalent of owning 1.8 trucks. They further cooperated to alternate the nights they stayed open late, thus keeping customers coming to their area.[223]

Constancy of Purpose

Deming wrote that it is management's job to determine the aims of the organization and to manage the whole organization toward the accomplishment of those aims. "Choice of aim is clearly a matter of clarification of values, especially on the choice between possible options." Deming defined constancy of purpose as a guiding principle for the management of the system as a whole. He said that an aim should never be defined in terms of a specific activity or method. It must always relate to a better life for everyone. He proposed an aim for any enterprise: to create something of value for all participants in the system, for everybody to gain over the long term—stockholders, employees, suppliers, customers, community, and the environment. Management's job is to help everybody win.[224]

Everyone in the organization must understand the aim of the system and how to direct their efforts toward it. Everyone must understand the danger and loss to the whole organization from a team that seeks to become a selfish, independent profit center. "Anything less than direction of best efforts of everyone toward achievement of the aim or aims of the whole organization is a directed verdict toward failure to achieve best overall results."[225] If an aim is to be achieved, there must be a method, and it has to be consistent with the organization's values. A goal that lies beyond the means of its accomplishment will lead to discouragement, frustration, and demoralization.

Deming distinguished aim from fact-of-life. The statement, "We will go out of business if we do not reduce our defective items to 3 percent by year end," is a fact of life not an aim. This fact could be translated into a goal or aim, but that requires a method to be planned and executed.[226]

Problems of today, said Deming, must be addressed, but management must not stay "bound up in the tangled knot of the problems of today, becoming ever more and more efficient in them," for example, by greater use of mechanized equipment. It is the problems of the future that require constancy of purpose and dedication to improvement of competitive position to keep the company viable and provide jobs. The absence of constancy of purpose is one of the "deadly diseases" that Dr. Deming diagnosed as a destructive lack of an essential management value. It is characterized by short-term thinking, a focus on immediate results, management by visible figures, making the bottom line look good by layoffs, buying cheaper tools and cheaper materials, deferring repairs and maintenance, and shipping everything produced regardless of quality. Quick profits and the next quarterly dividend are valued above the future existence of the company. Constancy of purpose means planning for the long term, including the methods to execute the plan, putting resources into innovation, research, education, and continual improvement in design of product and service. Do not think only in the present tense, on immediate results; think also in the future tense, he said.[227]

Two-Valued and Multivalued Mental Maps

Each one of us observes our individual *what-is* as we interact with people and things. When we eat a meal, for example, we have an ineffable sensory experience (i.e., one that is very hard to describe). Although we might not have the words to describe our experience of specific characteristics of the food, we might say that the food is bitter or sweet, soft or hard, dry or greasy. It is easier to place a value on our experience and describe the experience as good or bad, acceptable or unacceptable. When we evaluate something as good or bad, just or unjust, right or wrong, we are not describing the qualities and characteristics we initially abstracted from our sensations. We have gone beyond that to judge and evaluate our experience. The evaluation of goodness and badness is not in the process of observation; it is further removed from the observation. It occurs after the observation and then is projected back to the object.[228] If we are not aware of the separate processes of observation and then evaluation, we may confuse them. We may ignore the describing process and jump right to evaluation, and not even know or remember why we think things or people are "good" or "bad" once we have labeled them.

Mental maps contain abstractions that typically are in the form of language and cannot take into account all the details, nuances, and relationships in the territory. Therefore, our mental representation of the "real world" is simplified. One way we tend to leave out detail is by collapsing our view of the world into *either-or, is-is not* categories such as good *or* bad, yes *or* no, without any intermediate valuation. In the discipline of general semantics, this is known as a two-valued orientation.

Thinking with two values fosters an all-or-none contrast (e.g., things are either all good or all bad); people are either with us or against us. We tend to reduce our thinking to polar opposites rather than thinking in terms of degree, such as how bad and how good. We don't allow for alternate possibilities, for a middle ground. What is implied in this way of thinking is that if A is true, B must be false or contrary or opposite. If A exists, B cannot exist. If A wins, B must lose. Yet both can be true or false. A person or group may not be either for us or against us. Words that are opposites of each other, such as good and bad, and other labels and categories are artificial divisions. We create them in our mental maps and impose them on what we observe. When this happens, we have confused our observation with our judgment.

A person who sees the world as *is* or *is not* is blinded to life's possibilities. This two-valued thinking doesn't allow for a range of possibilities and choices. A multivalued orientation promotes total awareness, mindfulness, whole-system thinking. This allows individuals to see beyond the divisions created by imposing higher-order abstractions on the what-is.

The territory also may be divided into more than two categories when we label or categorize, but this still is a limited way of seeing the whole. Dividing the territory into smaller parts may be a convenient or a habitual mode of evaluation. It also can result from an inability of individuals in their daily living, or organizations in their policies and procedures, to use language to express the differences that exist in the whole-system. We give the same name to things that are different when we categorize and generalize. People are different from one another but are *reduced* to similar categories. We say that John and Mary *are* B+ or good employees, and Jean and Peter *are* C+ students. Is the label what they *are*? What do these different words or letters mean? Have we confused observation of performance with evaluation of a person? Is this a prediction of future performance or is it a permanent label attached to the person? Once we evaluate someone or something and can no longer see beyond that label, we may tend to set up a self-fulfilling prophecy (e.g., once we classify a person as a slow learner, he or she will be treated that way).

Why boil down a human being to a category in order to fill out an evaluation form that meets the limited structure of the organization's human resources policy? Is it because it is simpler to reduce the world this way, especially if the system applies pressure to do it, or is it that we don't have the vocabulary to express differences? How many of us like to think of ourselves as labels rather than as unique, individual human beings? Implicit in a two-valued orientation is the assumption that we can generalize about everyone to whom we have given the same label.

In the world of manufacturing quality control, process output is inspected and each item is classified as defective or nondefective, or as conforming or nonconforming, or as accept-reject. Such two-valued characteristics are called attributes. There are quality characteristics that inherently are two-valued—for example, whether a purchase order does or does not have the correct price, whether a container of medicine does or does not have the correct label, whether a screw is present or is missing on a part. There is no continuum along which the characteristic can be measured. Characteristics such as the diameter of a metal shaft, which can vary along a range of values, are called variables. They are multivalued.

However, these continuous characteristics often are reduced to two values. For example, the diameter of a shaft, which can be measured in inches or millimeters, may be compared to specifications and accepted or rejected. This seems analogous to the way we evaluate people, where characteristics that can vary naturally over a wide range are reduced to a few values.

John Betti, when he was a senior executive at Ford Motor Company, realized that American engineering and manufacturing was worried more about meeting specifications than continually working to improve production processes in order to reduce variation around a target or nominal value, which usually is at the center of the specification. I heard him ask how a measured characteristic that is just inside of a specification can be considered as good as others that also are inside the specification yet are much closer to a nominal or target value. How can those same parts that are just within the specification be considered to be better than parts whose measurements are also close to the specification but just slightly outside?

John Betti wanted to shift the thinking of engineers to one of target value. Dr. Deming also saw it that way. He believed that a better way to think about product quality is the *loss function* model of Dr. Genichi Taguchi, engineer and statistician who developed a methodology for improving quality and reducing costs. His loss function model is a multivalued approach. At the nominal or target value, there is minimum loss with loss increasing at further and further distances from the target. Another way to look at this is: how can a customer who gets a product that is barely conforming to specification be as satisfied as the customer who gets a product that is at the center of the specification?[229] The most important use of a loss function, said Dr. Deming, is to help us change from a world of simply meeting specifications to continual reduction of variation around a target value by improving processes. Deming explained this with an example of the losses in output, measured in dollars per hour, from the temperature in a room where people are working. Loss, shown on the vertical axis of a graph, increases as the temperature of the room, shown on the horizontal axis, departs from some optimum value, resulting in a U-shaped curve. The curve touches the horizontal axis at the target value where there is minimum loss. Dr. Taguchi called the loss a "loss to society."[230] I should note here that reduction of variation of manufactured product, of one piece to the next, does not have the same meaning when considering differences between people. The aim, for enterprise, is to produce more consistent process outcomes that are closer to a desired value. An aim for the management of people is not to make all employees alike but to respect and make use of their different talents and inclinations. Rather than classifying employees and students, leaders aim to improve the system as a whole.

Dr. Kosaku Yoshida, professor of statistics and former student of Dr. Deming, described Western concern with meeting specifications as an *acceptability* value. As long as the process output meets specifications, it is acceptable, whereas the Tauguchi model stresses *desirability*. The most desirable output meets target value. Output becomes less desirable as measured values move away from the target. The aim is to reduce variation in order to bring more process outcomes closer and closer to the target value.[231]

Intrinsic and Extrinsic Values

An object or activity that an individual values for itself rather than as a means to an end is said to have *intrinsic* value. An object or activity that an individual values not for itself but for the ends it will help to achieve is said to have *extrinsic* value. It also is called *instrumental* value since it is a means, an instrument, a method to achieve desired ends. Repairing a car has instrumental value for the mechanic who works in a garage as a means to earn money. If he really enjoys the work for its own sake, then the activity also gives him intrinsic satisfaction. People engage in a hobby, so called because it is enjoyable for its own sake, as an end in itself. People who find both intrinsic and extrinsic value in an activity are fortunate. This raises the question of how a job can offer both.

Ackoff gives an example of a company that refused to reduce costs by adulterating its product or abbreviating the production processes. Degrading the quality of its products would affect customer satisfaction but also would significantly reduce the satisfaction, the intrinsic value, that the managers derived from their work and which gave them pride in the company.[232]

The key question, again, is, what are our values and how do they limit or enhance our ability to develop as individuals, as organizations, as a society? Methods of process improvement used to reinvent government or reengineer business organizations and schools can be useful methods, but one could go out of business with a reengineered organization that does not operate as a whole system or has dismissed so many employees it has destroyed its ability to think. One has to ask how the methods are being applied, for what purpose and in what context? Often when Dr. Deming expressed his concern about the economic decline of the United States, many people initially became angry and defensive. Some took his remarks as too critical of American business. Others tried to refute him with personal examples, such as, "Wait a minute. My business is going great. I am selling all I can make, and I'm making a lot of money." Dr. Deming did not think there was anything wrong with making money or with living better materially. He appreciated the technology that helped him be more efficient and that gave him the ability to spend more time on creative work. However, he saw that our ability to have a better quality of life, to be economically healthy, required doing something other than more of the same. His plea, for example, to move the balance from extrinsic to intrinsic values came from both the logic and the values inherent in profound knowledge. He feared that individuals and the institutions of government, business, and education would continue to lose their capability to govern their future because extrinsically oriented values contribute to the fragmentation of the wholeness of individuals and organizations. In an organization managed with a balance of intrinsic and extrinsic values, people will question, challenge, explore. Knowledge will develop. In a system that is managed solely by extrinsic rewards and punishments, people will hide mistakes. They will be reluctant to share ideas.

Values and Prediction

Valuation, said C. I. Lewis, is a form of empirical knowledge in that value judgments predict the future and can be empirically tested.[233] If I value a certain food for its flavor, I anticipate that when I eat it I will enjoy it. Lewis wrote that the person who knows, for example, that he likes Bach and dislikes Stravinsky, even though he may be a musical ignoramus, knows what to expect when he looks at the concert program. Lewis then goes on to state his own value judgment: "At least half of the world's avoidable troubles are created by those who do not know what they want and pursue what would not satisfy them if they had it. And we could deal with the villains if it weren't for the fools."[234]

One's valuation of objects and people as means are predictors of future events. Ideas, objects, and methods are valued because they help to meet the needs of a person or organization. A value functions like a theory. To value, therefore, is to predict how well people, objects, and methods will meet needs to accomplish some ends. Whether they do the job is an empirical question, and the value can be validated by results.

Values that guide action to gain and apply empirical knowledge, as they do in planning and in Deming's PDSA cycle, are known in science as epistemological or epistemic values. These are criteria that guide scientific research, such as the power of a theory to facilitate imagination and to make discoveries, to produce accurate predictions, to enable the confirmation of predictions and the repeatability of findings in future studies.[235] The term "management science" implies a scientific objectivity by management in executing their responsibilities, yet science is *not* completely objective. Scientists make value judgments by choosing which criteria (values) they use to evaluate competing theories and which theory they finally choose. In this way, values affect the knowledge that is gained in science since scientists select the research area on both these epistemic, extrinsic values as well as the extent to which they intrinsically value doing the research.

An intellectual understanding of Deming's thinking can open the door to changing people's values as well as the way they value. Deming's teaching initiated the transformation of the values of a senior executive of a business. He told me that he signed up for Deming's four-day seminar at the request of the CEO who had attended a previous seminar. Under compulsion (extrinsic motivation), he went "kicking and screaming," not publicly of course. During the first two days of the seminar, he was uncomfortable and really had to control himself not to leave. However, by the third day something began to strike him. After the fourth day, he began to seriously question his own values and beliefs about employees and why he always blamed them for problems. He concluded, from his new knowledge, that there was a better way. His values reversed from "trust the system and blame the individual" to "trust the individual and change the system," from "work is an observable activity" to "thinking also is work and may not be observable," from "focus on short-term, numerical objectives" to "take a longer-term vision." "Nothing in my twenty years in business affected me that way," he said. He just couldn't argue with the correctness of Dr. Deming's message. He was redrawing his mental map, from the one Deming described in chapter 2 of *The New Economics* as management's "present practice" that produces heavy losses to one of "better practice." The change in values enabled him to see a new future and gain a new power, a new potential, and new possibilities for the organization that he hadn't seen before. His challenge was to gain the trust of employees, because whatever he said and did, they probably would question his motives when he returned to the company.

An intellectual understanding of Deming's System of Profound Knowledge may not open the door for some people. When I heard the executive explain this, I was reminded of something that Donald Petersen, when he was president of the Ford Motor Company, said to a gathering of company and supplier executives: the knowledge that helped many of the individuals in the room, and their companies, to achieve their current success would not guarantee success in the future. Petersen's statement seemed to shock many in the audience. It prepared them for the event to follow—Dr. Deming's four-day seminar.

A person may be defensive about past actions and continue to justify them based on the culture that shaped and reinforced them. After all, it was those practices and management style that got managers to their current positions. Individuals who see a need to change may have feelings of guilt, shame, and disloyalty to others with whom they shared these values. They may then convince themselves that what they did in the past was good and right and continue that tradition. Another option is to be a maverick, try to work on the system wherever and whenever possible and build support. When people begin to understand Deming's System of Profound Knowledge, they should not reproach themselves for the way they behaved or managed previously. In Deming's view, transformation is a process that helps people to "pull away from their current practice and beliefs and move into the new philosophy without a feeling of guilt about the past."[236]

Ackoff wrote that when a person has alternative means to produce the same end, you might think that one means should not be preferred over another. Yet we do have preferences based on aesthetic values. The satisfactions we derive from *what* we do—the means—*rather* than why we do it—the ends—may be a matter of individual taste. Some people may prefer black shoes, while others may prefer brown shoes, even though each are equally instrumental for walking.[237] Digital smartphones, for example, are produced in various colors to meet individual preferences even though they all are functionally the same. People have aesthetic preferences so that the means can have value in themselves. Albert Einstein included aesthetic criteria as important values in the conduct of science, values such as the simplicity, beauty, and elegance of theories in the sense of fitting observations together rather than solving a problem.[238]

Deming's Principles of Professional Practice

The distinction between the meanings of the words *ethical* and *moral* is not always clear, and often they are used interchangeably as synonyms. *Ethics* has been used to refer to a *system of values* or moral principles for a group or profession. "Medical ethics," for example, refers to the rules or standards governing the conduct of individuals as members of the medical profession. The "Puritan ethic" values self-denial and self-discipline as virtuous. When an individual does not act in ways consistent with the code of values of the group, the actions are said to be unethical.

Dr. Deming gave to each client at the start of their relationship a document that elaborated his code of ethics, the principles of professional conduct that guided his practice.[239] The document is a statement of the mutual obligations of consultant and client. I would add that this is a map that applies to both managers as professionals and the specialists they supervise by providing principles of practice to effectively apply knowledge. In his statement of principles, Deming wrote, "The purpose of this paper will be served if these suggestions provide some guidance in areas in which they are less directly applicable, or even if they only stimulate interchange of ideas that will lead to further work on professional standards." He also said, "Professional practice stems from an expanding body of theory and from principles of application. A professional aims at recognition and respect for his practice, not for himself alone, but for his colleagues as well." Deming continued that a professional person takes direction in technical matters, from standards set by professional colleagues and not from an administrative superior. A professional person will not follow methods that are indefensible, merely to please someone. Deming also stated in his code of ethics, "Allocation of responsibilities does not mean impervious compartments in which you do this and I'll do that. It means that there is a logical basis for allocation of responsibilities, and that it is necessary for everyone involved in a study to know in advance what he will be accountable for."[240]

Second Movement: Appreciation for a System

Chapter 9

Whole-System Thinking

> The world is a complex, interconnected, finite, ecological-
> social-psychological-economic system. We treat it as
> if it were divisible, separable, and infinite.
> —Donella Meadows[241]

Appreciation for a System

The traditional organization chart is a map of the separateness within an enterprise. The lines that represent each function do not show a direct path to travel between people and processes at the lower levels of the management pyramid. The lines for each function meet only at the top of the pyramid. The chart represents the organization as a collection of functions rather than as a system of interacting, interdependent parts. W. Edwards Deming, Jay Forrester, Russell Ackoff, and other systems theorists and practitioners have tried over the years to draw management's attention to systems thinking and its importance for leadership. Appreciation for a system is a theme that runs through Deming's entire System of Profound Knowledge.

Professor Jay Forrester, who developed the field of System Dynamics (initially called Industrial Dynamics) and taught it for many years at the Massachusetts Institute of Technology, decades ago recognized that managers must acquire a new way of thinking if they are to provide the leadership that enterprise requires in an increasingly complex world. In his book *Industrial Dynamics*, Forrester wrote: "Our most challenging intellectual frontier probably lies in the dynamics of social organizations, ranging from growth of the small corporation to development of national economies. As organizations grow more complex, the need for skilled leadership becomes greater."[242]

Forrester's prediction is even more relevant in today's global economy. He wrote that management has been an art for many centuries. An art relies on experience. Experiences were recorded, but common lessons were difficult to transfer. An applied science would provide the foundation to support further development of the art of management. Individual experiences, rather than being presented as a special case—as an art—could be translated into a common frame of reference, from which they could be applied effectively in new situations by other managers. The practice of medicine and engineering began as an empirical art representing only the exercise of judgment based on experience. Science helps to understand the basis for the art. The art develops through empirical experience but eventually stops growing because of the disorganized state of its knowledge. Science can help explain, organize, and distill experience into a more compact and usable form.[243]

Forrester went on to say, "The manager's task is far more difficult and challenging than the normal tasks of the mathematician, physicist, or the engineer. In management, many more significant factors must be taken into account. The interrelationships of the factors are more complex.[244] ... The task of the manager will become more challenging. His training will become more rigorous. The new professionalism will not bring automatic success. New tools used without proper understanding can lead to disaster. In the hands of those who use them correctly they become a new competitive advantage toward business success." [245]

Management Is Not Learned or Practiced as a System

Dr. Forrester looked forward to the development within enterprises of greater interaction and cooperation of managers in the various functions. However, programs of management education are not managed as a system of knowledge. Therefore they do not provide a systems model for managers. In Forrester's view, "Management education and practice have been highly fragmentized. Manufacturing, finance, distribution, organization, advertising, and research have too often been viewed as separate skills and not as a part of a unified system. Too often management education consists of gathering current industrial practice and presenting it to the student as a sequence of unrelated subjects. Similarly, in his work in industry, the manager specializes within departments where his experience perpetuates the atmosphere of unrelated compartmentalization."[246]

Russell Ackoff made the same point about management education. The profession is organized into separate disciplines in the same way subjects are taught in universities. However, the various disciplines do not represent different parts of the reality we experience; rather, they are different points of view about the same reality. The whole that is reality is artificially divided. There are no marketing problems or financial problems or production problems. Rather, there are points of view, not specific kinds of problems. Problems can be seen from many viewpoints. He gave the example of a marketing manager who sees a decrease in sales in the previous quarter as a marketing problem. Management tries to solve the problem by manipulating the variables that they can control, which is analogous to doing brain surgery for a headache when a pill will do the job. In medicine, a pill can be used because there is knowledge of how the biological system works, how the parts interact when a pill is swallowed and a chemical is released into the blood stream and carried to the pain center of the brain. We don't understand the functions of an enterprise as a system. Marketing may try to do the equivalent of brain surgery when a pill will do. Ackoff found that the vast majority of problems that management experiences are better solved someplace other than where they appear. Systems consist of interacting parts, and managers don't understand the interactions. This is due in large part to management education. Business programs present courses in marketing, production, finance, and purchasing as separate subjects; these courses and programs do not address how the functions interact as a system.[247]

Problems cross the boundaries of various knowledge disciplines. Since "the system" is a concept, an abstraction in a person's mental map, the whole-system can only be understood by viewing it from many perspectives, sometimes simultaneously. Seeing the whole is a continual process of minds interacting. Then when we see how the parts are connected and interact to produce the behavior and properties of the whole, we can find a better solution. Problems may be viewed separately but are not separable. They are interrelated, "a mess" as Ackoff called it.[248]

The eye at the top of the pyramid on a US dollar bill does not represent an all-knowing, all-seeing, omniscient management. The enterprise as a whole can't be seen from the top of the organization pyramid since seeing a whole is a collective affair. Also, it can be a long way from the top to the bottom of the pyramid, and detail of actions at lower levels can't be seen. Some people have suggested, in the spirit of participative management, to turn the organizational pyramid upside down. Yet, even if employees are imagined to be at the top of the pyramid, the organizational structure is still a pyramid, only upside down. Continuing the metaphor, the pyramid, which is precariously balanced on its tip, is susceptible to environmental disturbances that could knock it over. The structure doesn't reflect or allow the complexity and dynamics of the organization to be managed. There are more constructive and creative ways to conceptualize, structure, and manage the enterprise as a whole-system, such as flow charts and system diagrams. Some are discussed in later chapters. Gregory Bateson explained it this way: "The division of the perceived universe into parts is convenient and may be necessary, but no necessity determines how it shall be done."[249]

Parts, Wholes, and Boundaries

Ackoff defined a system as a whole that is connected to a larger whole by its function.[250] Each of its essential parts can affect the functioning of the whole; however, no one part separately can affect the whole. The properties and characteristics of the whole *emerge* from the interactions of the parts. None of these properties of the whole are in the parts. Synergy, a term created by the futurist and systems theorist Buckminster Fuller, means that the behavior of whole-systems is unpredictable compared to when the behaviors or properties of the components are evaluated separately. Synergy represents the integrated behaviors of a system rather than the differentiated behaviors of the parts taken separately. Dr. Deming made this point when he referred to this ancient Japanese poem:

Is it the bell that rings,
Is it the hammer that rings,
Or is it the meeting of the two that rings?[251]

New properties, behaviors, and capabilities emerge from the interaction of parts. Working together, they constitute a system. Consider six twelve-by-twelve-inch squares of wood, each one inch thick. None of them has the properties of a box. New properties emerge from the *interaction* of the parts when structured as a box with four sides, a top, and a bottom. It is rigid. It can hold things. Consider piles of bricks, lumber, and other materials on an empty lot. Architects, tradespeople, and others interact well, poorly, or not at all in a process that transforms a collection of parts into a system—a house with a level of quality that depends on how well the people fit together and how well the parts fit together. The house is a system with different properties from its parts. The collection of parts is static, but the house is a dynamic system because of the ongoing exchange of information between the parts that maintains a stable internal climate in the face of a variable, and perhaps turbulent, external environment. Such a property cannot be found in the furnace itself, in any of the parts of the furnace looked at separately, or in any of the other parts of the house looked at individually. A new property, something more and different, emerged from the *interaction* of the parts.

The properties, capabilities, and performance of the whole can't be predicted from the properties of the component parts, *analyzed* separately and then added together. The whole is something more and different from the sum of the parts. It is a synthesis. New characteristics and new behaviors emerge from the arrangement, relationships, and interactions of the parts. To describe an automobile as a system, you would have to *explain* how the parts interact to contribute to the purpose of the automobile. One might say that the whole *transcends* its parts, and yet, at the same time, the character and capability of the whole is *immanent* since it exists within the relationships between the parts that give rise to the survival, viability, and performance of that whole. If a system is reduced to its component parts and the parts are analyzed, those properties will not be found. The function of a system can't be carried out by any part of the system taken separately. If an automobile is taken apart, it loses its ability to transport people. An engine separated from an automobile can't move anything. An eye separated from the body can't see. Stafford Beer, the British systems theorist, put it this way: "Take a live thing apart to discover what life is. You will not find a component called life—and behold the live thing is dead. Shall we take a radio apart to find the voice? Or a car engine to pieces to find the speed?"[252]

System performance depends on the fit of interdependent parts. When the people in the system fit together well, the parts of the product and services fit together well. When people behave as a system, products and services behave as a system. When an enterprise performs as a whole, the experience of the customer is whole. Failure to understand that performance depends on how well interdependent parts fit together and can lead to unsolvable mysteries, wrong conclusions, and a waste of time. In the mid-1980s, a Japanese automotive manufacturer was producing cars with much higher levels of customer satisfaction than its American competitor. The American company tried to understand why this was so. The Americans analyzed the Japanese vehicle and their own vehicle by the following process: (1) each vehicle was completely disassembled; (2) specialists independently examined the parts (i.e., the engine engineers examined the engines, the body engineers examined the body panels, the chassis engineers examined the steering and suspension); and (3) the specialists wrote up their findings, which were submitted to an engineering manager, who combined the separate reports.

The results were puzzling. Part for part, the American car appeared to be better than the Japanese car (e.g., thicker gauge steel for the body panels). Why the puzzle? The method of *analysis* failed to get at the holistic experience of customers. Customers did not buy a collection of parts; they bought a whole-system, and that is what they evaluated. In their eyes, the experience of high quality was due to the way everything fit together, the way the parts of the vehicle interacted with each other and with themselves as customers, in terms of comfort and convenience of seats and controls, smoothness of the engine and shifting of the transmission, to produce the customer's whole experience.

The method of analysis of the American company—the independent actions of the specialists, the aggregation of the data by a manager— followed the same map, the same model as the method used to design the vehicle. Every part met engineering specifications. Every individual was doing his and her best, yet the vehicle as a whole did not have the expected quality. The American vehicle did not perform as a whole-system in the eyes of customers, because the people who designed and built it did not perform as a whole-system.

Scoring a Whole-in-One—Consider Golf

The word *whole* means "healthy," a coherent system or organization of parts fitting or working together as one. My friend Tom O'Connell, a PGA golf professional, when he was teaching in Scottsdale, Arizona, put wholeness into a context that might be familiar to many readers: "Every golfer has a model, a picture in mind that represents the proper swinging motion. Some models can produce excellent performance; others will produce poor performance. The model must be clear, complete, and in a harmonious relationship with the individual. The golfer should practice and play in an environment that is completely safe and free of intimidation."

The golfer's performance may be understood as a whole-in-one. The swing is produced by two whole-systems. First is the human system that contains the interaction of the golfer's physiological and psychological systems. Second is the interaction of the human system with the larger environmental system. Together they form *one* whole, inseparable performance system—a whole in a whole, a whole-in-one. While Tom was not a student of Dr. Deming, his professional understanding of the golfer's performance incorporates relevant aspects of some of Dr. Deming's 14 Points for Management, which flow from profound knowledge:[253]

- Point Number 8: Remove fear so that people may work effectively.
- Point Number 9: Break down barriers.
- Point Number 5: Improve continually the system of production and service.

Serious golfers are continually learning. They are able to experience that wonderful high, that magical feeling that comes when the swinging motion is a unified whole. Everything is just right, synchronized, working together. There are no separate parts—no shoulders, arms, hands, hips, legs, or feet. They all interact as one to accomplish the purpose of the activity, which is to propel the ball to the target. The hands don't try to dominate the feet. The arm swing doesn't dominate the body rotation. The eyes don't look wherever they please. Each part of the body that contributes to the purposeful action of swinging the golf club interacts harmoniously with the other parts and with the golf club in order to perform properly. It is as if the body as a whole knows what to do.

The interaction of the club with the ball and the consequent speed and direction of the ball is pure physics, but golf is not only a physical-mechanical process of applying force to the ball. It is an inseparable interaction between the physical, physiological, and psychological qualities of the system. The aim of the golfer is not to achieve a hole-in-one. Good scores will follow as a consequence of good process. A perfect score, although welcome, is not the goal. However, if all is proper, if the golfer operates as a *whole-in-one*, the chances of the ball going to the target are more likely, and a hole-in-one is possible. If one worries about the score, then he or she will tend to react to the result of each shot as if that result was due to the takeaway, weight transfer, swing path, plane club face angle, and so on. This can cause the golfer to overcompensate, reducing accuracy and consistency. Golfers need to guard against overdoing any one part of their swing.

If the golfer does not manage his or her play as a whole-system, performance will be disappointing, and the individual will feel frustrated and angry. This, in turn, will most likely cause the person to try to overcompensate even more, which will further degrade performance. To focus on the parts without regard to the whole is to ignore what produces exceptional performance. The quality of the relationships between the parts makes the difference in the quality of overall performance.

The golfer depends on the caddie; they are a team. The players have minimal interaction since they can watch and be influenced by the others, but they don't depend on each other. However, the golf game can be designed to create interdependence, such as in Ryder Cup international play or a scramble format in local play. In team sports activities, such as basketball, the nature of the interdependence between parts gives the game its unique character. Each player is like a specialized part of the body. The whole cannot perform without it, and the individual player has no purpose without the whole. The interaction between the players has to be orchestrated so that the parts can work together to optimize the performance of the whole. Methods to do this in any organization are discussed later in chapter 12.

The performing arts require the same kind of management of interactions, within each individual artist and between individuals of the group, such as a symphony orchestra, a choir, or a theater company. Just as performance of the golfer will degrade if one part of the body dominates the other parts, performance of the orchestra or chorus will be degraded if individuals play or sing louder or faster to gain attention for themselves rather than doing what is appropriate to optimize their interactions with the other performers.

Just as a golfer's swing follows from his or her mental model of the right swing, we are guided in our actions by the models, values, beliefs, and assumptions that are the content of our mental maps. In order for golfers to avoid penalties for going out of bounds in the physical game, they may have to go beyond the boundaries of their current mental model to better manage their performance. Golfers cannot improve their game unless they learn an appropriate model and then practice, continually learning to apply that model until a better one comes along. It is relatively easy to appreciate the fact that wholeness makes possible exceptional performance in golf and in the performing arts. It may not be as easy to appreciate this for other aspects of managing and living.

Systems Function within Systems

A system contains subsystems and itself is a subsystem of a system in which it is contained. Consider the human body. A biological system view reveals that the human body is a component of a larger whole. It is embedded in an external environment, which supplies nutrients and oxygen, and it contains its own subsystems, such as the digestive system. The parts of the digestive system in turn are subsystems—the mouth, esophagus, stomach, liver, and so on. Within each system are processes that convert food to energy. How the digestive system functions is described by these systems and processes. Why it functions is explained in terms of its function in its containing a supra system, the human body. The living and healthy human being has many functions in the containing environment, especially as part of various social systems. A subsystem may have a function in more than one system. For example, in the digestive system, the liver produces bile, which breaks up fat into smaller pieces that are easier to digest. In the circulatory system, the liver removes toxins from the blood.

We cannot see the whole-system at once since it is spread over various places and operates over time. Deming called this "temporal spread." The state of the system as a whole, therefore, can't be evaluated at any point in time or in any one locality, although various methods try to evaluate problems when and where they show up. Then the people and processes operating at that place and time are viewed as the cause even though actions and consequences may be widely separated in time and place. Interdependencies and the need to manage interactions are not always obvious.

A system is defined operationally for a particular purpose. We draw the boundaries for a particular purpose. We can share them with others in an organization by drawing them in various ways (e.g., flow chart of processes, embedded circles of systems and subsystems, and loop diagrams). Besides, we can never have complete knowledge and understanding of anything or everything. When we try, we see that the world is continually changing, with new patterns and relationships emerging.

System Level	Core System: System in Focus Contains sub systems and is contained in (a sub system of) a supra system.	Sub-system: Contained in core system	Supra System: Contains sub systems.
System Name	Automobile	Steering system	National Transportation System
Function Purpose	Personal transportation	Enable the operator to control the direction of the vehicle	Economic and security: distribute people, goods and services, for commercial, public and military needs
System Components (Parts or Subsystems)	Operating system (human operator or other controller), steering system, cooling system, powertrain system	Front tires, wheels, front suspension, steering gear, column, steering wheel	Automobiles, buses, trucks, rail cars, airplanes, highways and other roads, tracks, airports, gas stations, people operating and maintaining all of the above, government regulatory agencies

Table 9-1. Hierarchy of embedded systems

Table 9-1 illustrates how we might think about an automobile as a whole within a larger whole, as a whole-in-one, like little wooden dolls of different sizes, each one nested in the next larger size. The system of interest at a particular time is called the *system in focus* or *core system*. In the table, the automobile is selected as the core system whose purpose or function is personal transportation. The subsystems are described in greater detail, in sharper resolution than the containing system, as if they were being examined by a higher-power microscope.[254] An automobile contains various subsystems, including powertrain (engine and transmission), cooling, and steering. Each of these subsystems contains subsystems or components (e.g., the cooling system is composed of a radiator and other parts). The automobile, considered as a whole, is a component of larger supra systems, such as a national transportation system. (Dr. Deming questioned whether there actually was a national transportation *system* since an essential characteristic of a system is predictability and repeatability.) A system also may provide functions not essential to its primary function. An automobile also can be a status symbol.

Maps of Systems and Processes

The way enterprises are conceptualized has a very large effect on what
they do, and what they do affects the way they are conceptualized.
—Russell Ackoff[255]

Systems thinking conceptualizes relationships between things that are concrete and observable, such as a living organism or a business or something more abstract, such as an economic or political system. The term *systems thinking* applies to the particular model or methods of the systems thinker. Although models and approaches may differ, they share common system principles that, when studied, can provide a deeper understanding of systems thinking and how it may be applied. One common shared principle is that a system is a whole that loses its characteristics and properties if parts (subsystems) that it contains are removed or separated from other parts upon which it depends. This is because parts of a system do not have independent effects; they depend on or affect at least one other part of the system. The way our heart affects the whole, our body, depends on what our lungs are doing, and our lungs depend on what other parts are doing.

Peter Senge and his colleagues built upon the system dynamics model of their mentor, Jay Forrester, and integrated it into a system they call the Learning Organization.[256] Deming described a system in terms of purpose: "A network of interdependent components that work together to try to accomplish the aim of the system."[257] Stafford Beer's Viable System Model is based on a model of the human central nervous system where management is the brain that controls the enterprise, whose heart is the human being.[258] Russ Ackoff conceptualized an enterprise as a social system where people, who are components of the system, also have their own purposes. The approaches of these and other systems theorists may differ, yet much can be learned about managing the enterprise as a system. Ackoff and Beer were friends for many years yet disagreed on the model. Ackoff said, "I have learned more from my disagreements with Stafford than I have from my agreements with most others."[259]

Interactions with Environment

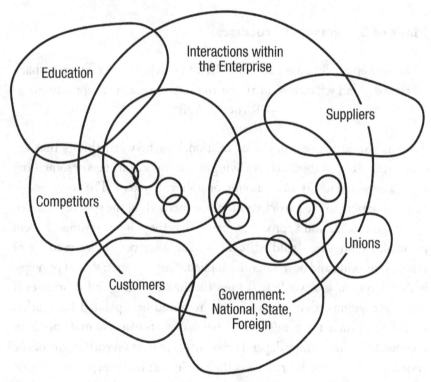

Figure 9-1. A systems view of enterprise

Figure 9-1 is one way to depict the enterprise as a system. The large circle represents the enterprise as a system contained within a larger whole, the social-economic-political environment—its supra system. The enterprise contains subsystems shown by the smaller circles, and within them are their subsystems. Along the enterprise boundary—the circumference of the circle—are the systems in its environment that interact with it. This does not show the dynamic, interactive nature of a system that we would see with feedback loops. Since a system is a conceptual map, in an actual organization, the map should synthesize the views of others in the enterprise, in its external environment, and in its subsystems and processes. This will enrich everyone's image of the whole. Seeing the whole is a continual process of minds interacting.

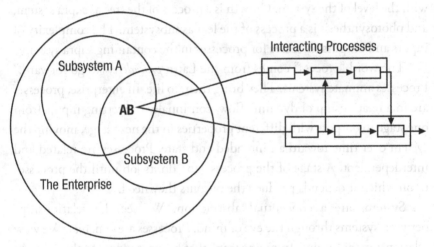

Figure 9-2. Interaction of subsystem processes

Figure 9-2 illustrates the interaction of two subsystems, A and B, within the enterprise. Their interaction occurs in the area where the circles overlap. Each subsystem contains processes that execute functions that transform inputs into outputs. Since the systems overlap, their boundaries are said to be permeable. Each of these subsystems also interacts with other systems.

A model of enterprise as a social system developed in the twentieth century as pressures from within and outside of enterprise forced, or enlightened, managers to consider the interests and purposes of employees in addition to those of the enterprise. We can view the social system as an ecology like a forest and other natural, living systems that must continually interact to remain viable, importing resources as inputs and exporting outputs. An ecology, such as a forest, is a web, a network of relationships of systems and processes of plant and animal life, nonliving and organic material, atmosphere, and moisture. In a forest ecology, a tree is a system. It contains subsystems, such as roots, a trunk, and leaves. The tree is a system that has a growth process made possible by the processes of its subsystems. The leaf, for example, is a subsystem that contains the process of photosynthesis, which uses sunlight to convert carbohydrates to sugar from carbon dioxide and water. That is one of many subsystems and processes in the system called "tree." There are others, such as moisture distribution, seed production, and decay. Processes, therefore, are aligned with the level of the system. Growth is a process of the tree as supra system, and photosynthesis is a process of the leaf as subsystem. The complexity of inputs and outputs increases for processes in the containing supra systems.

The word "process" comes from the Latin *procedere*, "to go forward." Processes animate systems. They bring them to life. In enterprise, processes are in a relationship of dynamic flow, continually converting inputs from one stage to outputs with different properties to the next stage, moving the system over time toward an intended end state. Processes are related and interdependent. A stage of the process can't do its job until the processes upon which it depends produce the outputs they need.

Systems are a conceptual abstraction. We see the relationships between systems through the eye of mind. Processes are concrete. We view relationships as outputs from one stage that become inputs to the next. As they function, they cross conceptual boundaries that define the systems, such as when financial and accounting processes cross into sales and marketing processes. Therefore, from a systems view, the responsibilities of people don't fit neatly into traditional top-down command and control structures. A process usually will contain elements that are simultaneously components of one or more other processes, just as plant decay is also a component of the soil-building process.

Deming wrote that processes are not individual entities.[260] Every activity, every job is part of a process. Process is a flow of interactions between internal suppliers and customers to the final customer in the enterprise's external environment. In each stage of the flow, there will be value-adding changes of state as input is transformed to output. Stages must work together as supplier and customer. Gipsie Ranney has observed that if a business enterprise is viewed as a system, profit is understood to be an emergent property of the enterprise as a whole. It then makes little sense to have interdependent parts of the organization work by themselves to increase profit or reduce costs.[261]

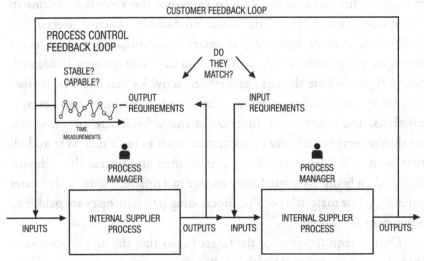

Figure 9-3. Internal supplier-customer interaction

Figure 9-3 shows a relationship between two interdependent and interacting processes in an enterprise's social system ecology. This was shown in figure 9-2 as an exchange between processes. In the model of an enterprise as a machine, we view employees as inputs to a process, as commodities. Employees may look at themselves that way too. In a meeting at a plant, a worker told Dr. Deming, "We are a commodity."[262] In an ecological systems view, employees preside over the process as a manager, not in the traditional sense of managing subordinates but in using their knowledge, skills, ideas, and energy to manage the process. Each process manager is a supplier-producer, converting input resources to outputs that are received as inputs by the next process manager who is an internal customer. This continues across the systems of the enterprise, where each process manager receives inputs, converts them, and sends them to the next process manager until the final internal or external customer receives the final products and services. "Presiding" has a range of meanings depending on the nature of the process. It can mean that the individual strictly follows procedures and executes tasks. It also can be at the other end of the continuum where the nature of the process allows the individual to exercise discretion and control and participate in process improvement with other process managers.

Every employee can be thought of and view him or herself as a process manager. This includes people who carry out the various functions in the system named "the plant"—the production operator, electrician, production control specialist, secretary, finance analyst, and other nonsupervisory, professional, technical, and clerical employees. Inside each box of figure 9-3 are the tasks and related activities that could be further detailed by a process-flow diagram. Inputs, such as machines, tools, energy, materials, and information, function in two ways. There are those that do the converting and may be consumed, such as tools that wear and oil that burns off. The inputs being transformed are process throughputs. Rather than being consumed, they emerge in a different state, with greater value (e.g., raw materials become functioning parts, invoices are paid, and equipment is serviced).

Output requirements are the target values that the supplier-producer intends to achieve to meet the customer's input requirements. These requirements, such as specifications, schedules, and budgets, consider not only the customer's needs but the supplier's capability. We can evaluate value added by the supplier by how well the customer's requirements have been met so that the outputs of that stage of the process can meet the next producer's requirements. Supplier output requirements must match customer input requirements. The feedback loop from the internal customer to the internal supplier provides information regarding the quality of the inputs received by the customer. Ongoing communication also may include other information for decisions about output (e.g., which characteristics to measure and how to improve the process). (See chapter 12 for discussion of a method for managing interactions.)

The producer as process manager has an internal feedback loop to control the process in order to maintain a stable, repeatable process by identifying and removing specific, identifiable sources of variation that produce adverse and undesired changes in the process. A statistical process control chart is used for this purpose. (See chapter 13 for more on this topic.) If a process isn't stable, it isn't repeatable; target values have no meaning, and the customer can't count on getting what is needed to function.

We also can use this model to represent the functions of supervisors and managers. A manager presides over a system that contains the process managers and processes that produce the products and services of that system. As we move to more encompassing supra systems, the measurements produced by the system are aggregates, composites of measurements produced by the subsystems of the enterprise. They are abstractions representing nothing specific, not representing anything concrete that we can point to.

Interactions Management to Optimize Enterprise Performance

"You think because you understand one you must understand two because one and one make two. But you must also understand *and*." Donella Meadows, a pioneer in environmental science, cited this ancient Sufi wisdom to make the point that when we have a whole-system view, we can see not just things but their relationships. She said, "When you see whole-systems, you start noticing where things come from and where they go."[263]

The effects of interactions on other systems and processes can be positive, negative, or neutral. Deming sometimes said that a person who steals second base with the bases loaded thinks he is doing a good job.[264] The coach who encourages the player to do this would be managing actions rather than interactions. Of course, this is not very likely on the ball field where the manager and coaches can observe the whole field of play. In enterprise, where the players are separated in time and place and the whole-system can't be seen simultaneously, *negative interactions*, as Deming called it, are more likely to occur. A system referee, if there were such a person in an organization, would call interference. Negative interactions can produce performance that is less than the sum of the parts taken separately. Deming warned that management produces negative interactions by fostering internal competition by rating, ranking, and rewarding employees based on performance attributed completely to them as individuals, without considering the contribution of the system. A system usually is the source of its own failures and other unintended and undesired consequences. The mismanagement of people discourages people from working together and destroys a system. Heavy losses result from internal competition between individuals and units within the enterprise.[265] Management is responsible for removing barriers and promoting cooperation to remove barriers.[266] In the complex social system of enterprise, necessary connections likely won't happen by themselves. A process is needed to identify and manage interactions.

Supplier (Sender)	Customer (Receiver)			
	A	B	C	D
A				
B				
C				
D				

Table 9-2. Interactions matrix of supplier-customer relationships

Consider this situation that might occur in a plant, among a staff, in a retail store, or in any enterprise with four process managers (A, B, C, and D), some or all of whom are in internal supplier-customer relationships and need to communicate with each other. Table 9-2 shows the complexity of a system with just four people, and interactions must be managed. We determine the number of supplier-customer relationships, R, by counting the number of cells on either side of the diagonal (shaded cells) in the table or by calculating:

$$R = 1/2 \ [n \times (n-1)] = \frac{1}{2} \ (4 \times 3) = 6 \text{ relationships (2-person interactions)}$$

We use the number n-1 because a one-person interaction (the shaded diagonal) doesn't exist, perhaps except for those individuals who argue with themselves. A relationship is an interdependence between two people or processes. As more interactions need to be managed, we can see from the equation how the number of interactions can grow. A system with five people will have ten possible two-person relationships; with six people, there are fifteen possible relationships. However, it is not likely that each person will depend directly, or indirectly, on all of the others.

A process to manage (orchestrate) interactions to optimize performance of the whole in different organizations is presented in chapter 12. Optimization can occur with the cooperation of people who depend on each other; otherwise the improvement of one process could cause problems for other processes by negative interactions. For example, sourcing parts to a lower-cost supplier may increase costs to other processes because of poor-quality parts. It might be that sourcing to a higher-cost supplier that provided higher-quality parts would reduce overall costs and increase sales revenues. People have to know how their actions affect each other. Working together requires a whole-system orientation, one that is not obstructed by hierarchical, functionally separated organization structures and evaluation processes that encourage individuals to maximize their individual performance to the detriment of others.

Sometimes processes are adopted from other organizations where they appear to perform well—without understanding why. Combining the "best" parts of different systems won't guarantee that the new combination will perform well or even be able to function. This has been a problem when companies benchmark other organizations. We may see this when exceptionally talented athletes from various league teams come together to form a team for a unique event like an All-Star game and overall performance is not as good as we might expect given the talents of the individuals. The "team" may perform more like a collection of parts than an interdependent, positively interacting system. The players initially can have difficulty blending and flowing together as one whole. When players are traded, they must learn to work together with their new team, and that depends on how their interactions are managed.

Leadership helps to make the interactions positive. Leadership can be obvious, as when the orchestra conductor or coach manages the playing, or less visible and more subtle as when jazz musicians manage their own interactions. Jazz saxophonist Joshua Redman has commented that the musician has to have rapport with fellow musicians off the bandstand as well as on. He went on to say, "Even though there is structure and form to jazz, the ideal in jazz is to express the moment spontaneously in terms of the group. There needs to be a feeling that all of us together are creating something which transcends that form."[267] Kareem Abdul-Jabbar, NBA Hall of Famer, made the same point when comparing jazz and basketball: "If you're a jazz musician, you have to be aware of your partners, your teammates, and react to them in time while you're performing. The same thing happens on the basketball court. You know, the whole idea of the solo, you want certain people to take a solo. In basketball, it's the shooting. You want certain guys to shoot and certain guys you don't want to shoot. You know, just figuring all that out and having a game plan and exercising that and being able to react to your teammates, it's a pretty interesting sport and discipline in that sense."[268]

Chapter 10

There Is No Accounting for the Costs of Suboptimization

> Economic logic is almost always applied toward the optimization of some aspect of a limited subsystem. It tends to downplay or omit those important qualities that are not quantifiable.
> —Willis W. Harman[269]

The central principle of chapters 10 and 11 can be summarized by the previously stated observation of Dr. Gipsie Ranney: If a business enterprise is viewed as a system, profit is understood to be an emergent property of the enterprise as a whole. It then makes little sense to have interdependent parts of the organization work by themselves to increase profit or reduce costs.[270]

What would be the result if the orchestra conductor were evaluated on meeting cost, productivity, and efficiency targets? The musicians would be encouraged to perform as if they were soloists, without regard to the music score or to what the others were doing. If musicians were evaluated on their individual performances, they would play as fast and as loud as they could in order to stand out above the rest. The conductor might be rewarded for the efficiency of the orchestra in completing the symphony in record time. Of course the result would be noise, which would not be a quality experience for the audience. Is this too farfetched as a metaphor for traditional management methods driven by financial targets and internal competition for rewards?

Anyone Can Reduce Visible Costs: Just Cut Things Out

Years ago, someone whom I thought was a friend offered to improve my car's performance by fixing the engine. He believed that he was a good mechanic, and so did I. He removed parts of the engine, fiddled around with them, and reassembled them. Some parts were left over. He said that they were not needed and did not know why these "extra-cost" parts were put there in the first place. The car then ran better than before—for one day. Then it died suddenly.

I thought about this years later when I learned that a large business had reduced the number of employees by 30 percent in order to lower costs. This made the numbers look good on paper—but not for long. As customers became increasingly unhappy with poor quality, late deliveries, and poor service, orders decreased and losses began to rapidly rise. The company decided to lower costs even more by removing larger parts of the system. It began to sell off some of its business units to raise cash, thereby accelerating the process of self-destruction. Deming observed that anyone can reduce visible costs if they cut out things and in so doing provide inferior products and services. The loss of profits can far outweigh cost reductions.[271]

Financial accounting processes aim to reduce cost in order to improve the bottom line. It can be helpful to remember Gipsie Ranney's counsel that costs are not causes; costs come from causes. In other words, costs are ends, not means, not methods. Dr. Tom Johnson, professor of accounting, put it this way: "A business organization cannot improve its long-run financial results by working to improve its financial results. The only way to ensure satisfactory and stable long term financial results is to work on improving the system from which those results emerge."[272]

What Cost Accounting Misses: The Losses from Separateness Thinking

The word "corporation" derives from *corpus*, the Latin word for body. Financial management models view the corpus as made up of separate parts. Accounting processes measure performance of the whole enterprise by adding the performance of the separate departments. The theory is that if each part is individually doing its best, the results of the whole enterprise will be best. Willis Harman, a systems engineer and futurist, put the systems view of the human body into a management accounting context.[273] He explained separateness by asking us to imagine what would happen if the stomach "thought" it could pursue its self-interest independent of the well-being of the whole human. It would justify its appetite with rationalizations such as, "What's good for the stomach is good for the whole," and "The business of the stomach is the growth of the stomach." It would try to maximize its own absorption of nutrients and minimize the amount going to other parts of the body. It would evaluate its performance with indicators such as "market share of the food value" and "gross abdominal product." The stomach would not survive, nor would the human being who contained that stomach. Both survive because the stomach performs its function with regard to the whole body—the supra system in which it is contained—and the supra system in turn meets the needs of its subsystems for nutrients and protection.

A whole-system is held together by interactions of the parts that give the whole its viability, its life. The whole cannot exist (function) without its parts, and the parts cannot exist (function) without the whole. This is as true of social organizations as it is of biological life. The character and performance of a whole-system emerges through interaction of parts and not from adding the performance of a collection of separate parts.

The age-old story of the blind men and the elephant emphasizes the defects of separateness thinking and acting. In the story, a group of men, who can't see because either they are blind or in darkness, each touch an elephant to learn about it. Each one touches a different part. When they each describe the elephant, of course they do not agree. An enterprise is more and different than the sum of its separate parts, just as a painting is more and different from its lines and paint.

Deming recognized that visible figures are important, such as payroll, taxes, and invoices from suppliers, yet we cannot be successful by managing only with visible figures. "He that would run his company on visible figures alone will in time have neither company nor figures." The most important figures that management needs are unknown or unknowable, yet management must take account of them. These include factors such as employee pride in work, cooperation between internal and external suppliers and customers, the effects of performance appraisal and other processes of evaluation, feedback, and compensation, sourcing to the lowest-cost supplier to reduce the costs of purchased materials, and the multiplying effect on sales from happy or unhappy customers.[274] In other words, the popular saying, "if you can't count it, it doesn't count," is wrong.

Management accounting relies on visible figures. Profit, revenue, and cost numbers of an enterprise are produced by the activities of people, processes, and management styles and systems. Enterprises are essentially social systems—human performance ecologies—with transactions between people: customers with suppliers, designers and engineers with purchasing, lawyers with regulators, and so on. However, models that measure performance don't explicitly take into account that performance results from the quality of the interactions between conscious, thinking, reflecting, feeling human beings who want to be respected for doing a good job. Dr. Deming told the controller of a large company that the visible costs that the financial system measured were trivial compared to the hidden costs and to the lost opportunities for profit. It quickly became obvious that this was not what the controller wanted to hear.

Status	Engine	Transmission	Both
Present	$100	$80	$180
Proposed	$130	$0	$130
Savings	Per Unit		$50
Annual Savings	1,000,000 Units		$50,000,000

Table 10-1. Cost of powertrain electronic components

The three tables, 10-1, 10-2, and 10-3, illustrate Dr. Deming's point. Table 10-1 is based on the experience of a motor vehicle manufacturer.[275] The engine and transmission each had electronic components. An engineer found that a redesign of the engine components would eliminate the need for electronic components on the transmission and save eighty dollars but would require adding thirty dollars to the cost of the engine. The management of the division that manufactured the engine rejected the proposal. Since they operated as a profit center, they would be penalized for adding cost. Their job was to reduce the cost of manufacturing an engine, not the cost of manufacturing a vehicle. What incredible suboptimization! The company manufactured one million units per year; therefore, the unrealized annual savings was $50 million. If the company were producing a return on investment (ROI) of 5 percent, it would require an investment of one billion dollars to earn this amount!

Similar examples can be found in other enterprises. I encountered a situation in which the customer service department needed to replace a twenty-year-old vehicle. However, since the cost of a new vehicle would have been charged to their budget and a complete overhaul of the old vehicle would be charged to the budget of the maintenance department, they chose to have the vehicle overhauled at greater cost than replacement!

Traditional models increase total cost when they don't consider the effects of local plans and actions on other parts of the enterprise. This thinking reflects the widely held assumption that the performance of the whole is the simple sum of the performance of each of the parts considered separately. Consequently, each person and unit is urged to do its best so that the whole will be best. Pressures from meeting local objectives tend to interfere with working together to reduce costs by optimizing enterprise relationships.

(1) Manager	(2) Expected Results	(3) Actual Results
(2) Purchasing	+	-
(3) Engineering	+	-
(4) Assembly	+	+
(5) Overall Results	+3	-1

Table 10-2. Performance under traditional assumptions

Table 10-2 illustrates the calculation of performance expected under the traditional assumption that the whole will be its best if the individual units do their best. This is shown for three interdependent organizations: Purchasing, Product Engineering, and the Assembly Plant. Typically, each unit, or department, independently establishes plans and objectives that will satisfy the global goals or objectives of a higher-level manager. Objectives usually are quantified. Each unit plans to accomplish the local objective for itself, as indicated by the + in column 2, rows 2, 3, and 4. The + indicates positive performance in terms of revenue, sales volume, or cost reduction. The effects in any cell indicated by a plus or minus are assumed, only for this illustration, to be the same. The plans, which are expectations (predictions) of performance, are aggregated up the management pyramid into the overall objective of the senior manager of the function or business unit. Throughout the year, management compares actual performance to plan—the budget. Management discusses negative deviations (variances) from the plan and takes corrective actions. Each manager is rated at the end of the year according to department performance and rewarded or punished accordingly.

There is an assumption implicit in this method that each individual has control over the performance for which he or she is held responsible. Therefore, if we are doing our best, working hard, then we should succeed. The problem is that attempts to meet local objectives and maximize local performance may very well produce actual performance that is worse than we would expect by adding up the separate plans.

Table 10-2, column 3 shows not only that actual results were less than expected but that there was an overall loss, even though each department planned and acted to produce positive results for itself. The reason for this can be seen in table 10-3, which expands table 10-2 to show the effects of unplanned interactions between units. (The results in table 10-3, row 5 are the same as in table 10-2, column 3.) This may help to explain how senior management can be promised, say, a 15 percent gain from each unit, but at the end of the year receive much less, perhaps even a loss. This paradox results from traditional assumptions and methods that hide the source of gains, costs, and losses.

(1) Department Actions	(2) Effects on Purchasing	(3) Effects on Engineering	(4) Effects on Assembly	(5) Effects on Whole System
(2) Purchasing: Sources to supplier with lowest price, but no engineering capability.	+ Reduces expenditures by 10%.	- Hires engineer to work with supplier, Purchasing, and Assembly to solve problems.	- Parts unusable or hard to assemble. Can't meet production schedules.	-1
(3) Product Engineering: Redesigns product and replaces many individual parts with fewer subassemblies.	- Purchasing spends much time with Engineering to help supplier produce subassemblies.	+ Higher quality and reliability, better appearance.	+ Fewer product parts have less variability. Easier and faster to assemble than previous design.	+1
(4) Assembly Plant: Retools assembly process for new product design.	- Supplier's parts cause problems in assembly process. Buyer "lives" in plant.	- Engineering spends much time in plant with supplier and buyer.	+ Faster to assemble product. Lower labor costs.	-1
(5) Results Attributed to Departments	-1	-1	+1	-1

**Table 10-3. Maximizing local performance
lowers overall performance**

Table 10-3 shows that overall performance suffers when individual departments work to maximize their own performance locally and do not work together to optimize performance of the whole-system. The independent plans and actions of each department appear in column 1, rows 2, 3, and 4. Each department influences results in the following ways:

(1) Influences its own performance. The effects appear in the shaded cells on the diagonal. Each department has developed plans and acted to produce a + for itself. These results also appear in table 10-2, column 2, where an overall result of +3 is expected:

Purchasing (table 10-3, row 2, column 1), in order to meet cost reduction objectives, sourced one of the subassemblies to a supplier with the lowest price, even though the supplier had no engineering capability. This helped the Purchasing department save 10 percent in expenditures for purchased parts. It gets a + for itself (row 2, column 2).

Product Engineering (row 3, column 1) redesigned the product to replace many individual parts with fewer, more complex assemblies. It gets a + for itself (row 3, column 3) because the new design improved overall product quality, reliability, and appearance.

Assembly (row 4, column 1) retooled to assemble the larger subassemblies. It replaced some workers with robots to speed up the process and reduce labor costs. It gets a + for itself (row 4, column 4).

(2) Influences performance of other departments, and they, in turn, affect it. These interaction effects are shown in the nonshaded cells of rows 2, 3, and 4 in columns 2, 3, and 4. For example:

Purchasing (row 2) negatively affected Product Engineering (row 2, column 3) since the lack of supplier engineering capability made it necessary for Engineering to hire an engineer to work with the supplier. Purchasing also negatively impacted Assembly (row 2, column 4). Both of these effects, in turn, negatively impacted Purchasing since it now had to spend more time in meetings with Engineering (row 3, column 2). Purchasing also had to send a buyer to "live" in the supplier's plant (row 4, column 2). These interactive effects illustrate that the organization does not operate according to a model in which units act independently with no effects on each other.

The effects of one department on another may be positive. The redesigned product was easier to assemble (row 3, column 4), although this gain was offset by the poor-quality subassemblies that the plant received (row 2, column 4).

The totals in row 5, columns 2, 3, and 4, show the results that would be attributed to each department. Purchasing, for example, appears to produce a negative result (row 5, column 2). The Purchasing manager would be held accountable for this result, even though performance of the department was negatively impacted by interactions with Engineering (row 3, column 2) and Assembly (row 4, column 2). The result (row 5, column 2) will form the basis of performance feedback and evaluation of the purchasing manager.

The effects of each department on the system are shown in column 5. Purchasing (row 2, column 5) and Assembly (row 4, column 5) each caused a loss to the system even though they met their own local objectives (shown in shaded cells). Product Engineering produced an overall positive effect on the system (row 3, column 5). Overall, the interactions between departments produced a loss. The bottom line is negative. The attempt to separately optimize each department suboptimized the system as a whole.

The quality of the interactions affects the visible results, but how that happens—the dynamics of the system—is not visible to the financial management system. Results produced by any individual or department alone, as well as those produced by positive or negative interactions, can't be separately measured. Most performance evaluation methods, however, are based on the assumption that performance is produced and controllable where it appears. Interaction effects are not explicitly considered.

The False Promise of Management by Objectives

Harry Artinian, a former associate of mine at Ford who has a background in finance, was able to look at administrative, service, and support processes with two maps—that of Deming's System of Profound Knowledge and that of management accounting. He saw what many of the accountants either did not see or were unwilling to admit seeing. When problems appeared, management added layers of inspection, review, and approval in order to maintain tight financial control and ensure that expenditures remained within budget. Rather than diagnosing and fixing the process, as described in chapter 7, where operational definitions improved the claims process, management reviews and approvals were imposed to compensate for process problems that appeared locally within the process, even though they could have causes upstream. Tight financial controls do not make a process capable of meeting specifications or targets or capable to perform as intended. Instead they can disrupt the smooth flow of the process. The question that we can ask of any activity is, what value does it add for others in the system who are internal customers, and especially for the external final customer?

Traditional financial control systems are known by various names, such as management by objectives (MBO), management by the numbers (MBN), and management by results (MBR). The focus is on process outcomes and how well they meet financial targets. Performance of the enterprise is calculated by adding together the results of the separate organizations, as illustrated in table 10-3. MBO as practiced leads to loss when management does not account for the interdependence between components with their positive and negative interactions. The dynamics of these interactions are not recognized when (1) financial objectives are distributed *down* the organization rather than being collaboratively established by internal suppliers and customers of a process and (2) methods to meet objectives don't exist. It is assumed that if every component accomplishes its share of the company's objective (target, goal, or quota), the whole company will accomplish the objective. This can't occur when the components are interdependent because attempts of a component to maximize its own performance likely will be at the expense of some other components. In Deming's view, MBO is no substitute for leadership.[276] He also warned of the invisible costs of trying to improve the bottom line by reducing visible costs such as maintenance of equipment and squeezing suppliers without consideration of the effect on production.[277]

Management accounting systems, by measuring labor, materials, and other costs, do not shed light on how to meet cost targets. Costs result from a system of processes. Information about costs does not provide knowledge about what occurs within a process. It is the responsibility of people in the operations to have and apply process knowledge. Pressuring managers to reduce costs and meet budgets does not help when processes are not capable of doing so. A budget is a prediction that requires stable and capable production processes. When such processes are in place, then average results or a range of results can be predicted. Better yet, then the process can be improved and processing costs reduced. Even fixed costs can be reduced (e.g., if accidents are reduced, insurance premiums may be lowered).

A problem inherent in MBO is associated with the frequent reporting of performance to objectives. Managers are pressured to explain and correct negative deviations. Those who understand the inherent variation of a process may respond that results "were due to chance" or "are within the limits of normal variation, and I predict the process will meet targets by year end." These statements can be substantiated with understanding of Deming's theory of variation and statistical process control charts. Both the accountants and the operations managers must understand this; otherwise, operations employees will be pressured to respond to and compensate for negative deviations from target as if they had identifiable and locally correctable causes. Local overcompensation produces problems for people in other parts of the system. It is highly disruptive and adds cost. This aspect of MBO and MBR is discussed in detail in chapter 14.

There is another way to make the numbers. Pressured by fear of poor performance reviews and consequent effects on compensation, people may act to assure that the numbers are positive. Some managers or employees may manipulate the numbers, and some may cause the system to be manipulated. For example, sales agents who are paid when they book a sale rather than when the company is paid may try to pull forward future sales and encourage potential customers to sign contracts long before orders will be processed. Sales numbers will increase even though revenue won't be realized until the company gets paid. Production will face a sudden increase in orders beyond their capability to process them. It is likely that quality will suffer, shipments to customers may be late, and customers will go elsewhere. Manipulation and distortion of the system can occur in any organization. We hear of situations in schools where administrators and teachers adjust test scores from pressures on them to have their students meet and exceed test standards and have the school receive a high ranking.[278]

The pressure of meeting financial objectives was a factor that threw the global economic system into chaos and affected most of us in our businesses and daily lives. The great recession, which revealed itself when the housing bubble burst around 2007, resulted from a complex interaction of many forces, including government objectives to increase home ownership by making mortgages more affordable. Mortgage brokers, who originated the majority of mortgages before the financial crisis, were under pressure to increase sales and revenues from brokering home loans. These loans could then be broken into pieces, repackaged, and sold by the lender to investors as mortgage-backed securities. On behalf of lenders, they signed contracts with borrowers who were high-credit risks and most likely would not be able to repay the loan. Since mortgage brokers were not a bank, but more like a sales force for the lender, they were not accountable if the loan defaulted. Many of these subprime loans were adjustable-rate mortgages. The house of cards began to collapse in 2007 when borrowers had difficulty making the payments. This happened at the same time as the low adjustable-rate mortgages they made a few years earlier began to revert to higher interest rates and monthly payments increased.

Having objectives and goals sounds good. However, objectives don't contribute anything without a plan, a method to achieve them, and relevant information generated by processes used by the manager of those processes. If the system is stable (i.e., repeatable within limits of its historical variation), an objective beyond the capability of the system will not be achieved. If the system is not stable, there is no way to predict what the system will produce. It has no capability. An objective by itself doesn't contribute anything.[279] The financial management system looks at ends, not means. When managers told Dr. Deming about their objectives, ones that often were admirable, he always asked them his famous question: "By what method?"

The Transformed Map of a Recovering Management Accountant

Dr. Tom Johnson, an economist and self-described "recovering management accountant," is well known for his early contributions to the traditional accounting profession. His books *Relevance Lost*,[280] coauthored with Robert S. Kaplan, and *Relevance Regained*[281] focused on improving the information available to management accountants. Johnson underwent a transformation of his own thinking and for more than two decades has been working to help others in the accounting profession understand that traditional financial management tools of MBR, by trying to optimize performance of individual departments and functions, suboptimize the performance of the enterprise as a whole.

I spent four days with Professor Johnson in June 1992 at one of Dr. Deming's seminars. He is a proponent of Deming's System of Profound Knowledge and especially of a whole-system ecological view of enterprise. He proposes that business and economic organizations should be viewed as natural living systems, with all that this view implies for financial management.[282] In his writings, especially in his book *Profit Beyond Measure*, coauthored with Anders Bröms, Johnson presents this view as an alternative model for accounting and financial management professionals. In that book and other articles (e.g., "Manage a Living System, Not a Ledger"), Johnson explains that better cost information, such as activity-based costing (ABC), will not provide a long-term method of reducing manufacturing costs. The focus must be on managing work activities as components of an ecosystem. Based on the assumption that financial results emerge from complex interactions and nonlinear feedback loops, in the way that outcomes arise from the interrelated parts of a living system, attempting to control those results with linear accounting information is both wrong and possibly destructive to enterprise in the long run. Johnson therefore recommends that management view financial results as the outcomes of operations that behave according to the principles that govern a natural living system.[283]

Processes are the means to achieve ends. Managerial accounting focuses on the ends. "Managing by Means" (MBM) is the term that Johnson uses in _Profit Beyond Measure_ to describe financial management thinking that comes from an ecological map of the enterprise as a living system. The philosophy and methods of management change dramatically from using financial targets to _drive_ results to how and why results are going to be achieved. Johnson explains that MBM can produce quantitative measurements, but it helps to understand that those measurements have emerged from a system of relationships. Accounting models must be able to evaluate the contribution to performance of the quality of interrelationships between different activities and functions in a business. Methods to achieve this are explained in _Profit Beyond Measure_.

Johnson is not alone in his challenge to the management accounting profession. Professor Joseph Castellano and his colleagues at the University of Dayton recognized years ago the importance of Deming's System of Profound Knowledge for accounting theory and practice and the validity of Deming's concerns about the effect of management practices, such as MBO, that suboptimize enterprise performance. They have written a number of articles that appeared in management accounting publications with recommendations similar to those of Johnson.[284] For example, they cited Deming's warning in Point 11 of his 14 Points for Management that goals and targets contribute nothing to the accomplishment of work without methods and capable processes.[285] Rather, numerical targets that are beyond employees' capability create fear with their consequent manipulation and distortion of the numbers. Where there is fear, the numbers can't be trusted.

Dr. Castellano and his colleagues are concerned that Deming's warning has been largely ignored both in the business press and in most management and accounting textbooks. In addition, these textbooks should include knowledge of variation and its associated tools, such as statistical process control charts. They are necessary for management to know the effect of their own actions and those of others on process performance. They also point out that management may not realize that MBO and MBR are obstacles to teamwork, cooperation, and harmonious relationships.

There's No Accounting for the Costs of Provincialism

The financial *control* system compiles revenue, cost, and profit information from separate parts of the business in order to measure the overall financial results of the business. It also uses the results from the individual parts of the business to evaluate how well they are meeting financial targets. However, tables 10-1, 10-2, and 10-3 illustrate the principle that in an interdependent system, results that appear in a given place at a given time can't be separated from activities that occurred elsewhere in the system and at a different time. Although the accounting system attaches results to the function where results appear, it can't trace the results to the system of processes that produced those results. Yet pressures are applied locally to contribute to profit by increasing revenues or reducing costs.

In *Profit Beyond Measure*, Johnson and Bröms describe the management accounting model associated with MBR that drives these suboptimizing actions.[286] Information is compiled by separating revenue, cost, and profit and then treating them as independent. Profit is calculated from the equation: Profit = Revenue − Cost (P = R − C). It is assumed that cost and revenue are independent and additive. To increase profit, one can increase revenue, or reduce cost, or both. Profit is conceptualized as what remains when cost is subtracted from revenue. Any amount of cost that is reduced is added directly to profit. For example, if cost is reduced by 25 percent, that amount is added to profit. This could be expressed as R − .75C = P + .25C. The model does not tell management how to reduce costs or increase revenue, nor does it care. Management can reduce costs, for example, by removing parts of the system (as my mechanic did when he removed parts of my car), by laying off people, or by deferring maintenance. The equation doesn't account for any detrimental effect of specific actions on revenue and profit, as illustrated in table 10-3. Alternatively, management can increase revenue by sales promotions or rebates. Revenue and cost are independent in the equation. Therefore, they show up in the bottom line without identifying any link between the costs of activities that raised revenues, or cost reductions that reduced revenues. R, C, and P can't be traced to the activities that affected them. Johnson and Bröms point out that this occurs because it is customary for accountants to collect revenue and cost information in separate sets of accounts, which they close into a profit and loss account. The income statement calculates profit from these separate accounts. The authors explain that detailed information to link process activities to financial measures is available from the order that each customer places with the company. Order lines include quantity sold, revenue earned, direct and indirect costs.[287]

Tracing the source of aggregated financial measures down to specific activities is similar to a process suggested many years ago by Stafford Beer that he called "cone of resolution."[288] The process is analogous to giving management a microscope for focusing on the detail of various subsystems and processes and relating them to enterprise financial results.

The authors have no problem with using accounting data to *describe* the overall financial results of a business. The problem occurs when this model is used to set and evaluate numerical objectives and direct and control the operations without information about the capability of the systems and processes that produced those results. All it can do is describe with financial quantities the end results that emerged from the various processes and systems, not how people, processes, and systems interacted to produce those outcomes. Operations management needs information that comes from the interdependent processes and systems (i.e., the means that produce the ends, such as the order line). The order line can refer to an entire product, such as an automobile, or subcomponents or services, such as maintenance contracts. Order-line information makes the flow of profit visible with each item ordered.[289]

When the Accounting Tail Wags the Dog

Organization cultures are subject to the same dynamics as occur in the cultures of civilizations. Larry Miller, consultant to corporations on creating high-performing cultures, in his book *Barbarians to Bureaucrats*, cites lessons learned from the historian Arnold Toynbee that cultures rise and fall in historical life cycles.[290] Businesses are subject to the same life cycles as civilizations. Many begin their assent energized by a creative motivation, even when there is not much of anything else. Eventually they may become economically successful. When growth and acquisition of more wealth become the primary goal, the enterprise tends to become bureaucratic and loses its energy and creativity. Quality declines. Employees feel alienated and separated from the organization. Dissatisfaction of employees and customers puts the organization on a downward slope, which continues unless leadership revives the organization by getting it on a path that transforms and renews the energy and creativity of its employees.

Any highly successful enterprise can enter the downward slope of the life cycle. It has more to do with management's goals and mental maps than with aging. The Toyota Production System (TPS) has been a model of quality and efficiency for years and was studied by American engineers and operations managers. They visited Japan, and when they returned to their companies, they began to copy various manufacturing practices, such as just-in-time delivery of parts. Deming told these managers they could not just copy what they saw because they didn't understand the system as a whole, especially the financial control system, and the theories that made such practices possible and successful. Tom Johnson studied the Toyota Production System for many years and found that it was successful because it operated according to the principles espoused by Deming and other systems thinkers. In the early 1950s, Deming taught these principles to Japanese engineers and managers, including Mr. Kiichiro Toyoda, the founder of Toyota Motor Company. These are principles that American management chose to ignore in a growing consumer market. Thus, accounting played an entirely different role in Toyota than it did in American firms. The Toyota management system had been quite different from that of American business. Financial results of their activities, such as revenue, cost, and profit, were understood to be outcomes of well-run processes and not targets to be reached or used to control results. It was the systems and processes themselves that had to be the source of improvement by providing information that could identify error, delays, and other dynamics that produce waste and cost. Therefore, Johnson, in

Profit Beyond Measure and other writings cited in this chapter, encouraged the financial management community to study the Toyota model.[291]

When Toyota began to have quality problems beginning around 2010 and had to recall vehicles, it looked like the rug was pulled from under the feet of those who promoted the Toyota management system. The problem was that Toyota pulled the rug from under its own feet when it began to ignore the management systems that made them successful over five decades. During the 1980s, Japanese companies were sending young managers to study at American business schools. They returned home with MBAs and the lessons they had learned to receive the degree. Deming had publicly warned them during his own seminars that if they continued to study American management practices, "trouble lies ahead," and it did. In Johnson's view, the problem began in early 2000 when Toyota management decided to surpass General Motors and become the world's largest automaker. They ignored the practices, which Johnson calls "management by means," that had made them successful for five decades. They adopted American practices of financial management and established goals of growth. They believed this would enable them to achieve the scale and size to have more control over market prices, decrease costs, and improve profits. Such a goal, wrote Johnson, not only diverts focus on the longer-term consequences to the company, but endless growth is not logical or possible and eventually will destroy the system.[292]

Measurement Maps and Process Territory: What Do the Numbers Mean?

Mental maps contain both numerical and verbal abstractions that represent the territory. Numbers are abstractions (symbols) that we use to count and to measure. We can point to the numbers on a spreadsheet but not to what they represent. Looking at numbers, such as cost, profit, and revenue, is like looking at the description of a meal on a menu or a photo of someone. The menu is not the meal, a photo of a person is not the person, and the numbers are not the process that produced them. Looking at the number that is the measured weight of an individual is not the same thing as looking at processes such as the person's diet, exercise, and metabolism. The number doesn't provide information about how the person got to weigh that amount. Although it may indicate that the person's process of living may have to change, it doesn't say how. That may require the expertise of a physician or other professionals with special knowledge. The professional manager, as physician concerned with maintaining the health of the organization, will be alert to Deming's warning that warranty costs are visible but do not tell the story about quality since anyone can reduce the cost of warranty by ignoring customer complaints.[293]

Johnson has advised managers not to think that they can rely solely on abstract financial quantities to explain and control financial results rather than supporting the human activities that cause those results. Accounting information is descriptive, not prescriptive. It can describe financial outcomes, such as revenue, cost, profit, and investment, but it doesn't help managers better understand how to improve costs or financial performance.[294]

Another consideration is that figures used in reporting financial, quality, productivity, and other results, especially as they are aggregated up the levels of management, are not very helpful for action at that level. The methods that generated the numbers are rarely questioned. Even if they were questioned, it would be difficult to be specific since the figures often are aggregates of numbers from separate parts of the business, which removes them even further from the processes that produced them. They have no actionable meaning as composites or averages.[295] The results of arithmetic manipulations on the combined numbers, such as averages and percentages, are higher-level abstractions that are even further removed from the processes that produced them and what is observable. While you can observe the individual whose weight you have measured, you can't observe the average weight or average intelligence when looking at the group of people whose individual measurements were averaged.

When the figures for different objects are combined, such as three oranges are added to a basket that contains two apples, information that there are five fruits in the basket tells us nothing about the particulars of the contents of the basket, other than the abstraction that there are five pieces of fruit. The equation $2 + 3 = 5$ doesn't care what the numbers refer to, just as the numbers representing the outcome of a process tell us nothing about how they were produced. In a world where performance outcomes emerge from the interactions of various forces, aggregations provide a poor basis to make process-related decisions.

Chapter 11

~

Accounting for the Enterprise as Ecosystem

Effective corporate management must focus on the interactions of its parts rather than on their actions taken separately ... Supervision and command are the management of actions; coordination and integration are the management of interactions, and this requires leadership.

—Russell Ackoff [296]

When things are not working well, management seeks improvement by manipulating the behavior of the parts. People are externally controlled by their financial and other objectives and associated incentive and compensation systems. In the early 1990s, reengineering, which essentially was a method to achieve short-term cost reductions by removing parts of the system, primarily the people, began to spread rapidly throughout business organizations. These methods fit right in with management's accounting model. Instead, management should be moving the enterprise in a direction away from the stifling effects of the kinds of mechanistic thinking reflected in methods such as reengineering and toward *de-engineering*, as Margaret Wheatley called it. [297]

In her book *Leadership and the New Science*, Wheatley asks management to consider alternate models from subatomic physics and molecular biology. Order and pattern are created not by externally imposed structures such as can be seen in command-and-control organization charts that define relationships vertically but through principles inherent in the natural processes that allow the autonomous interaction of the individual parts of an ecology. [298]

Relationships That Optimize System Performance

Russell Ackoff observes that when an organization is conceptualized as a machine, management considers the purposes of people to be irrelevant to the way the people are managed and the way the enterprise behaves. This inhibits effective adaptation of the enterprise in turbulent, chaotic, unpredictable environments. However, when enterprises are conceptualized and managed as social systems, and individuals have the kinds of freedom of conscious and purposeful choice that they are able to exercise responsibly in the larger democratic society, the enterprise will be much more able to act effectively. It will have a greater capability to respond to unpredictable environmental changes that already have occurred—to passively adapt—as well as the ability to innovate and shape the external environment—to actively adapt. Such an organization is better able to perceive opportunities and take advantage of them.[299]

Performance could be improved dramatically if the enterprise learned to operate as a whole-in-one with interdependent rather than separate parts. The enterprise corpus is whole when the people that it contains are whole. However, the policies, procedures, and methods of evaluation, reward, and punishment can divide the enterprise's systems, processes, and people into separate parts that act independently of the other parts and suboptimize performance. Enterprise components need to function in ways that enable the enterprise to operate as one indivisible organization that works together to optimize performance.

When the system is optimized, there is greater gain for all. This logic extends to relationships between competitors. Dr. Deming observed that a poor competitor can hurt you as well as himself, can ruin your name as well as their own. When one company, for example, offers the customer price rebates in order to stimulate sales, competitors are pressured by their own sales organizations, who also are driven by market share and revenue, to do the same. When everyone is offering rebates, sales and market share of each company will eventually average out to their previous levels, since rebates no longer differentiate products.

Customers may think that lower prices are great, but eventually they also can lose. Price wars can reduce profits of all the competitors. When the price war ends, companies may raise their prices to make up for lost profits and to recover their increased costs. This can further reduce sales and profit. All of this results in less funds available to develop new products and services, and customers will have fewer choices in the future. The competitors, in the heat of battle, also may badmouth each other. This can cause consumers to lose confidence in the products and services of all of the companies and seek alternatives, if possible. In the long run, no one in the system wins, unless an upstart competitor sneaks in with innovative alternative products and services while the others are fighting it out.

Optimization is a process of working to achieve the full capability inherent in the whole enterprise by blending the talents and knowledge of people. Table 11-1, in contrast to table 10-3, illustrates how performance can be optimized when people have the information they need and are willing and able to work together for the good of the enterprise as a whole. This means understanding the consequences of one's plans and actions on other parts of the organization.

(1) Department Actions	(2) Effects on Purchasing	(3) Effects on Engineering	(4) Effects on Assembly	(5) Effects on Whole System
(2) Purchasing: Selects new supplier able to engineer and produce subassemblies.	- Higher piece price includes amortization of supplier engineering capability.	++ Lower cost to engineer subassembly.	+ Better quality parts make assembly easier and faster.	+2
(3) Product Engineering: Redesigns product replacing many small parts with fewer subassemblies.	+ Fewer parts to purchase, fewer suppliers to work with, less problems to solve.	+ Longer-lasting design. Fewer revisions needed.	+ Fewer parts to assemble, fewer part numbers to receive and track, less total variability and better fit.	+3
(4) Assembly: Retools process for subassembly parts and just-in-time (JIT) delivery.	+ JIT delivery reduces supplier inventory cost; piece price is reduced.	+ Engineers spend time improving design for better assembly rather than solving problems.	- Incremental cost incurred to retool for larger subassemblies and JIT delivery.	+1
(5) Overall Results	+1	+4	+1	+6
(6) Credit Given to Departments	+2	+2	+2	+6

Table 11-1. The economics of cooperation

The partners in the relationship plan together to optimize the larger system that contains them. This may mean that one or more of the parties may have to incur what traditionally may appear to be a loss. In table 11-1, we see that Purchasing (row 2, column 1) and Assembly (row 4, column 1) each selected actions that would affect themselves negatively in the short term (shaded cells of rows 2 and 4) in order to enable the whole enterprise to do better. The end result is optimization of the whole-system, which produces a gain of +6 (row 5, column 5). This contributes to profit and can be used to develop new products and services, improve existing ones, and reinvest in the enterprise in other ways.

Financial results also may be shared, but it would not be logical to try to identify the separate contribution of system participants. Purchasing and Assembly intentionally have added cost or otherwise have taken a loss locally to help the system, while Engineering has shown a gain because of this. Since all departments are interacting and inseparable parts of the system, they share the credit equally for the total results (row 6). This follows from the analogy to the functioning of a body. The various components of the body cannot be individually and separately credited for their contribution to the health of the body as a whole. Failure to equitably recognize contributions to performance not only violates system logic but also demoralizes individuals and creates internal competition that will jeopardize the cooperation needed to continue to perform in an optimal manner.

Equity in profit sharing doesn't mean that there are not differences in compensation for engineers, buyers, and other system participants. Salary is determined by factors such as market rate, level of education, seniority, experience, and knowledge. Salary increases should be kept separate from recognition and performance feedback.[300] If profit sharing is used, it has to be managed in a way that does not create a dependence on extrinsic incentives, nor degrade the contribution that people make because they believe it is intrinsically right to help the enterprise and to provide something of value to society.

Managers often are disappointed with overall results. When they pressure individuals to achieve local numerical objectives, this can produces disorder rather than a smooth and integrated process flow because people do not work together for the good of the enterprise and may work at cross-purposes. This increases costs and reduces quality. However, managing according to the principles seen in life's natural systems can enable everyone—suppliers, consumers, investors, employees, and the enterprise and society as a whole—to come out ahead. Gregory Bateson, anthropologist and social scientist, asked us to learn from the natural world, to let nature teach us, to think as nature thinks.[301] There are useful lessons that management can apply from the ecologically sound functioning of natural systems. An essential one is Russell Ackoff's suggestion to replace cause-and-effect models with the concept of producer-product.

Economist Michael Rothschild argued throughout his book, *Bionomics: Economy as Ecosystem*, that the natural ecological systems of the biological world, such as a rain forest with the interdependencies and adaptation capabilities of the life contained within it, offer a better way to think about the dynamics of human interactions in a free market economy than do the Newtonian mechanical laws of the physical world. Life in natural ecological systems functions and survives not through predictable sequences of cause-and-effect processes but rather through the dynamic, interactive exchange of information that enables organisms to regulate themselves in the context of what is happening around them. This self-regulation occurs within the system, not from outside of it. Organisms in a rain forest are in a continual process of growth and adjustment. A free market economy functions in the same way. A spontaneous order emerges not from central planning but from the interactions of self-interested buyers and sellers who adjust to shifting prices and other changes in the environment. Individuals cooperate because it is in their best interests to do so.[302]

The fact that the principles of a free market economy seem to align with the understanding of biologists about the way ecosystems work is more than coincidence. Rothschild notes that Darwin studied economics, including Adam Smith's book *The Wealth of Nations*, prior to formulation of his theory of natural selection. Darwin learned that a viable economy was possible because of the wide variation in the talents, inclinations, and interests of people. Individuals can earn a living by using their special talents to produce goods and services that they sell or trade for goods and services that they can't produce. A viable economic system is a continual interaction between consumers and producers. If there is no demand for one's products or services, the associated skills, knowledge, and technology are replaced by those in greater demand. Over time, the character of the system as a whole changes. It is a self-selecting, self-regulating process.[303]

Darwin may have had Adam Smith's ideas in mind during his observations in the Galapagos Islands, but Smith and Darwin did not think ecologically. Gregory Bateson writes that Darwin looked at the survival of single individuals or groups of individuals such as a family unit. He did not consider the relationship between the individual and the environment.[304] In order to understand what is going on, one cannot look only at the individual; rather, one has to look at the system as a whole and see the individual-within-its-environment. The unit of survival is a whole-within-a-whole. This gets to the heart of the argument made earlier about the body and its parts, that the contributions of the individual and the systems of the enterprise are inseparable, just as a person's biological and psychological makeup interacts with the containing environment.

Fritjof Capra, in his book *The Web of Life*, makes a similar point when he compares *holistic* and *ecological* views. A holistic view of, say, a bicycle (his example), enables one to see the bicycle as a functional whole and to understand the interaction of its parts accordingly. An ecological view considers, in addition, how the bicycle is embedded in its natural and social environment: where the raw materials that went into it came from, how it was manufactured, how its use affects the natural environment and the community that uses it, and so on.[305]

Adam Smith believed that when people pursue their own interests, both they and the society benefit. Individuals led by an "invisible hand" often promote the interest of society, even though that is not their intention, and perhaps contribute even more than when they intend to promote the public good directly.[306] But in today's highly interdependent social-environmental ecology, where local actions can have dramatic global effects, which in turn have local consequences, what does it mean to act in one's self-interest? How can one know whether one's actions today will not eventually harm the sustaining natural social-economic ecology and hence come back to harm the individual tomorrow? It seems to me that self-interest can be achieved only when the individual behaves according to the guiding principle that one's own health and well-being are intertwined and inseparable from the health and well-being of the containing whole. If the whole ecology does not survive, the individuals within it will not survive. We can see in the deep economic recession that began around 2007 what happens when there is tampering with the natural ecological functioning of a free market.

According to Capra, Adam Smith's invisible hand is a metaphor that describes the self-regulatory processes in social life. But the invisible hand cannot function effectively unless individuals have relevant information to evaluate the potential consequences of their actions. This can come through cooperation.[307] Michael Rothschild, looking at the economy as a whole, writes that mutually beneficial relationships, common among species in nature, can lead to mutual profitability in business. However, this viewpoint is at odds with the popular notion, erroneous yet eagerly applied in almost every type of enterprise, that in the natural world, competition pits species against species to assure "survival of the fittest."[308]

The concern is with destructive competition. Alfie Kohn, in his book *No Contest: The Case Against Competition*, cites the thinking of Stephen Jay Gould, who presents evidence that natural selection occurs without any discernable struggle and that competition actually discourages survival. Survival in nature is more likely when individuals of the same or different species work with, rather than against, each other.[309]

Accounting for Systems Behaving Naturally

The notion that cost should be minimized or profit maximized within a fixed epoch leaves right out of the count other factors which are vital to the future viability of the business ... Costings are short-term control instruments, and will not detect the mismanagement of latent resources ... until it is too late.
—Stafford Beer[310]

Management that governs the enterprise as a living ecosystem (ecosystem can be read as ecological system and economic system) would need a compatible management accounting model. In *Profit Beyond Measure*, Johnson and Bröms provide one that is aligned with the dynamics of a living ecosystem. Rather than the linear, mechanistic model of MBR, which treats revenue and cost as independent, they present a model that recognizes that revenue and cost interact to produce profit (i.e., that profit emerges from the relationship of revenue and cost).[311] Years earlier, Stafford Beer pointed out that what seems to be a marketing question, such as the number of lines of product that should be sold, is not separate from the cost of production in the factory. It is incorrect to assume that the factory's costs are independent of the product mix.[312]

Table 11-1 represents a segment of an organization's ecosystem. It illustrates how profit can emerge from relationships that aim to optimize the system as a whole. It shows, for example, that a higher-cost supplier who produces high-quality parts that are easy to assemble by the customer can reduce costs of manufacturing that outweigh the higher-cost parts. In the case of appearance items, a creative supplier can work with engineering to produce designs and materials that are more inviting to customers. Management accounting must recognize that tradeoffs have to be made to optimize the system as a whole. Natural systems seem to be able to do this without measurement systems external to their processes. Perhaps, as Tom Johnson suggests, "Our business and economic organizations should be viewed as life systems."[313]

Chapter 12

~

Leaders Can Make Music:
People in Organizations Playing in Concert

A good manager is like a symphony conductor ... trying to
bring out of that group a wide range of simultaneous and
harmonic tones and sounds. It is a dynamic process.
—General (Ret.) Robert T. Herres[314]

A score of a musical composition can be viewed as a map for the
musicians and the conductor. The score, as map, facilitates interactions
between the players and with the conductor. It may be as detailed as the
score for a traditional symphony orchestra, or it may be more of a guide,
a schematic, for jazz musicians that outlines how the performance may
evolve. Whichever the case, the score enables the musicians to produce a
pattern of sounds that they intend for listeners to perceive as music.

A Music Score Integrates the Players into a Performance Ecosystem

Daniel Puig, engineer and analyst, applied Gregory Bateson's thinking
about the concept of map and territory to understand the whole group of
musicians and the score, especially in jazz where the music emerges from
improvisation by the musicians. In jazz, the musicians interact by listening
to each other and responding to the playing of others. The interaction
of the musicians with each other and with the score produces a whole

performance, a pattern of relationships with properties of the whole that are not contained in the parts. These properties emerge from the dynamic connections between the parts without disregarding the qualities of the parts. The system of musicians and score is a social ecology, which Puig calls a "performance ecosystem."[315]

Herb Alpert, a successful musician and composer for many years, sees it this way: "When you're blowing the horn, sometimes everything works, and it's a tremendous feeling. Especially I think jazz is a phenomenal creative force ... but it's a collective thing, what you're doing. You're listening to all the musicians around you and you're working within that structure. I think we need more of that as human beings. We need to be able to appreciate each other's differences and I think jazz really takes us in that direction."[316]

There are different models for leading a musical performance. They range from a conductor on a podium leading a symphony orchestra of up to a hundred musicians to that of a self-managed string quartet or jazz combo. The Orpheus Chamber Orchestra rotates its members in the role of leader to match the piece performed.[317]

Regardless of the structure and leadership model, the quality of an organization's performance, of its product or service, emerges from the quality of human interactions. It depends on how well the players fit together, whether in the symphony orchestra or string quartet or jazz combo, or in the manufacturing plant, in engineering, in the restaurant, in the school, in the hospital, or in any other enterprise. Gregory Bateson writes, "The right way to begin to think about the pattern which connects is to think of it as primarily a dance of interacting parts."[318]

Many of the words that musicians use connote whole-system relationships. *Harmonious* means that the parts are agreeably related— that is, they are characterized by accord in sentiment or action. Harmony is a means of joining, of fitting things together, such as when notes are combined in an aesthetically pleasing manner to produce a chord. *Chord* is a short version of *accord*. *Concert*, the verb, comes from the Latin roots *com*, or with, and *certare*, to strive, hence, "to act together in cooperation, to bring into agreement." The performers join together, united by purpose into a whole that is one intelligence, one consciousness, one mind, one heart. The Latin origin of *accord* meant heart-to-heart.

Performing artists are able to see how their role or function contributes to the whole performance. What would be the quality of an orchestral performance if one or two musicians were removed from each section in order to reengineer the process and reduce costs? Imagine a management climate where the emphasis is only on productivity to the exclusion of quality, and there is internal competition to be seen as best. Would musicians play without regard to what the others are doing and loud enough to gain attention of the conductor? There would be maximum efficiency with zero quality. Quality is evaluated in use, in the interaction between the product, the users, their expectations, and the service they can get in case the product fails or requires maintenance.[319]

In the theater or concert hall, artists interpret the plan—the script or musical score—without worrying that an outside disturbance might interfere with the artistic performance. In other kinds of enterprise, especially business, people need to be in a state of readiness to face changes in the environment from government legislation, competitors, or failures anywhere in the world economy, which can occur overnight. Jazz musicians have more freedom to improvise around the theme or purpose of a piece than do musicians in a symphony orchestra.

Unlike playing in a concert hall or theater, players in business organizations may not be physically together. Harmonious interaction can be difficult. Imagine a live performance of a symphony orchestra where the strings, the winds, and the percussion section each are in a different part of the building or even in different cities. This is a problem performing arts enterprises ordinarily do not have to face during a concert. The performers and the theater audience (customers) are in the same place, and the customers are continuously consuming the product as it is being produced. Failure to behave as a whole-system can't be hidden behind numbers or compensated for by costly inspection and rework.

In organizations, customers and suppliers, internal and external, usually are separated in time and place. The challenge to management is how to orchestrate the performers, who are in different locations, into one whole-system. Technology can help, but it also can cause delays in responding that can disrupt interactions. It can even separate people who used to work together. This has happened in the music business where technology has decreased real-time togetherness between musicians. The musician Dave

Koz described how technology has fragmented the way recorded music is created. In prior years, musicians spent more time playing together in the studio and in concerts. There was a lot more fellowship and musicianship. They could get to know each other and their unique styles, such as their phrasing. People today work in different studios and send music files back and forth to each other. He prefers having all the musicians together in the studio where they can interact and play off of each other.[320] Koz's description of the process of adding separate performances together to get the whole performance reminded me of the process of management by results.

Leadership That Connects

Art, as in *artisan*, originally referred to the skill needed to join things together. Norio Ohga, former Sony president and chairman, also was a talented musician, conductor, and chairman of the Tokyo Philharmonic Orchestra. He often compared leading a company to conducting an orchestra. A company president must draw on the talents of the people in the organization, just as a conductor does.[321] Ohga also said, "The conductor must allow the orchestra to express the music. At the same time he must make the performance a finished product in a short period of time. That is the same at Sony."[322]

Max DePree, in *Leadership Jazz*, describes the concepts that guided him in his leadership role of orchestrating human expression while he was chairman and CEO of Herman Miller, Inc. He asks leaders to "think of achievement as a collaborative and synthetic result" and to recognize that most of a leader's work "depends heavily on the quality of our relationships."[323] He writes: "An organization's cultural harmony is fragile. I'm talking about the sweet music that emanates from diverse and productive groups of people. Leaders certainly have a hand in creating the atmosphere where this kind of harmony can exist, but they don't direct it or mandate it or control it."[324] He also said that jazz-band leaders know how to integrate the "voices" in the band without diminishing their uniqueness.[325]

Unlike Max DePree, some managers believe that abandonment of tight hierarchical control can only lead to chaos. They see any alternative to top-down control as laissez-faire management and therefore an abdication by management of its responsibility to maintain order. Yet control absolutely exists in the performing arts. It may be obvious, as when the conductor stands on the podium in front of the orchestra. It may be subtle when the function of leader resides not in a single individual, such as the conductor, but in the interactions that create the whole. This can be seen in a jazz or a string quartet, or in a chamber orchestra with thirty musicians. Whether the function of leading and conducting is visible or invisible, control comes from within, very much in the manner of mutual adjustment that characterizes the performance of other professionals.

The performing arts validate the principle that individual freedom, guided by responsibility _to_ others (not _for_ others), leads not to chaos but to creative order of the whole. Peter B. Vaill, professor of human systems and organization change theorist, writes in _Managing as a Performing Art_ that the performing arts provide a framework to appropriately discipline the creativity and personal expression of each performer both during solos, which are performed within a system of support from others, and during ensemble parts when everyone is playing or performing together.[326]

Scoring without Numbers

The healthy functioning of the human nervous system requires the functions of synapses. A synapse, which comes from the Greek word that means "fasten together," is a structure that enables a neuron—nerve cell—to communicate with other neurons and other cells by sending an electrical or chemical signal. In an analogous manner, communication connections must be made for the healthy functioning of the enterprise as a social performance ecosystem. Healthy, whole, robust, and vigorous have similar meanings. The health of an organization can be maintained and improved by enabling synapses to be made between people.

A score in sports and games is a number. In organizations, management uses numbers to evaluate enterprise performance. A score in a musical composition is a map that shows the arrangement of the vocal and instrumental parts as a coherent whole. In a social ecology, people need something analogous to a musical score to know where they fit in so they can govern themselves and their interactions with other people. The quality of human relationships cannot be meaningfully quantified; however, relationships can be orchestrated into a score that enables synapses to be made between people.

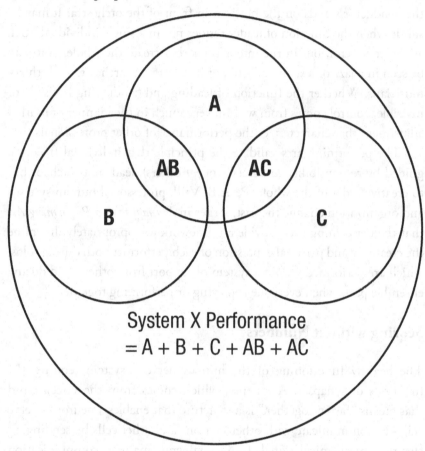

Figure 12-1. Three individuals in two relationships

Figure 12-1 illustrates the relationships between individuals, A, B, and C, in System X. A relationship is a mutual dependence between two people or processes. Three two-person relationships are possible: A *and* B, A *and* C, B *and* C. Let's say that A and B need to work together, and A and C need to work together, and B and C don't have to work together, then only two of the three possible two-person relationships actually exist. The number of two-person relationships possible, R, as described in chapter 9, is calculated using the formula for combinations, $R = 1/2 [n \times (n-1)]$, where n is the number of individuals in the system. For example, if there are two people in the system, only one relationship is possible obviously since R = 1/2 [2 × (2–1)] = 1; if there are three people in the system (this case), R = 1/2 [3 × (3–1)] = 3 possible two-person relationships; if there are four people, then six two-person relationships are possible, since R = 1/2 [4 × (4–1)] = 6; and so on. Performance of System X therefore depends on the individual abilities and actions of A, B, and C, and the two interactions A *and* B, A *and* C (*symbolized* as AB and AC). Therefore, System X Performance = A + B + C + AB + AC. All possible interactions usually are not necessary since every person usually doesn't depend on every other person. In addition, some are indirect (e.g., although B and C could be indirectly related through A's relationship with C, i.e., B's relationship with A may depend on what C does). Since complexity expands geometrically, critical interactions and interdependencies must be identified and managed. This is necessary for the enterprise to function as a performance ecosystem with an optimal capability to remain viable while living in a competitive environment with its continual changes and disturbances.

Orchestrating Interactions in Manufacturing

An engine manufacturing plant of a large automotive business was plagued with a variety of problems such as product defects and late deliveries to its customer, the assembly plant. The plant manager wanted to improve cooperation in order to eliminate these problems. He knew that continuing to exhort people to do better or holding more problem-resolution meetings would not help. Although some of the plant's problems were related to suppliers and to product engineering, he felt that the plant had to clean its own house before he could ask others to improve.

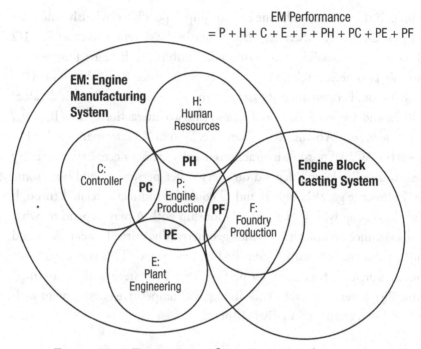

Figure 12-2. Engine manufacturing viewed as a system

Figure 12-2 illustrates an engine manufacturing system, EM. Four of the contained systems, called "departments" on traditional organization charts, are located in the engine plant: Production, Human Resources, Plant Engineering, and the Controller. Engine Block Casting is located in the foundry. Performance of the system, EM, depends on the following:

- actions within each department in the engine plant: P, H, C, E
- actions within the production department in the foundry: F
- interactions of P with the other departments: PH, PC, PE, PF

The same kind of map can be applied to look at the sources of performance within any of the contained systems, such as the Controller, or Plant Engineering.

Interactions Matrix

The plant manager asked an internal consultant to help.[327] A two-day planning session was held off-site with department managers and superintendents. The plant manager explained that setting more aggressive objectives would not help the situation because the plant did not have a method to accomplish those objectives. They would have to identify the ways they could support each other. The process started with the manager of Production who described the difficulties he faced every day to produce high-quality engines and meet the production schedule. He then asked the others how they would help him. Each of the other department managers then proposed, in turn, what they would do to support Production. This was an initial commitment that would continue to be refined as learning occurred. For example:

- The Plant Engineering manager offered to work toward developing a maintenance schedule that would minimize downtime.
- The controller offered to change the reporting format to move away from micro-reporting of performance on each machine or production area to overall production reporting. The Production manager was given the discretion to develop any kind of measurement and information management system within the department that would help him operate better.
- The Human Resources manager offered to schedule training in statistical process control (SPC).

(1) Department	(2) Production Support Actions	(3) Plant Engineering Support Actions	(4) Controller Support Actions	(5) Human Resources Support Actions
(2) Production (Receiver)	Within Production	Meet maintenance schedule.	Accept Production's report format.	Provide SPC training.
(3) Plant Engineering (Receiver)	Shut down machines and clean the area.	Within Plant Engineering		
(4) Controller (Receiver)	Provide data in graphical, time-ordered format.		Within Controller	

Table 12-1. Engine manufacturing interactions matrix

The initial commitments of these three managers (Foundry Production was not yet involved in this process) to support the Production department are shown in row 2, columns 3, 4, and 5 of the interactions matrix, table 12-1. Commitments were more detailed than presented here. Only a portion of the matrix is shown.

The process continued as each of the other departments had the chance to explain their situation and receive commitments of support from the others. For example:

- Plant Engineering explained that it was difficult to maintain equipment because there was oil or water on the floor. Also, sometimes they would arrive at the scheduled time and Production would refuse to shut down the machine. The support actions to help Plant Engineering are shown in row 3. Production (row 3, column 2), for example, agreed to shut down the machines and clean up the area before the scheduled time for maintenance.

- Production (column 2, row 4) offered to provide information to the controller in time-ordered graphical format. This would enable the controller to see at a glance whether plant performance is stable and predictable and, therefore, be better able to plan.

After the session, each department manager presented the interactions matrix to the supervisors and others within the department. The initial commitments that the manager made on behalf of the department were discussed. In order to develop their capability to meet their commitments, an interactions matrix was developed within each department.

The plant operated for two weeks, with each department working to fulfill its commitments to support the others. Daily meetings with the plant manager moved from frustration and defensiveness to an evaluation of how the system was working. Then the managers met again to discuss the commitments they had made. They modified commitments based on what they learned or feedback. This became an ongoing process of feedback and mutual adjustment and replaced the daily problem-resolution meetings. Managers no longer were working on problems; they were working on the system to dissolve problems. The role of the plant manager now was one of orchestrating the interactions of the department managers.

Likewise, the role of each department manager was to help orchestrate the interactions of people in each department and to facilitate their interactions across departments.

After learning how to operate with this process, the manager of the Engine Plant asked the Foundry manager to use the process. The Foundry did so with success. Eventually the Foundry and the Engine Plant used the process together. The interactions matrix was expanded to include the Production department of the Foundry.

You may think that this is a lot of work. It is not as much work as continually dealing with the continual supply of problems and pressures that characterize an organization that is not managed as an interdependent system. After a while, this process becomes second nature and doesn't take much time, certainly not as much time as problem-resolution meetings. The clarification of commitments by asking questions, such as "What do you mean by clean up the area?" and clearly providing and listening to the response saves time by avoiding conflicts later on.

A Retail Furniture Business in Concert

Gallery Furniture of Houston, Texas, is owned and managed by Jim ("Mac") and Linda McIngvale, the couple who started the business in 1981.[328] Even before learning from Deming, they had grown the company into one of the most successful retail furniture businesses in the country. They accomplished this feat by perfecting the traditional methods of selling furniture and managing the sales force. Mac brought the customers into the store. He became one of the best-recognized personalities in the city mainly because of his frequent appearances in television promotions. Once customers entered the store, it was sell, sell, sell. Mac's operating philosophy at that time was "make any sale by any method as long as it's legal."

Mac's management methods assured that this philosophy was followed. He rewarded or punished sales associates according to their performance in meeting Mac's numerical sales targets. He held daily contests, with bonuses for the best performers. He ranked employees at the end of the month, with rewards for those in the top 10 percent and punishment for the bottom 90 percent. The individuals who occupied these positions changed from month to month, so it was actually a lottery, as Deming explained to him and as Mac later understood. This ranking process encouraged sales associates to focus on meeting their own needs, not those of the customers. It promoted game playing, such as forcing out deliveries to meet quotas, even if furniture had to be temporarily stored in the sales associate's garage. It encouraged internal competition, such as sales associates failing to wait for their turn (the batting order) to greet a new customer entering the store. Mac thus ensured that each sales associate worked as an independent agent. Salespeople were afraid of having to face Mac if they did not make their targets, not only because of the lost compensation and other penalties, such as moving to the end of the batting order, but also because Mac could be very intense when he expressed his displeasure. Turnover of sales associates averaged 15 percent a month. Mac had a large budget to continuously advertise in the classified section of the Houston newspapers for sales associates.

Why did customers tolerate the high pressure? Besides the fact that they would face a similar situation in most furniture stores that carried similar merchandise (moderately priced to moderately high priced), Mac offered customers an advantage over the competition. The store provided same-day delivery to the Houston metropolitan area.

Constraints on Performance Become Obvious

What changed? Unlike the situation that faces most managers who seek new methods to save them when the business is on the decline, this enterprise was financially successful. However, the store seemed to have reached limits for further growth. Forty-three percent of all customers entering the store purchased goods, compared to an industry average of 25 percent. Mac was unable to increase this number, no matter how hard he pushed or cajoled employees. Revenues also had stabilized. Mac wanted to continue to grow. His location prevented him from adding floor space. In addition, he was the main reason most people shopped there; many customers asked to see him when they came into the store. Mac therefore ruled out opening another location at that time since he could not be in two places at once.

About this time, Mac became aware of Dr. Deming's ideas that numerical quotas and financial incentive schemes discourage cooperation and cause loss. Mac and Linda, together with their managers, attended numerous Deming seminars. Deming helped them to understand how they could go beyond the constraints of their current capability, without adding resources. They were able to envision a business where employees helped each other to sell. They could accomplish this by cross-training sales personnel in a variety of jobs so they could fill in other areas of the business to meet changing needs. They could sell in the store on weekends and holidays when customer volumes were highest or help out in Receiving during vendor deliveries. Employees would see themselves as part of a larger whole—the business and the Houston community. Mac and Linda understood that a deep change in the management system and enterprise culture had to be undertaken. This had to start with Mac himself, but it also required all employees to learn. The first lesson was why it was necessary for sales associates to move from commissions to salary.

Mac's friends warned him that if he did this he would lose the business. Most of the managers and sales associates were afraid of such a change, even though they wanted to be free of the pressure from Mac. They were afraid that they couldn't guarantee success for themselves if they had to depend on others. They had learned well from Mac that *they* were totally responsible for their own performance. Some people worried that others would slack off and not carry their weight. Ironically, each person who worried about someone else also was the target of someone else's worry. Management worried that the superstars, the few consistently high-volume sellers, would leave. Yes, they might, but Mac had come to believe that the overall gain from cooperation would be greater than the losses from exiting superstars. He also understood that the visible gains produced by high-pressure superstars are most likely offset by costs such as when merchandise is returned or when customer service representatives have to visit the customer to repair damaged merchandise. There also is the loss of repeat customers and all the potential customers that these unhappy customers can persuade to shop elsewhere.

Although Mac had grown the business in the traditional way, he was no longer willing to operate with a system and style that he could now see constrained the potential of the business. He would rather face the problems of change than continue to face the problems produced by the current system.

First a Hop of Faith, Then a Leap

Sales associates and the other employees began attending Deming's seminars. They participated in discussions with Mac and Linda in order to think through the advantages and disadvantages of changing the operating philosophy and management system. In particular, they considered the benefits to the enterprise and to themselves of salary pay for sales associates. Mac then took a "hop of faith," as he described it. He eliminated sales quotas. Some sales people left, as expected. Within a few months, it became obvious that the company was still in business and that even the small increase in cooperation did raise closing percentages and sales revenues. Fortified by these results, Mac then took a "leap of faith" and replaced commission and bonus pay of the sales force with salary pay. Current employees were given a salary based on their prior-year earnings and seniority. New employees were given a starting salary, which had been established by Mac and a study team from the sales department. Even though the new compensation system included profit sharing and medical benefits, more sales people left. Those who stayed still may have had some reservations so early into the change, but they found that they liked the predictable income versus the weekly and monthly ups and downs they experienced under commission pay.

One consequence of this change was a self-selection process. Individuals who stayed, as well as new hires, were able to work more cooperatively. These individuals also were able to easily move away from hard-sell tactics and take on a more professional approach of helping to identify and meet customers' needs. The character of the system was indeed beginning to change.

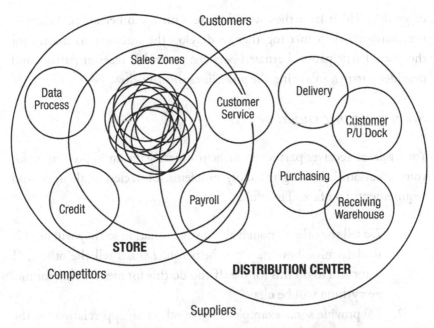

Figure 12-3. Furniture business viewed as a system

Mac, CEO and general manager of the store, and Linda, general manager of the distribution center, met with employees to discuss the business as a system (see figure 12-3). This discussion helped management to see that they had to identify critical interdependencies so that they could establish critical working relationships. Consistent with the ending of sales quotas for individuals, management's role would move away from the management of the actions of individuals to achieve sales objectives, toward an orchestration of interactions that would benefit the business as a whole. Everyone agreed that every aspect of the customer's experience must be very positive. Customers must feel "wow" in every interaction they have with any part of the business.

Interactions Matrix

Store managers met with the consultant[329] to discuss the process of interactions management that would be used to develop a system of mutual support and cooperation. Managers then met with their area (Sales Zones, Credit, Data Processing, etc.) to prepare a description of what they faced every day, which later they would share with the other areas. Mac and the managers then met together to develop the interactions matrix for the store. Participants alternated between two roles, receiver-partner and provider-partner, following the guidelines shown below.

Receiver-Partner Guidelines

Your role as receiver-partner is to help others gain an appreciation for your situation, including the daily problems, obstacles, challenges, and requirements you face. Therefore:

1. *Do* tell the others enough about your situation so they will be able to determine how they can help you. *Do not* tell the others, "I want you to do this for me. If you do this for me and that for me, everything will be okay."

2. *Do* provide some examples to give others an appreciation for the general situation you face and the consequences to the organization. *Do not* develop a long list of problems. The point here is not to list every problem that you face. Your specific problems are symptoms of a broader system problem, which this process is trying to define and dissolve.

3. *Do* prioritize your concerns in order of importance. *Do not* try to overwhelm the others with the incredible difficulties you face, as if your situation were worse than theirs.

4. *Do* raise issues that you really think are out of your control to influence, where you really need the help of others. *Do not* raise issues that are within your control to influence. (You may not see this at first.)

5. *Do not* point fingers, assign blame, or shift the burden to others. You are part of the system, and so are the others. Remember, most of what happens is produced by the system. Bad things happen even when people want to do a good job and try their best. *We are trying to get at the system problems.*

Provider-Partner Guidelines

Your role as provider-partner is to offer support actions to help others, in the context of the larger system. Therefore:

1. *Avoid* thinking, *Yes, I would like to help, but ...* Initially, do not put limits on how you can help others. You may think you do not have the ability to help others, but after preliminary development of the matrix, you may find you can do more because the others will support you in new ways. You certainly do not want to overcommit, but you should try not to under-commit.
2. *Avoid* the self-fulfilling prophecy where each individual is afraid to trust the other. *Do* trust others.

After reviewing the guidelines, each manager had a chance to explain the situation in his or her area, using the information each had prepared earlier. For example:

- The Credit Department manager explained that information often was missing from the credit application that Sales submitted to them. When this happened, Credit had to chase down the sales associate before they could complete the credit check.
- A common problem was revealed after the Sales Zone managers described their situation: Customers were turned over from one sales zone to another without introducing the customer to the sales associate in that area. Customers were annoyed at having to answer the same kinds of questions each time they moved to another area of the store.

After a manager described the situation for his or her area, the others offered ways in which they would help, following the guidelines for the role of provider-partner. A portion of the interactions matrix for the store is shown in table 12-2. The Bedding Sales Zone (row 2, column 1) is supported by the actions of the other Sales Zones (row 2, column 2) and by Data Processing (row 2, column 3). Part of the situation that Data

Processing faces each day can be seen in the shaded cell (row 3, column 3). Sales offered to help Data Processing (row 3, column 2).

(1) Area or Department	(2) Sales Zones Support Actions (Provider Partner)	(3) Data Processing Support Actions (Provider Partner)
(2) Bedding Sales Zone (Receiver Partner)	Ask customers if they have been to Bedding. If not, ask if they would like to be escorted there.	Remind customers, if they purchased lamps, to take them with them. Ask customers who purchased bedroom furniture if they need a new bed frame or mattress.
(3) Data Processing (Receiver Partner)	Put correct SKU#s on work sheets and complete all items. Give priority to pages from Credit.	Within Data Processing Work sheets illegible and incomplete. Sales associates slow to respond to paging.

Table 12-2. Store interactions matrix

The process used within the store was repeated with the management of the distribution center. A portion of the interactions matrix is shown in table 12-3.

(1) Area or Department	(2) Customer Delivery Support Actions (Provider Partner)	(3) Purchasing Support Actions (Provider Partner)
(2) Customer Service (Receiver Partner)		Order only merchandise that manufacturer will service, not one-time-only merchandise.
(3) Receiving Warehouse (Receiver Partner)	Identify exchanged or returned merchandise on paperwork as "return to vendor" or "restock."	

Table 12-3. Distribution center interactions matrix

After management and the employees learned how to operate according to these mutual commitments, management expanded the matrix to include interactions between the store and the distribution center.

A Leap of Performance

The transformation of the system, which included the orchestration of relationships described here, produced dramatic improvements in performance in the three years after making these changes. For example, sales revenues nearly doubled, closing percentages and inventory turns were up, the cost of sales decreased, and turnover was nearly eliminated. The flexibility to move employees on and off the sales floor to meet changing situations made it unnecessary to hire just-in-case sales people. Conversely, since many sales associates were trained in other functions (e.g., delivery and customer service), they were able to help out during slower sales periods. Other costs inherent in the old management system began to disappear, such as merchandise returns and other costs due to overselling the customers. Employees and management spent more time on work that added value. The time that Payroll needed to administer the pay system was reduced from ten hours for commission to one hour for salary pay. In addition, Payroll no longer had to deal with a continual stream of phone calls from sales associates asking if they made quota. Profits increased and were shared with employees. Customers felt less pressured and helped more.

Ongoing Learning of Individuals and Evolution of the Enterprise

This was a momentous change not just for the business but personally for Mac. He was fully aware that occasionally he reverted back to his old, hard-driving style, but this happened less often as time went by. Yet it was still a source of fear in the organization. A key role of the external consultant was to help Mac become aware of this tendency to revert, understand its source, see its potential to destroy the new system he put in place, and work on minimizing it.

People began to identify themselves not so much by their function but as a part of Gallery Furniture. The thought, *That's not my job*, was disappearing. People were making decisions jointly on issues in which they were involved. Seasoned sales associates helped new ones. Instead of spending time pouring over computer printouts of sales and commissions, people had time and energy to work on improvement and standardization of processes, and to improve their personal sales techniques. Mac also began to introduce these practices to his suppliers through in-house seminars.

A Custom Job Shop in Concert

This privately owned company designs and manufactures vinyl extrusions to meet the needs of window and door system manufacturers who supply the commercial and home building industries. The company has the capability under one roof to custom design a product, custom design and manufacture the tools and dies, and then manufacture the final product.

The CEO, president, and all of the managers attended one of W. Edwards Deming's four-day seminars. They came to believe that the management principles and methods that he presented would help the company to improve. The company advertised this to the world in its public statements and marketing literature, which read in part: "We follow the principles of the late Dr. W. Edwards Deming … Dr. Deming's teachings guide us to focus on continual improvement of product quality and customer service … The most important relationships are supplier-customer interactions, as well as the relationships between the people of (company name)."

Management had decided that in order to continue to grow and differentiate itself from its competitors, it had to produce at least one new die each day to accommodate the schedules of its current customers and meet commitments to new customers. This fact of life, this reality of the business, had been translated into a numerical objective for the manager of Tooling Design and Manufacture. The capability to consistently achieve this objective had not yet been demonstrated.

The manager of Tooling Design and Manufacture met once or twice a week with his boss, the company president, to evaluate how he was doing with regard to the objective. They weren't seeing any progress. The department manager was quite frustrated, first, because he knew the importance of meeting the objective, and second, because every day he encountered obstacles to meeting the objective. He knew that performance would improve if there were more cooperation between departments—for example, if he could get more frequent access to production equipment to test the dies before releasing them to production. Since the production manager was under pressure to meet his own numerical objectives, he was not very willing to give up machine time.

Every day there were many interactions between members of management, mainly in the form of meetings, mostly ad hoc, except for the weekly management meeting with the president. These interactions were not as cooperative as they needed to be to improve the performance of the business. Occasionally an attitude of provincialism surfaced as one department revealed its belief that it was more important than the others, or had a more difficult job than the others, or that the others were not doing their job.

Production Tooling: The System in Focus

The external consultant and one of the managers drew a picture, shown in figure 12-4, to illustrate how the various departments influence the capability of the company to produce dies.[330] The system in focus is the Production Tooling System. The Advanced Tooling Development System is also shown to illustrate that people usually participate in more than one system.

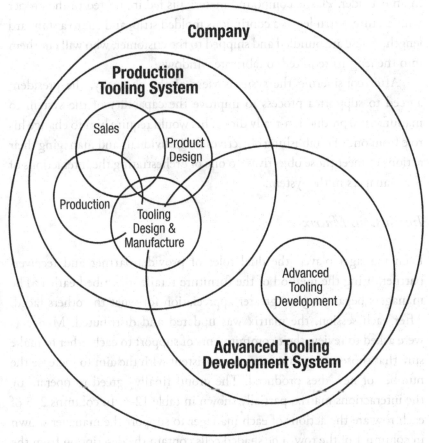

Figure 12-4. Production Tooling System

The system generally operates in the following manner. A sales person interests a new customer, usually a window manufacturer, in the capabilities of the company. Then Product Design works with the customer and uses computer-aided design (CAD) to develop a design that meets that customer's requirements. Product Design then submits their design to the Tool Design and Manufacture department, where they translate it through CAD to a blueprint, which will be used to manufacture the die. Highly skilled technicians, who use computer-controlled, high-precision metal-working equipment, manufacture the die. They test the die on production equipment. Then they send the die to production, where it is used for the initial and subsequent customer orders. The die is placed in an extruder. Plastic compound material is fed in, heated to the proper temperature, extruded as a continuous molded strip, and cut to a standard length. These are bundled and shipped to the customer, who will cut them into the lengths required to fabricate windows.

After considering the systems view of the company, the president agreed to support a process to improve the capability of the system to manufacture production-ready dies. This would require him to change his role from one of establishing objectives for individuals and managing their actions to meet those objectives, to one of orchestrating the interactions of the managers in the system.

Interactions Matrix

Each manager played the dual roles of provider-partner and receiver-partner, using the method of the furniture retailer described earlier. The managers began to get a greater appreciation for what the others faced. After each session, the matrix was updated and distributed. Managers were asked to review their commitments of support to each other to make sure that those commitments were consistent with the aim to increase the number of new dies produced. The group finally agreed to operate by the interactions matrix, partially shown in table 12-4. In columns 2–5 of each row are the actions of each manager to support the manager shown in column 1 of the row. The shaded cells contain the description from the manager of the situation within the department.

(1) Department	(2) Sales Support Actions (Provider Partner)	(3) Product Design Support Actions (Provider Partner)	(4) Tooling Design & Manufacture Support Actions (Provider Partner)	(5) Production Support Actions (Provider Partner)
(2) Sales (Receiver Partner)	Not well informed about production schedule changes in order to manage relationships with customer.	Simplify designs to speed up tool production and meet customer schedule.	Provide current tool schedules to Sales and update on progress.	Plan for flexibility to meet short lead-time requests.
(3) Product Design (Receiver Partner)	Work with customer to minimize customer changes to design.	No relief to deal with post-approval design changes by customer, Tooling, or Production.	Provide feedback on tooling feasibility for product design.	Provide production samples of prior designs to show produceability of a proposed design.
(4) Tooling Design & Manufacture (Receiver Partner)	Communicate possible changes to schedule by customer.	Work with Tooling and customer to simplify product design for tooling.	Production extruders not available to test tools.	Coordinate with Tooling to make extruders available to test tools.
(5) Production (Receiver Partner)	Work with customers to develop realistic timing.	Work with Tooling and customer to simplify product design for tooling.	Use SPC on tool cutting equipment to build better tools.	Dies need frequent maintenance.

Table 12-4. Production tooling interactions matrix

Managers and employees noted improvement in results and in relationships between departments. Daily interactions and the weekly management meeting with the president reflected a new sense of "being in it together." The meeting was a chance for them to evaluate how well they and others in the company were working together as a system and to update the matrix. Management agreed to extend this method to other systems.

A Corporate Staff in Concert

This enterprise is composed of subsidiary companies that provided a variety of telecommunications and information products and services. These were primarily local and long-distance phone service, mobile-cellular products and services, directory information, and advertising. A central staff provided corporate policies and guidance and carried out other corporate functions. Senior management wanted the company to become adaptable and flexible in dealing with an external environment of dramatic change of regulations, technology, and competitors. Internally, these executives sought to develop collaboration, teamwork, listening, and trust. The two executive vice presidents, who presided over the corporate staff, wanted to see these values operationalized throughout the company so that the firm could take greater advantage of the information, knowledge, and talent that existed in the separate parts of the enterprise. They wanted the enterprise to operate as one interrelated business (see figure 12-5), rather than as independent parts in the manner of a holding company.

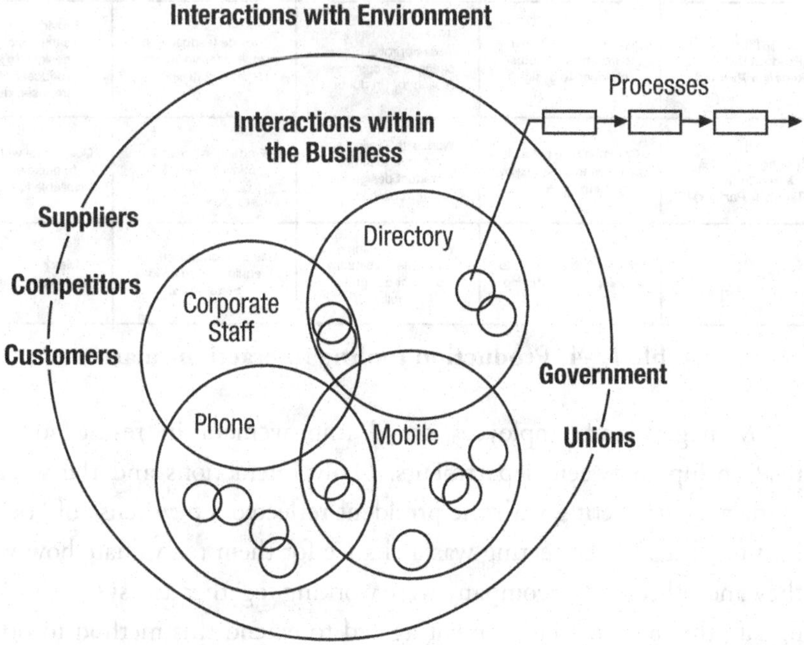

Figure 12-5. A whole-system view of the business

The two staff executives recognized that they could not simply preach to others about change; change had to start with themselves, as individuals and as an organization. Therefore, the executive staff first would have to learn how to operate according to the values and principles that they wanted others in the company to follow. Interactions between staff functions tended to occur only by way of requests to other staff departments for information, or responses to such requests from those departments. Management agreed to proceed with development of a process to identify and manage key relationships within the staff.

Interactions Matrix

Participants were the two staff executive vice presidents and their department heads. They followed a process similar to that described in previous examples given in this chapter. Each individual participant played the roles of provider-partner and receiver-partner. The commitment of the senior staff executives made it possible to bring together, in the same room at the same time, the management of the whole-system. When the process started, the managers did not quite see themselves as dependent on other departments.

An initial session was held to develop mutual understanding of interdependencies. After the session, the discussion was summarized in the form of a preliminary interactions matrix, which then was distributed to the participants. They were asked to complete the matrix regarding their own needs for support from others and their commitments to support others. The matrix then was modified to include this new information. A second meeting was held with all of the managers to review the updated matrix.

Table 12-5 presents a portion of the matrix for three areas. The shaded cells show the requirements within a department. A nonshaded entry shows the commitment of support by the manager, indicated at the top of columns 2–4 to another manager, indicated in rows 2–4, column 1.

(1) Department	(2) Treasury Support Actions (Provider Partner)	(3) Human Resources Support Actions (Provider Partner)	(4) Investor Relations Support Actions (Provider Partner)
(2) Treasury (Receiver Partner)	Timely information on long-term and short-term plans of each business area. Knowledge of risks inherent in plans.	Involve Treasury early in design of new compensation and benefit programs.	Assist in evaluation of external information sources.
(3) Human Resources (Receiver Partner)	Provide information and analysis to support development of compensation plan.	HR policies and processes must support business strategy and corporate values.	Provide employee seminars on stock investing.
(4) Investor Relations (Receiver Partner)	Provide information on financing plans and activities. Cooperate in shareholder related activity.	Identify significant HR initiatives to enable effective external positioning within the investment community. Respond effectively to HR related questions.	Maintain credibility with external analysts and investors. Respond quickly to ad hoc questions from other departments.

Table 12-5. Corporate staff interactions

Hidden Critical Interdependencies Are Revealed

The Human Resources director, whose purview encompassed the entire staff, examined the completed interactions matrix. He concluded that more interdependencies logically should exist but had not been revealed. He thought that each manager might find it easier to identify additional interdependencies if four generic staff activities were considered:

(P): Planning Organization-Wide. Develop plans that affect all of the business or all of the corporate staff.

(R): Regulating. Develop and monitor rules and regulations (e.g., company policy).

(S): Stakeholder Positioning. Influence external stakeholders (e.g., government, investors, the public).

(D): Service Delivery. Provide a service to another staff department or subsidiary business.

(1) Department	(2) Business Planning Function-Process	(3) Accounting Function-Process	(4) Public Relations Function-Process
(2) Business Development	P, R, D	—	D
(3) Controller	R, D	P, R, S, D	—
(4) Public Affairs	S	—	P, R, S, D

Table 12-6. Function-Process activity matrix

The Human Resources director developed a function-process activity matrix, partially shown in table 12-6. Three departments are shown in column 1, rows 2–4. Three functions, or processes, appear in columns 2–4. The entries within each cell indicate which generic staff activities each department in column 1 has to perform to do its work. The shaded cell in each row indicates that the department has the primary responsibility to carry out the function listed at the top of the column. It therefore engages in most of the generic staff activities in order to manage that function or process. Business Development (row 2, shaded cell) performs activities P, R, D. The nonshaded cells indicate an overlap of staff activities. Public Affairs (row 4) performs a business-planning function (column 2) through its activities, indicated by S, to influence external stakeholders. Therefore, Public Affairs and Business Development should be able to help each other.

Partnerships Are Formed

The function process activity matrix helped to reveal the basis for additional relationships. A partnership concept was developed to enable those managers in the most critical interdependencies to work together, as shown in table 12-7. The managers decided to limit their participation to a maximum of three partnerships at any one time. Figure 12-6 illustrates the partnerships identified in table 12-7.

Managers Participating	Partnership X	Partnership Y	Partnership Z	Number of Partnerships that Contain the Manager
A	•	•		2
B	•		•	2
C		•		1
D			•	1
E		•		1
Number of Managers in the Partnership	2	3	2	7

Table 12-7. Formation of staff partnerships

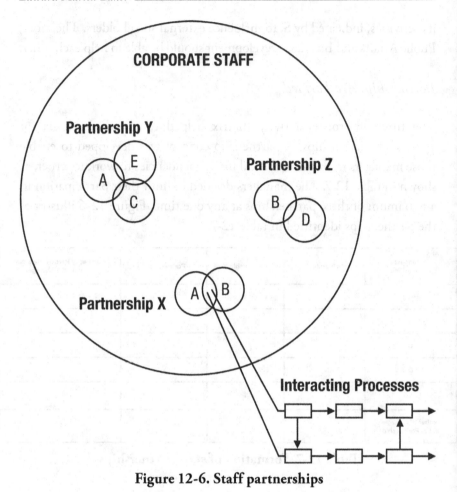

Figure 12-6. Staff partnerships

Learning Continues

Partnerships that are unaffected by changes in the environment will exist for a relatively long time. Others will be formed to adapt to specific changes in the environment since the company is very much affected by communications technology and by government policies and regulations. Staff management held regular meetings among themselves to share information about partnership activities and developments in the environmental supra system that could change interdependencies and therefore require new partnership arrangements. They also discussed how to handle various interaction management issues, such as how often to meet and how to manage the process as it starts to involve more employees within each department.

Orchestrating Interactions for a Whole-in-One

The interactions management process described in these organizations is an application of theories and principles of a whole-system-performance ecology. It should suggest the question, "If I apply system principles in my organization, how can I provide the leadership to help the organization function as a social performance ecology and how can I learn from it and sustain it?"

The next chapter begins a discussion of Deming's map of variation. This component of the Deming symphony provides insights that have profound implications for understanding and managing a system.

THIRD MOVEMENT: KNOWLEDGE ABOUT VARIATION

Chapter 13

~

Deming's Map of a Theory of Variation

> Statistical theory and methods are creating a science of
> management and of administration through their ability
> to aid in the discovery of causes.[331] The central problem
> in management, leadership, and production is failure to
> understand the nature and interpretation of variation.[332]
> —W. Edwards Deming

Systems and processes vary over time. One of Deming's powerful questions is, "What do the differences mean?" Deming related a conversation between a plant manager and his boss who asked every morning about the production numbers from the previous day. Deming evaluated the question this way: "One thing [is] sure, it was higher than it was the day before, or it was less. So what? What does the up or down mean?"[333] What action is appropriate and constructive when management observes differences in production numbers each day, or variation in the characteristics of materials received from a supplier, or differences between individual employees assessed in a performance review; when teachers and parents see changes in student scores from one test to the next? Deming's theory of variation makes it possible to rationally understand the source of differences over time in the outcomes of processes and what action to take.

My undergraduate introductory statistics course nearly turned me off to the subject, as it may have done to you. It did not give me an appreciation for the profound ways we can view and affect the world, as does Deming's map of variation, also known as statistical thinking and statistical theory.

His map is intertwined with and inseparable from the other components of profound knowledge. Deming's theory of variation is a basis for rational thinking about differences that occur within an organization, from the shop floor on up, and within life in general. Application of the theory through the use of tools such as control charts where measurements are available is essential, but unless we understand the theory, the methods have limited usefulness, and results are likely to be misinterpreted.

Undergraduate introductory statistics classes that do not at least create an awareness of Deming's ideas are missing an opportunity to provide content that students will find relevant to their lives. The material can be made interesting and fun and inspire students to additional study. Deming did this in his seminars and his teaching at Columbia University and New York University.

Deming directed some of his writing on statistical theory and methods to business executives and to experts in psychology, engineering, law, accounting, consumer research, and other professions. He also remarked that perhaps statisticians have even a greater need for such knowledge.[334] I accompanied Dr. Deming on visits to the chairperson of the statistics department of a number of colleges. He tried to interest them in revising their curriculum, but in most cases he did not prevail. Perhaps, as with most people who are not open to considering new ideas, they were too comfortable with the way things were, or maybe their attachment to their beliefs and models (their map), which they shared with others in their profession, was a barrier to seeing other possibilities.

Students in high school and even lower grades are capable of gaining an appreciation for statistical thinking. Deming wrote about one student, Patrick, who at age eleven plotted the arrival time each day of his school bus. On *only* two days, the bus was late. We might have a tendency to generalize and think, *Why is this bus* always *late?* or *What's wrong with the driver?* Rather, Patrick, without making calculations, saw evidence from the pattern of plotted arrival times that on the two days that the bus was late, the causes could be identified. It turned out that the delay on one of the days was caused by a new driver, and on the other day by the door closer not working. Differences in arrival times on the other days were normal variation for which specific causes could not be identified. It was variation due to a system of causes, including variation in traffic and time for students along the way to board the bus.[335]

The Failure to Understand Variation in Everyday Life

In a statistics class, you may have been taught that if the likelihood of a head or tail on a single toss was equal when flipping a coin, then in a long series of flips we would expect to see approximately half of the coins come up heads and half come up tails. However, the theory of probability that produced this expectation would apply to actual flips made in a vacuum, and therefore process variables such as the human or machine flipping the coin, air currents, and other environmental factors would have no effect. However, we typically don't flip coins, or do anything else, in a vacuum. Yet the theory of probability is useful just as are plane geometry and spherical geometry, the normal curve and other theoretical models, which we can apply to understand the world in which we live.

Even when flipped in a vacuum, for the coin to be "unbiased" it would have to be manufactured perfectly without any irregularities that would cause heads or tails to be favored. Any manufactured coin will differ from the design concept of the ideal (perfect) coin, if only by a very small and sometimes undetectable amount. Variation in manufacturing can be caused by wear of tools and dies and the chemistry and composition of the metal mixtures. The long-run results of flipping the coin may approach an equal chance of heads or tails, but to actually achieve the same proportion of heads and tails in the long run is an abstraction and exists only in the mind, especially when the _long run_ is taken to be infinity. Plato wrote more than 2,500 years ago that perfection is an idea.[336] Perfection exists only in the invisible world of thought and not in the visible world of everyday living. This is true of objects such as a circle or, in the social realm, concepts such as the good, justice, and fairness.

Variation is a fact of life in the empirical world. Years ago in a presentation delivered at various meetings to mechanical engineers, business and industrial executives, and university faculty, Deming said:

> All things exhibit variability. People and peas vary. Not
> all people like the same things or do equally acceptable

work, or work best under any one set of conditions or hours. Moreover, the performance of any one person or machine varies from hour to hour ... There is no such thing as constancy in real life. There is, however, such a thing as a *constant-cause system*. The results produced by a constant-cause system vary, and in fact may vary over a wide band or a narrow band. They vary, but they exhibit an important feature called *stability* ... It is the *distribution* of results that is constant or stable. When a manufacturing process behaves like a constant-cause system, producing inspection results that exhibit stability, it is said to be in *statistical control*. The control chart will tell you whether your process is in statistical control ... The control chart helps to formulate rational courses of action by showing when the variations in the inspection results may safely be left to chance, or whether it will pay to assume the existence of an assignable cause and do something about it.

Deming went on to say that when acting on these problems, we should be thankful that there are only two kinds of mistakes that can be made, and:

The question is when to act as if there were an assignable cause, and when not. If you look for trouble or increase the amount of inspection because you think there is an assignable cause (one you can find) when actually none exists, you will only go on a wild goose chase, waste time and money, and probably make trouble. And when you fail to look for trouble or to recognize a spotty condition arising from an assignable cause when one actually exists, you waste time and money again.[337]

Profound knowledge of variation applies to all aspects of living, not only managing processes in organizations. Deming wrote that the application of control charts on the shop floor is only a small fraction of the needs of industry, education, and government and that the most important application of such knowledge is in the management of people.[338]

Deming's books are full of examples of the failure to understand variation. Here are two from *Out of the Crisis*:[339]

"In general, we have been with above-average leadership, said Robert K. Murray, who is tabulating the responses of 970 historians questioned in the survey. 'We've been remarkably lucky, considering the relatively haphazard way we select a president. Historians have determined that almost one out of every four has been great or near great, and over half are above average,' said the professor of history at Pennsylvania State University" (*San Diego Union*, February 21, 1983, p. C-2).

"Nuclear reactors at 15 of the nation's 50 nuclear plant sites have failed on a Nuclear Regulatory Commission 'report card' and will get closer attention from federal inspectors. The NRC staff, based on studies concluded at the end of last year, found the 15 power plants 'below average' in overall performance, including maintenance, radiation and fire protection and management control. An NRC spokesman said '... the purpose of the study was to make sure we focus our inspections on plants showing below-average performance'" (from a *Wall Street Journal* report of an NRC Report, October 1981).

Dr. Deming commented that the aim of management of nuclear power plants or anything else should be to improve all plants. No matter how successful this management, there will always be plants below average. Specific remedial action would be indicated for special (specific, assignable) causes of variation. You can probably think of examples, your own and that of others, considered to be good management, such as a goal to reduce the proportion of salaries above the median salary or attempts to have all stores perform above average by eliminating those that perform below average. It should be obvious that when below-average performers are removed from the system, they will be replaced eventually by those who once were above average.

Eight plants reported to the general manager of a large manufacturing operation. Before visiting a plant, he had ranked the eight plant managers according to each plant's performance. When he visited a plant and discussed its performance with the plant manager, he would try to motivate the lower-ranked managers by comparing them with the other plant managers, telling them they were below average, or if above average, worse than some of the other plants. This enabled him to use the technique on seven of the eight managers. Of course, he could always use this method since half of the plants always would be ranked below average, no matter how well they did.

Profound Knowledge of Variation Has Broad Applications

Statistical theory is independent of any particular experience (i.e., it exists before [a priori] the experience). The theory doesn't care whether it will be applied to manufacture pharmaceutical products, to test materials, to evaluate consumer responses, or to compare methods of farming. It doesn't care what process produced the numbers.[340]

According to Deming, "The theoretical statistician is the practical man since he has a better guide for practice than the errors of his forefathers."[341] He applies the power of theory to his work. The practical statistician, on the other hand, practices the errors of his forefathers. Deming, who described himself as a consulting statistician in the sense of the theoretical statistician, redefined "practical" as guided by theory.[342] He wrote, "The day has past when 'theoretical' means impractical."[343]

Deming stressed in his teaching that statistical problems are solved only by statistical theory, not by management, engineering, or any other area of knowledge. Knowledge of variation and its methods, on the other hand, are not a substitute for expert knowledge in engineering, chemistry, economics, marketing, medicine, psychology, economics, and other fields. It will not in itself determine the right question or right answer. It will not determine the operational definition of passed, failed, good, bad, occupation, age, or education. Statistical theory is an aid to management. It extends expert knowledge by helping to measure differences in performance in order to isolate and regulate the causes of variation and departures from a standard.[344]

Statistical Theory and Practice as a Moral and Spiritual Undertaking

There is evidence that Deming saw his teaching as a moral undertaking. He did not label his teaching as moral philosophy, but on his office wall was this framed statement by Florence Nightingale:

It is by the aid of Statistics that Law in the social sphere can be ascertained and codified, and certain aspects of the character of God thereby revealed. The study of statistics is thus a religious service.

His appreciation of Nightingale's quote, and perhaps her life, may be seen as underscoring the spiritual foundation of his work. Nightingale viewed statistics as a moral science. Her profession was nursing. She combined her knowledge of medicine with her knowledge of statistics to convert health data to statistical charts and diagrams, which could be used as powerful arguments for medical reform. She believed, as did Deming, that a manager could be successful only when guided by statistical knowledge and that the legislator and the politician often failed for lack of this knowledge.[345]

Dr. Deming's Parable of the Red Beads

Dr. Deming taught that there is no substitute for knowledge. This is especially the case with his theory of variation. So many people behave without this knowledge in their lives every day. This results in costs, economically to organizations and to the spirit, mind, and heart of individuals who suffer from their own ignorance, as do those with whom they interact and manage. Here, for example, is a statement from a woman who participated during one of Dr. Deming's seminars in a demonstration he called the "red bead experiment." She was one of the volunteers from the audience who participated as "willing workers" in a simulated factory production line managed by an autocratic supervisor, played by Dr. Deming.

"When I was a Willing Worker on the Red Beads, I learned more than statistical theory. I knew that the system would not allow me to meet the goal, but I still felt that I could. I wished to. I tried so hard. I felt responsibility: others depended on me. My logic and emotions conflicted, and I was frustrated. Logic said that there was no way to succeed. Emotion said that I could by trying. After it was over, I thought about my own work situation. How often are people in a situation that they cannot govern, but wish to do their best? And people do their best. And after a while, what happens to their drive, their care, their desire? For some, they become turned off, tuned out. Fortunately, there are many that only need the opportunity and methods to contribute with."[346]

When I recall Dr. Deming's demonstration, the memory of it has taken on the abstract quality of a parable, an allegory, with moral and intellectual lessons. I thought of the dialogue between teacher and student in Plato's "Allegory of the Cave" in his book, *The Republic*. Dr. Deming conducted his red bead demonstration on day two of his four-day seminar. It was theater. He asked for participation from the audience. There were volunteers for various roles: six production ("willing") workers, two inspectors, another as inspector general to verify the count of the inspectors, and a recorder of results. Deming acted as a tough supervisor, a role he appeared to enjoy and played exceedingly well. The demonstration made it possible for Dr. Deming to help the audience gain some powerful insights necessary for managing, leading, and living that can't be learned in traditional statistics courses. I will describe it briefly, but a video has to be seen for full effect.[347] I haven't seen anyone who can make the case the way Deming did.

Once they are on the stage, Dr. Deming, acting as supervisor, asks the six people to verify that they volunteered to be "willing workers," and he asks one of them to volunteer to be the "average worker." A willing worker volunteers to be average. He tells the others that they all are above average. Each worker's name is recorded, and instructions are given.

Deming tells the workers that the firm manufactures beads. The customer wants white beads. Red beads are defective. Their job is to make white beads. (The lessons are relevant even if you only provide services and don't manufacture beads or don't manufacture anything.) As their supervisor, Deming tells the workers that continuation of their job depends on their own performance so they must put forth their best efforts. If their performance slips, they may not have jobs. Their jobs are entirely up to them. No one can resign, but they can be fired.

The equipment consists of a rectangular paddle that has fifty (5 x 10) beveled depressions. The raw materials consist of a mixture of red and white beads that are contained in a rectangular box. The worker first has to mix the materials by pouring the contents of the box into a second rectangular box, and then pouring it back into the first box. The worker then is to scoop the beads, filling the paddle. They are told that their objective is to select only white beads since the customer will not accept red beads—a zero-defect objective. Since 20 percent of the beads are red, it is almost impossible to select only white beads. Deming doesn't tell the workers of this percentage, which he knows from a previous count of all of the beads, but they can easily see that there are red beads. After each scoop, the inspectors counted the number of red beads in the paddle, the inspector general verified the count, reported to the recorder, and the fifty beads were returned to the box.

Deming, the supervisor, tried to get the willing workers to scoop only white beads from the box. He chided a worker for a scoop with many red beads and gave a bit of praise when the red bead count was low. We will see later, when Deming constructed a control chart from the results, that reward, punishment, and threats of firing had no effect on the results produced by the workers, who obviously were trying their best to meet the goals of defect-free production.

This part of the demonstration simulated four days of production. At the end of day four, the supervisor carried out what he called a "fantastic plan of management." He fired the three worst workers based on results of the previous four days. On day five, the demonstration continued with the three "best" workers (Jim, Marilyn, and Teresa in figure 13-1). Again, the results were similar and disappointing.

Record of the number of defective items by Willing Worker, per day. Lot size 50, each Willing Worker per day.

Willing Worker	Day 2D					
	1	2	3	4	All 4	5
Jim	7	9	5	8	29	9 5
Shirley	5	7	14	14	40	
Francine	17	8	12	8	45	
Marilyn	6	11	7	6	30	8 7
Teresa	14	5	9	5	33	4 11
Judy	4	11	11	8	34	
All 6	53	51	58	49	211	44
Cum x̄	8.8	8.7	9.0	8.8	8.8	x x %

$$\bar{x} = \frac{211}{6 \times 4} = 8.83$$

$$\bar{p} = \frac{211}{6 \times 4 \times 50} = .177$$

$$\text{UCL}_{\text{LCL}} = \bar{x} \pm 3\sqrt{\bar{x}(1-\bar{p})}$$

$$= 8.83 \pm 3\sqrt{8.83 \times .823}$$

$$= \begin{matrix} 16.92 \\ .74 \end{matrix} \longrightarrow \begin{matrix} 17 \\ 1 \end{matrix}$$

Wooden beads
Census count,
one by one
Total 4000
Red 800
White 3200

Paddle No. 4

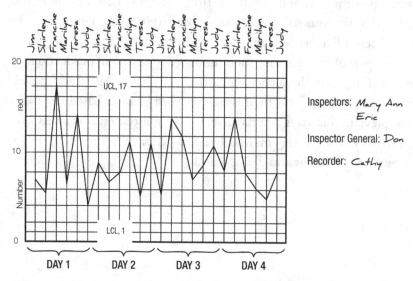

Inspectors: Mary Ann
Eric

Inspector General: Don

Recorder: Cathy

Figure 13-1. Control chart from Deming's red bead demonstration

During the debriefing of the demonstration, Deming constructed a statistical process control chart, a graphical representation of process outcomes. Figure 13-1 shows the chart from a demonstration conducted for a client during a seminar in which I participated.[348] Results varied around the average (centerline) of 8.8 red beads and were *within* the control limits, which ranged from a lower control limit (LCL) of one to an upper control limit (UCL) of seventeen with one questionable result. One worker on day one scooped seventeen red beads. The number seventeen falls on the UCL. It is unusual yet possible for a point in control to fall on a control limit. Deming had managed the process to assure that it was executed according to his rules. He had watched each worker scoop the beads and verified that the count was correct. Therefore, he concluded that the point on the control limit was part of a pattern of common cause variation and that the process was stable (i.e., repeatable and predictable). The variation between workers and from day to day was produced by the process, which included the management style of the supervisor. The workers were not at fault. They had no ability to influence the outcomes, yet the supervisor blamed them for the results and fired them. Performance on day five with the best workers was like the other days since "best" is always in the past. These employees also were fired, even though, as the demonstration showed, performance was beyond their control.

There are various types of control charts depending on the nature and availability of data. Some processes generate data frequently; others take a longer time to produce outputs. Some charts plot measurements ("variables data"), while others plot qualitative ("attributes") data. Figure 13-1 is a chart of attributes data. Red beads (defectives) for each production period were counted and plotted on the chart, and averages were calculated.

During a break after the demonstration, people came up to Dr. Deming and told him that he used an extreme example, that the world isn't that way. Deming wanted to show that the management system and the production process were the dominant forces in the behavior of the individuals. He used a strict autocratic management system to make it clear that everyone is constrained by the system in which they work and the system in which they live. It is the system that influences the actions of people, whether in organization systems or other social systems. Senior management may be more constrained in their actions, at times even more than others in enterprise, because what they plan, say, and do affects the future of the entire enterprise.

Red Bead Demonstration: Lessons for Management

The demonstration illustrated the absence of leadership. The supervisor had awarded merit increases in pay for good results and put employees on probation for poor results even though employees had no control over the outcomes. Procedures were so rigid that the employees had no chance to improve performance or even to offer suggestions for improvement. For example, they could not replace a red bead with a white one or scoop the beads a second time. One of the employees was fired for emptying the paddle and scooping a second time. Management didn't do its job to improve the system (e.g., work with the supplier of the beads to try to reduce the proportion of red beads in the incoming material).

One responsibility of management is prediction. On day five, management kept the place open with the "best" workers. Management had no rational basis to evaluate one employee as better than another or to predict that the three workers who were best in the past would be best in the future.

The supervisor also was a product of the system. The performance objective given to him was unattainable. His performance appraisal also was dependent on the performance of his unit. All of the variation in the demonstration, the differences between the results produced by each employee, came entirely from the process. The process was shown to be in statistical control—that is, stable and predictable. This conclusion was based on intimate knowledge of the procedures prescribed and followed by the six production workers, as well as on study of the chart. The employees, initially willing to contribute, continued to try their best under the circumstances, yet they could do no better than that shown in the control chart of figure 13-1.

Operational Definition of Common and Special

The control chart applies to any process whether on the shop floor, in the office, in the classroom, in the hospital, or any other process where data can be collected over time. The control chart doesn't care what process produced the numbers. It will provide information to improve the process and system, from mass production and job shops, to service processes and professional sports, and to our own individual performance. As an example, Deming provided an example of how a control chart can show how lessons have lowered a golfer's score and improved consistency of play.[349] Even if data are not available to construct a control chart, profound knowledge can guide us to evaluate, decide, and act from an appreciation for the dynamics of a system and its sources of variation.

The Deming-Shewhart control chart provides an operational definition of the types of causes, or producers, of process variation. If data points are not within the control limits, the process is defined as not stable. There exists what Deming called *special* causes (Shewhart called them *assignable* causes) since they are *specific* to the time when those data points outside of one or both control limits were produced. They do not occur on a regular basis. When there are signals of the existence of special causes, the process is not in statistical control. If the source is found and corrected, the process should return to a state of statistical control, a stable state.[350] Special causes often can be identified and removed by employees who work in the process. Other patterns, such as trends, also may indicate special causes.[351] Deming warned that a search for patterns can be overdone.[352]

There is no evidence of special causes in the control chart of figure 13-1. Since there aren't any data points beyond the control limits, the process appears to be in statistical control (i.e., stable). This means that the differences in results over time for each willing worker and between workers were due to a system of causes common to all results (Shewhart called them *chance* causes). These causes are inherent in the system. They continually influence results. Although data points vary from each other, the variation is stable and therefore predictable within the control limits. We can conclude, with a high degree of belief (degree of belief can't be quantified), that future results will be like the past results, unless a special cause acts on the process or the system changes. Whether the conditions under which the data were collected will remain the same in the future is not a statistical question; rather, it requires knowledge of the process and the factors that might affect it. The control limits can be extended into the future, if it was judged that changes would not occur. Without a change in the process—the material and paint of the beads, the paddle, the supervisor's procedures—the process will continue to produce the same average proportion of defects and vary within the control limits. However, it is management's responsibility to improve processes and systems by improving the equipment, working with suppliers, giving employees more discretion to make changes, and in maintenance schedules and procedures.

The red bead demonstration is an example of how numerical goals cannot achieve desired results without an accompanying capable process. The statistical control limits are not imposed by engineering specifications or by management goals or targets. They are calculated from the data produced by the process. Management's attempt to meet specifications and targets by continually adjusting the process can make things worse. Deming called this "tampering," and it is discussed in the next chapter. Better performance can come only from improving the system and its processes.[353]

Importance of Time-Order

One often sees in business meetings, research reports, and media stories results displayed in the form of a histogram. What rarely, if ever, is discussed is the stability of the process that produced the histogram and which forms the basis of conclusions. A histogram can hide instability, such as drift—the gradual shifting of the distribution results over time. A histogram can have a symmetrical shape and look like a normal curve yet not be stable. The problem is that the time variable is collapsed in a histogram such that drift and other special causes can be hidden. Deming's theory of variation tells us that any conclusions drawn from a histogram are questionable without knowing if the process is stable. A process is not capable if it is not stable, and stability can be evaluated only from a time-ordered pattern of data, such as that seen on a control chart. [354]

Types of Errors When Using a Control Chart

Statistical methods in practice are not tests of hypotheses. Walter Shewhart developed the control chart to minimize loss from inappropriate actions. The decisions and actions guided by the principles of the control chart have an economic basis. They minimize loss from making adjustments too often and from failing to make adjustments often enough. Shewhart wrote, "By the elimination of assignable (special) causes of variability we make the most efficient use of raw materials, maximize the assurance of the quality of manufactured product, minimize the cost of inspection, and minimize loss from rejections."[355]

Sometimes, but rarely, there are false signals on a control chart, but it still is economically advantageous to be guided by the chart. There are two types of errors possible when we make decisions from the control chart. This is much like a medical doctor making a diagnosis or an aircraft controller detecting the presence of aircraft from an airport control tower.

- Miss (false negative): The control chart does not indicate a special cause is present when actually it is. All points are within control limits, even though a special cause is present. The chart has missed a special cause and results in a decision not to do anything when action should be taken to identify and remove the special cause.
- False alarm (false positive): The control chart indicates a special cause is present and that the process is out of control when the process actually is in statistical control. This results in a wasted attempt to identify a special cause that doesn't exist.

These types of errors are rare when using a Shewhart-Deming control chart, but they can't always be avoided. It is possible to get a result beyond a control limit with a stable process. I was present at a Deming seminar when a willing worker drew a sample of twenty red beads, a result that turned out to be beyond the control limit of nineteen. Deming judged this result to be a false signal since he knew that procedures were strictly followed and that such an event can occur, although rarely.[356]

The problem of accuracy of observation, measurement, evaluation, and decision errors surrounds our lives. False-positive and false-negative errors are not limited to control charts. They can, and do, occur in all areas of human observation and decision making, such as crime investigation, medical diagnosis, and monitoring of people by airport TSA inspectors.

If an inspection process is too sensitive, it may increase the chances of a false alarm; if it is not sensitive enough, it can miss problems. Sensitivity is a tradeoff between the costs of such errors and the costs of avoiding them. Most airline passengers would like to reduce as much as possible the time taken for inspection as well as the methods used by airport TSA inspectors but are willing to make some tradeoff for the security benefits. The TSA would like to assure that no one who poses a threat to passengers gets through security, but passenger discomfort and disruption of airline schedules should be considered.

If process managers use a Shewhart control chart, they will minimize the overall loss from both types of errors. If they try to minimize misses of special causes by bringing the control limits closer together, more data points will be outside the limits and therefore will be taken as signals of special causes. Investigation will most likely not lead to correct identification of special causes and will have led to confusion and a waste of time. Widening the control limits beyond those recommended by Shewhart and Deming will result in fewer false alarms but will increase the frequency of misses since fewer points will be outside of the control limits. Deming warned that once the control limits have been calculated, they should not be moved to change the sensitivity of the control chart.

Deming's Profound Insight about Sampling

After the red bead demonstration, Deming said that the container from which the willing workers took samples of fifty beads (which were replaced in the container) contained 4,000 beads—800 red and 3,200 white. He asked the audience to predict the average number of red beads the process would produce over time. Most of the audience thought about it in the following way: since 20 percent of the beads are red (800 of 4,000), then the number of red beads sampled over many demonstrations should average out to 20 percent, and 20 percent of samples of 50 beads in the paddle will average out to ten red beads.

Deming congratulated the audience on their arithmetic but told them that if they ran their business from that theory, they would be in trouble. He explained that they applied a relative frequency definition of probability. Such a theory would work if the fifty beads were chosen each time by random numbers. However, the sampling method used by the workers was mechanical. Probability theory does not consider the forces impinging on the process, particularly the characteristics of the paddle— its shape, size, material, and so forth. Knowledge of the proportion of red beads in the incoming material is not a basis for prediction of red beads in the output. The demonstration is a process of mechanical sampling, not random sampling. Deming notes that a sample is neither random nor not random. It is the selection procedure that is so labeled.[357] With random sampling, using for example a table of random numbers, probability theory predicts an average of ten red beads. Probability theory does not apply to mechanical sampling. The long-term average of red beads obtained by mechanical sampling is unpredictable from probability theory.

Let's look at the red bead demonstration not as a simulation of process in a factory but as a process itself. The equipment, materials, methods, and people in the process interact to produce the stable results, results that vary but whose range and average can be expected to repeat over time. There are various contributors to performance variability. The wooden beads used in the demonstration, being manufactured, are not all exactly the same. Then they are painted red and white. Red pigment is different from white pigment. It may be heavier or lighter. The size, shape, and material of the container have an effect. Room temperature, humidity, and static electricity may also have an effect.

Deming used four different paddles over the years. Table 13-1 is based on Deming's discussion of the demonstration and shows the results with the four different paddles.[358] Differences in paddles produce different results.

Paddle	Paddle Material (Sampling Tool)	Cumulated Average Number of Red Beads Over Many Years of Demonstrations	Change in Average Number of Red Beads from Previous Tool
1	Aluminum. Different beads were used with Paddle No. 1 than with Paddles 2, 3, and 4.	11.3	—
2	Aluminum, but smaller and easier to use	9.6	-1.7
3	Apple wood. Bulky	9.2	-0.4
4	White nylon	9.4	0.2

Table 13-1. Red bead demonstration paddle history

Mechanical sampling produced average results over time that differed from the results that would be obtained by random sampling—an average of ten red beads. If differences like these occurred in an actual manufacturing process, predictions based on theoretical probability rather than empirical results could be the difference between profit and loss. Sampling on the basis of a table of random numbers is independent of the process; it filters out the effects of any process or external environmental factors, yet we must know these factors to effectively manage the process.

The four paddles differed from each other. The material sampled—the beads—also was different when Deming used Paddle 1. The average number of red beads (defectives) "produced" was different for each of the four processes. These changes show the sensitivity of the process to equipment and materials. We can assume that Deming's management style did not change. Over the thirteen years that I observed him conduct the demonstration, he did not soften his autocratic, controlling, directive behavior.

The red bead demonstration is what Deming called an *analytic* study. The aim of such a study is to predict future process performance. Data obviously do not come from the future, yet management's job is prediction. If a process it is stable, then past results can be used to predict future results. However, the prediction does not come from statistical theory. Prediction comes from substantive knowledge, such as engineering, chemistry, economics, and psychology, as well as knowledge of the dynamics of a system. A subject-matter expert knows something about the factors that may or may not cause the process to perform differently in the future and can judge whether the conditions—the common cause system of interacting forces—under which the process produced the past data will continue to be the same. If the expert judges that they will be the same, then prediction that the future will be like the past can be made, and the results of a control chart can be extended to the future. Such knowledge can't be certain or quantified since changes, intended or unintended, can occur.

In order for Deming to make his point about the difference between mechanical and random sampling, he had to know what was in the container. He counted all of the beads. This was what he called an *enumerative* study, to find out what proportion of beads in the container were red. An enumerative study is not concerned with future performance. Rather, it answers the question "how much" or "how many" exist right now. A 100 percent count often is not practical when there are a large number of items to count or if it is too costly. Instead, random sampling usually is used in an enumerative study. The people or objects in the sample are selected by using a table of random numbers.

Deming described the random sampling of iron ore pellets in order to estimate how much iron was in a particular shipload of ore.[359] It was that particular shipload of ore that was of interest, not other or future shiploads. An enumerative study is conducted to take action on the objects or people studied, such as how much to pay for that shipload of ore. Enumerative studies could answer questions about the number of males and females that work in a certain occupation or the number of products that are sold in a region.

An enumerative study uses what statisticians call *probability sampling* since random numbers are used to select the units of interest (people, materials, teaching methods, medical treatments, lots, etc.) to be evaluated and probability theory applies. Since the samples are selected randomly, the probability of the estimate of an error can be calculated.

Random sampling could be used to estimate the proportion of red beads in the container—if that were the aim. The beads would be individually identified with different numbers, and a table of random numbers would be used to select samples of fifty. Then probability theory would provide an appropriate way to estimate the average number and proportion of red beads in a sample of fifty beads as well as the probability of being wrong. Since we know what actually is in the container, we would expect the average proportion of red beads obtained by random sampling to be .20 and the average number ten. Of course, we couldn't know that before conducting an enumerative study.

The probability of being in error can't be calculated in an analytic study since random sampling is not used and therefore probability theory doesn't apply. This is why the term statistical significance to characterize a point beyond a control limit is inappropriate. A control chart does not provide a test of significance; rather, its use is to achieve and maintain the stable state of statistical control. This also is the reason that the probability of false or missed control chart signals can't be determined. We can't be more precise than verbally describing the risk, for example as low, moderate, or high.[360]

It is common practice for researchers to use tests of statistical significance to interpret results. Studies published in scientific and technical journals often contain statements regarding the statistical significance of a difference between treatments or methods or processes. For example, researchers may structure a study so that a proposed method is hypothesized to be better than another method. If a difference is found that seems to favor the proposed method, the researchers question whether this could have occurred by chance. A test of statistical significance is applied to the data in order to decide whether the observed difference in favor of the proposed method is greater than a chance occurrence (i.e., is "statistically significant"). The researchers may find statistical significance to be $p < .05$, which is a way of stating that the probability that the difference in results found between the two methods is due to chance is less than five in one hundred. They then reject the hypothesis that there is no difference between the methods and recommend that the proposed method be adopted. A statement about probability may also be used to quantify degree of belief in the results. For example, "I'm 95 percent confident that the proposed method is better."

It may elude most readers of research findings that statistical significance is not a predictor of performance. It does not tell us whether the difference found in the study will hold up in the future in other places and conditions. Two methods that have shown no statistically significant difference under one set of conditions may differ greatly under other conditions, and conversely, a large significant difference found in the study may not occur under other conditions. This is not a statistical question; rather, it is one that requires subject-matter knowledge. In addition, a test of statistical significance won't tell the researcher the practical significance of a difference. A difference that will make a practical difference should be known in advance. This requires subject-matter expertise to judge whether the size of the difference matters in practice and whether the results will apply in the future and under what conditions. For example, a question that has practical significance is whether Process A will produce greater benefit, such as more production, than Process B by a difference that justifies the increased cost of Process A. In any study that compares methods, when more than one measurement is made, differences will be found. Any study can find a statistically significant difference if the sample size is large enough, even if the difference has no practical consequences. Again, the issue is what the differences mean for practice.[361]

Deming was appalled by the inappropriate application of statistical theory and methods to describe and evaluate the important problems, challenges, and opportunities facing humankind. Reviewing a study of differences in the hearing levels of children by demographic and socioeconomic characteristics, Deming commented that a study of differences *in any characteristic* between these groups of children would find statistically significant differences if the study was big enough. What is important, he commented, is not whether the groups differ but whether the difference exceeds some magnitude, some quantity fixed in advance by clinical knowledge, not statistical knowledge. How big would a difference have to be to indicate something of importance to medicine, sociology, and learning? A study should not be conducted to learn whether some difference is statistically significant since you can find statistical significance if the study is large enough.[362]

Management, as a profession, is like medicine in that key indicators of organization health can be monitored. These indicators are the professional manager's tool for diagnosing system and process stability. Even if the method is not easily applied, or if numbers are not available, understanding the concepts of common and special causes and stable and unstable systems can point individuals in the direction of improvement. It can avoid wasted and destructive actions, such as blaming an individual when the system is at fault. Management should think in terms of analytic studies and the continual improvement of processes and systems. The book *Improving Quality through Planned Experimentation* by Moen, Nolan, and Provost provides methods to conduct analytic studies.[363] The practical reason for conducting a study is for action to shape a better future. This could be done with performance reviews, but instead of using the data to learn how to help employees and to improve the system to yield better performance, employees are judged, rated, and ranked. Deming felt test scores should be used in schools to evaluate which students need special help.

While data can't be interpreted without theory, theory can be used without numerical data. Even if numerical data can't easily be obtained, one can still use the theory in thinking about people and processes. Deming reported the thinking of a supervisor in a corporate accounting department who observed that an employee was consistently having trouble with an assignment. Applying the theory, the supervisor concluded that the employee's performance was consistent (i.e., stable). Rather than giving him a poor performance rating, he trained him to do a different kind of work, which the employee was able to master.[364] This supervisor understood, from knowledge about a system and variation, that repeatable performance associated with an individual can't be separated from the influence of the system. In an enterprise managed as a social performance ecology, the system will influence performance in a totally different way than in the red bead demonstration. For example, mavericks, rather than given a low rating, will be encouraged to create and innovate.

Sampling in the Processes of Living

> Statistical theory (theory of probability) as taught in the books for
> the theory of sampling and theory of distributions applies in
> the use of random numbers, but not in experiences of life.
> —W. Edwards Deming[365]

Deming said that in life we make judgments based on samples. We may, for example, form an opinion about a restaurant based on one or two visits, or of a hotel after a short stay, or about a geographical area based on a short trip.[366] Deming's observation suggested to me a connection between the red beads sampling process and the ones that we use every day in our lives.

The purpose of mechanical sampling in the demonstration was not to estimate what was in the container. If it were, random sampling would have given a more accurate estimate of the contents of the container, since, as explained earlier, it would not influence selection of the things being sampled as did the paddle design. Rather, the purpose was to know what we would get in a real-time sampling from the container—the external environment. Mechanical sampling, not random sampling, provides that knowledge.

Life is like mechanical sampling, not random sampling. We live in an environment that contains a continual stream of moments that can influence us. In living, we sample those moments from the environmental container. The red beads represent the negative events and things and circumstances that we do not want to occur, but they sometimes appear in our sample. The white beads represent the positives that we want to occur and strive to achieve. The paddle represents the mental map, with its models, beliefs, and values that influence what we select in our sampling.

Do we have to accept what we get in our sampling, what life presents to us? Do we have to be like the willing workers who were so constrained by the system that they had to accept what sampling presented to them and could not reduce the amount of red beads they obtained from the container? We can reduce the negatives (red beads) and increase the positives (white beads) by changing paddles (i.e., improving our mental map with profound knowledge). In so doing, we can gain more valid empirical knowledge about the container, about the larger whole, about the environment, about the systems with which we interact—which we influence and that influence us.

This will give us greater control over our lives, over our decisions and actions.

Chapter 14

∼

Tampering

Do that which consists in taking no action and order will prevail.
—Lao-tzu

One of the main causes of loss in organizations results from a practice that is known as management by objectives (MBO) and other names (see chapter 10). The practice typically consists of managers periodically asking the people who report to them how they are doing compared to the performance targets (objectives, goals) they were given. Depending on the level of the manager in the organization, and whether the manager is on staff or in the operations, this questioning can occur as often as every week, and even daily or hourly. Performance is reported as deviations—variances—from targets or goals, which typically are expressed as quantities such as costs, schedule, number of design changes, engineering specifications, production numbers, and sales numbers. When deviations are considered unacceptable, there is pressure to get back on track. So action is taken to correct the situation.

Brian Joiner, an associate of Dr. Deming, wrote that the effects of this questioning down the chain of command is like the action of connected machine gears.[367] When a big gear is connected to a smaller one, a slow turn of the big gear will cause the smaller gear to turn more quickly. Senior management in an organization is like a big gear. When it asks, "What happened?" and says, "Get this corrected," it moves the next management level—a smaller gear—to action. This smaller gear rotates faster, which in turn moves the next lower level—even smaller gears—to rotate even faster in order to answer the boss. In this machine analogy of an organization, the bigger gears are drivers, and the smaller gears are driven.

Pressure to perform starts with the method of assigning objectives. Overall objectives are developed at the top of the organization, based on competitive strategies and other considerations. They are then separated into parts, such as objectives for Finance, Sales, Engineering, Purchasing, and Manufacturing. These objectives are not supposed to conflict. They are further divided as they move down to each lower level of the hierarchical pyramid. The individuals or units may not have a method for meeting the objectives, or the system itself may present obstacles to meeting the objectives. Yet it is assumed that performance is totally within the control of the individual managers and employees who are held responsible for meeting the objectives.

The process is reversed on the way up the chain as data are combined when performance to objectives is reported. An engineer told me about the reporting process of the engineering department where he once worked. Employees were required to submit regular reports of their progress. Their personal calendars read: "Monday, Tuesday, Progress Report Day, Thursday, Friday." Each engineer reported accomplishments of the past week in writing to their immediate supervisor, who in turn prepared a summary for their supervisor, who then summarized it for the department manager who, in turn, summarized (edited) the main points for the assistant chief engineer. He told me, "Where it went after that, I honestly don't know."

Questions about results, especially during an individual's performance review, typically are based on the assumption that the person being evaluated has complete control over achieving performance to target. The assumption that an individual is totally capable to meet targets is most evident on the shop floor where process output is a measurable physical product. Equipment operators, encouraged by supervisors, may continually adjust the machine when specifications are not met and defects are being produced. Everyone involved becomes frustrated and angry when instead of getting better results, the adjustments increase the variability of the process and make it more unpredictable. If a control chart were being used, these effects would be evident by wide swings in the data. Higher up the organization, the effects of these ad hoc actions are not evident since there usually is not the immediate link in time and place between action and results that can be seen, whether on a control chart or in the coping behavior of people.

Equipment with automatic controllers can also make things worse. Some machines are programed by engineers to self-adjust when parts are out of specification. Since the stability of a process doesn't depend on whether or not the specifications are met but rather on the nature of causes—common or special—in the system, these automatic adjustments also can destabilize a process and add variability. This is explained in the rest of this chapter.

Tampering

Tampering is the term Deming applied to the human tendency to overreact to undesired performance. It can be thought of as overcontrol or overadjustment, as meddling and pestering people in what otherwise could be a smooth-running process.

The cultural imperative to tamper is captured by the often-heard statement, "Don't just stand there; do something." Yet that action rule can do harm rather than good. It produces many of the problems that occur in most organizations and in our own lives. The theories that underlie tampering have been confirmed by simulation and experiment to be excellent predictors of the resulting patterns of undesired performance and loss.[368]

Better results might be produced by knowing when to follow the rule, "Don't just do something; stand there." This can be a difficult rule to follow for those of us who see ourselves as problem solvers, as people of action. It is especially hard when pressure is applied to meet objectives, to make the numbers. Deming's theory of variation and the dynamic behavior of a system inform us that there are times when not acting is the most productive policy. The application of theories and tools, such as the statistical process control chart and feedback loop diagrams of system dynamics, can help us to understand the effects of tampering and end such behavior.

Deming illustrated the effects of tampering with a demonstration he called the funnel experiment.[369] A funnel is positioned above a flat surface that contains a cloth marked with a target. A marble is dropped multiple times through the funnel, which has been aimed at the target. The location on the cloth where the marble comes to rest is marked, and the process is repeated enough times to see the pattern of results. The experiment is conducted under various action rules with the funnel either fixed in place or adjusted based on results of the drop. Another way to illustrate tampering is by the sighting and aiming of a rifle in target shooting. Both of these exercises try out different action rules to try to accurately and consistently hit the target. (In a seminar room, the marble-drop exercise actually can be done with the equipment, but the target-shooting exercise is better done as a thought experiment.) They are analogous to the behavior associated with management by objectives. It is as if a shooter—an operator or manager—who is under pressure to hit the target is trying to do well but can't. The operator may have technical knowledge about the process but no theory or the wrong theory about how to control process accuracy and variation.

Consider a marksman using a process of sighting a rifle in order to consistently hit the center of the target. Action Rule 1 is described in table 14-1 for both the funnel experiment and the sighting and aiming of a rifle. Under Rule 1, the rifle is sighted and then fixed in place. In seminars, people are asked at the start of the exercise what action to take after seeing the result of the first shot, simulated in figure 14-1a, or dropped marble (simulated or actually done). Most people think that they can reduce the variation and get closer to the center of the target by resighting after each shot. They want to reaim the rifle or funnel and to continue adjusting after each shot. They think that since the rifle is fixed, the only source of deviation from target is where the rifle is aimed. An expert marksman told me that novice shooters are likely to shoot quickly and continually make adjustments, resulting in a chaotic scattering of shots. People may not understand that the process of rifle sighting, marble drop, or any repetitive process has various forces that interact to produce the outcomes. When the method of continual adjustment was shown not to work, some people suggested, more serious than in jest, to move the target.

Action Rule 1	Results	Other Actions That Will Produce Similar Results
Rifle Sighting Place the rifle in a fixture, aim the rifle at the target, tighten the fixture so the rifle cannot move. Fire enough shots to define the shot group pattern. Do not adjust. **Marble Drop** Place the funnel in a fixture, aim the funnel at the target, then do not move the funnel. Drop the marble through the funnel enough times to see the pattern of variation. Mark the spot where the marble comes to rest after each drop. Do not adjust.	Figure 14.1a shows the performance of what appears to be a stable process. Stability could be confirmed by plotting the data on a statistical process control chart. The pattern of results appears to be random, i.e. the position of any individual shot is unpredictable. The variation defines process capability. Depending on the equipment and other process factors, Rule 1 might result in greater precision (less spread), as shown in Figure 14.1b.	When the process is stable, technical knowledge can be applied to improve the process. In the case of rifle sighting, the expert knows which variables affect accuracy and precision, such as: Equipment: rifle, type and condition of the sight, ammunition, protection from weather, light, wind. Operator: cleaning the rifle bore, avoiding eating and drinking that impede relaxation (e.g., caffeine). The marble drop process might be improved by lowering the funnel, using a fuzzier tablecloth, replacing the marble with a steel ball and placing a magnet under the target.

Table 14-1. Action Rule 1

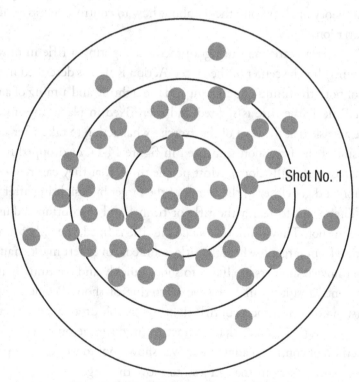

Shot No. 1

Figure 14-1a. Variation under Rule 1

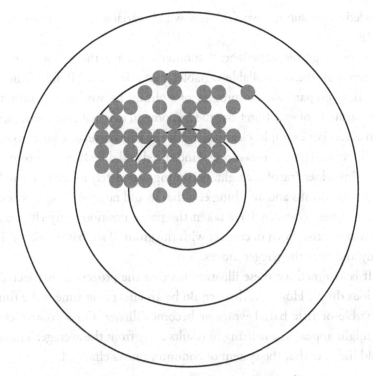

Figure 14-1b. Less variation under Rule 1

Figures 14-1a and 14-1b both illustrate the variation expected from successive shots of the rifle or marble drop when following Rule 1. The figures show that the process, when left to run without the constant interventions from adjustments after each shot, appears stable. A control chart (discussed in chapter 13) should confirm this. Figure 14-1a indicates that the average shot is on target with lots of variation around the average. Figure 14-1b shows the results that could occur under Rule 1 for a different process, such as a different rifle or weather conditions. The pattern is tighter with the average (center of shot group) above and to the left of the target. Shooters who have experience and maintain their equipment would not need many shots to sight the rifle, perhaps only five shots or less. They would know that even under Rule 1 and with proper preparation, the process still is subject to sources of variation. The only way to improve accuracy (get closer to the target) and consistency (with less variation) for either process is to work on the system of common causes. The knowledgeable shooter would know which variables affect accuracy and precision.

Knowledgeable experienced shooters manage the whole-system of sighting—all the controllable variables that affect aim. Before firing the rifle, they prepare for the process of sighting by working to minimize system sources of variation from the equipment, external environment, and themselves. For example, cleaning inside the rifle barrel (the bore) to make sure there is no grease, measuring wind speed and direction as information for the initial setting of the sight, becoming completely relaxed by avoiding caffeinated drinks and anything else that would raise heartbeat, checking to ensure they correctly have taken the prone position (only elbows and body from waist down in contact with the ground) so that the rifle is held steady and only the trigger moves.

It is assumed for these illustrations that the process is unaffected by previous drops. However, there could be an effect over time if the funnel or marble or rifle barrel wears or becomes dirtier. On a control chart, this might appear as a drifting of results away from the average. The drift would indicate that the system of common causes changed.

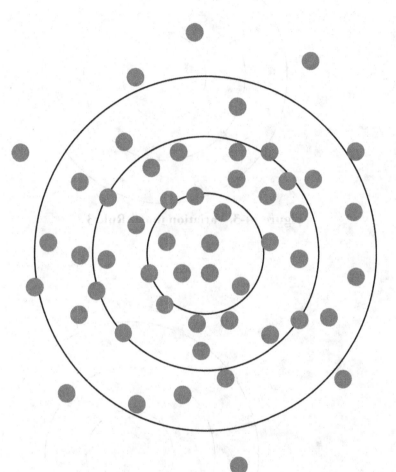

Figure 14-2. Variation under Rule 2

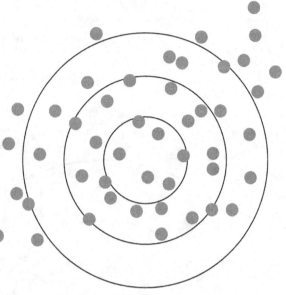

Figure 14-3. Variation under Rule 3

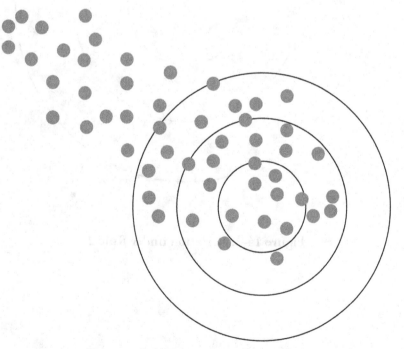

Figure 14-4. Variation under Rule 4

Action on the process after a single shot or marble drop will make the process more variable, as can be seen in figures 14-2, 14-3, and 14-4, which result from following the action rules in tables 14-2, 14-3, and 14-4. The patterns show that variation has been added to the random variation by adjustments made to compensate for unwanted results. It is as if management is trying to outwit randomness, to rephrase an idea in Nassim Taleb's book, _Fooled by Randomness_.[370] The process manager behaves like a blackjack player who doesn't stick to the strategies that would allow them to win more often in the long run.

Action Rule 2	Results	Some Other Actions That Will Produce Similar Results
Rifle Sighting Before each firing of the rifle, compensate for the deviation (error) of the previous shot from target. Adjust the rifle sight from its present position to a position that will aim the next shot in a direction opposite of the previous error and the same amount as the previous error. For example, if the shot is 30 cm northeast of the target (at 1 or 2 o'clock), move the sight so that the rifle is aimed at 30 cm southwest (to 7 or 8 o'clock) from its present position. **Marble Drop** Before each new drop of the marble, compensate for the deviation (error) of the previous drop from target. Adjust the funnel from its present position in the equal and opposite direction. For example, if the marble comes to rest 30 cm northeast of the target move the funnel 30 cm southwest from its present position.	Figure 14-2. shows that variation has been added by adjusting the process after each shot or marble drop. If left alone, the process would have produced less variation, as we saw under Rule 1. Under Rule 2, the variability of results has been increased, but the process still appears stable. Under Rule 2, tampering actions may not occur immediately after the previous result. The operator or manager may wait for more results to come in, or there can be delays in feedback as described in the next column in actions 2 and 3.	1. Operator adjusts the process when a piece goes out of specification. 2. Supervisor or operator resets a process at start of shift based on last shift results. 3. Customer adjusts orders to suppliers based on current inventory without considering orders supplier has shipped but customer has not received due to delays in transit.

Table 14-2. Action Rule 2

Figure 14-2 shows that Rule 2 also appears to yield a stable process. This would be confirmed by a control chart. We see in figure 14-2 that the variation has increased with greater deviations from target center. The center of the pattern—the process average—has not changed. The process still appears to be stable, but the variation—the deviations from the average shot—has increased.

Action Rule 3	Results	Some Other Actions That Will Produce Similar Results
Rifle Sighting Before each firing of the rifle, make the following two adjustments: 1. Adjust the rifle sight to the center of the target (target becomes the reference point, the origin), then 2. Adjust the rifle sight from the target in an equal and opposite direction to compensate for the last deviation from the target. For example, if the shot is 30 cm northeast of the target (at 1 or 2 O'clock), move the rifle sight to aim 30 cm southwest (to 7 or 8 O'clock) from the target. **Marble Drop** Before each new drop of the marble, make the following two adjustments 1. Move the funnel over the target (target becomes the reference point, the origin), then 2. move the funnel from the target in an equal and opposite direction to compensate for the last deviation from the target. Figure 14.3 shows that the successive shots swing back and forth. Once in a while a few successive shots or drops swing back and forth with decreasing amplitude, followed by resumption of ever-increasing amplitude.	Figure 14.3 shows that the successive shots swing back and forth. Once in a while a few successive shots or drops swing back and forth with decreasing amplitude, followed by resumption of ever-increasing amplitude.	1. Enforcement of illicit drugs improves. Drugs become scarcer. Price increases. More drugs are imported Enforcement improves. Cycle continues. 2. Gambler increases bet to cover losses. Losses may decline in short term with some short-term wins, but will increase in long term since odds favor the casino. 3. Escalation and retaliation in price wars and wars between nations.

Table 14-3. Action Rule 3

Fig 14-3 illustrates the effects of Rule 3, given in table 14-3. The rifle shots and marble drops move further away from the target center, swinging in one direction and then the other.

Action Rule 4	Results	Some Other Actions That Will Produce Similar Results
Rifle Sighting Before each shot, adjust the rifle aim to hit the last shot. (A marksman actually would not do this.) **Marble Drop** Before each drop, set the funnel right over the position where the marble came to rest at last drop.	Figure 14-4 shows that the pattern of results eventually will, as Deming liked to say, head toward the milky way.	1. History, unwritten, passed down from generation to generation. Folklore. Gossip. 2. Each employee trains the next employee based on what was learned from the previous employee. 3. Manufacture each new batch of paint to match the color of the previous batch. Cut a piece of wood to match the length of previous piece.

Table 14-4. Action Rule 4

Rule 4 in table 14-4 has the objective of consistency, not accuracy, from shot to shot. Figure 14-4 shows that the shot or drop moves further away from the target in the manner of a random walk of a man who has had too much to drink. As Deming describes it, he wants to go home but doesn't know which direction is which. He takes a few steps, stumbles, gets up, takes a few more steps, stumbles, gets up, and continues in this manner.

He moves further and further away from his destination.[371] Likewise, succeeding marble drops and rifle shots move further from the target.

Examples of tampering are all around us. You probably can think of some of examples of your own tampering or have seen it from others. Don't try to identify the particular tampering rule that applies. The point is to show that ad hoc interventions in reaction to undesirable results rather than improving results most likely will make them worse.

An *open-loop system* provides feedback to the process manager, but the data are not used to continually adjust or regulate the process when targets or specifications are not met. Rule 1 is followed in an open-loop system. The process manager, as controller in an open-loop system, recognizes that the results will vary over time and therefore doesn't assume that each deviation from target has a special, specific, identifiable cause that an adjustment can correct. When a stable process consistently produces output that is not wanted (e.g., specifications or targets are not met), the system as a whole has to be improved. When the control chart provides evidence of a special cause, action is taken to find and remove the cause. Other than addressing a special cause, a stable process that is producing intended results can be left alone to run. Depending on available resources, improvement could be considered.

A *closed-loop system* provides feedback about process output that allows the controller—human, machine, or other method—to adjust the process according to a rule or model to correct or compensate for deviations from target or specifications. Rules 2, 3, and 4 illustrate methods to control process output in a closed-loop system. One of the other methods was used by the psychologist B. F. Skinner who successfully trained pigeons to guide a ballistic missile by continually correcting deviations from the target. However, the government canceled the project in favor of electronic guidance systems.[372]

The point of the funnel experiment is to show the losses from overadjustment, from acting as if variation that came from the system was due to a special cause.[373] Deming told us that "gadgets" or other methods that try to guarantee that there will be no defects will make things worse. They will drive losses and costs to a maximum by applying Rules 2, 3, or 4. They do not help to improve the process.[374]

The Shewhart-Deming statistical process control chart is not intended for closed-loop systems. The chart is based on the assumption that successive outputs (e.g., a marble drop or rifle shot) is not affected by the previous ones (i.e., they are independent, not correlated). This is the assumption behind Action Rule 1. Rules 2, 3, and 4 have a built-in correlation between successive drops. The output variation is a combination of random variation and deterministic variation. We know from the design of an adaptive controller that compensating adjustments are built in and that if we plotted the data on a chart, we would see evidence of special causes. Compensating adjustments increase variation and can move the average. We know this from theory of variation, without using a control chart. If you are walking by a machine with a graphic or digital display, just watch it for a while. It may be displaying process variables such as temperature, or output measurements such as weight or some dimensions. If the patterns fluctuate up and down widely and wildly, you would probably be correct to think that overadjustment is increasing the variation. Theory informs you that a person or device is overcontrolling the machine, adding cost and degrading quality.

Automatic, adaptive control systems such as the thermostatic control of room temperature by a furnace or air-conditioner seem to operate according to Rule 2. A temperature sensor gives feedback to a thermostatic switch. Room temperature will vary slightly above or below a target level ("set point value," e.g., 68°F), warmer if the sun shines through the windows and heats the room, or colder if someone opens a door and a draft comes in. When the temperature deviates from target by a specified amount, the furnace is turned on or off in order to maintain room temperature at the target level. The addition of nonrandom variation from the compensating adjustment increases the spread between drops or shots, as shown in figure 14-2, but the process is stable.[375]

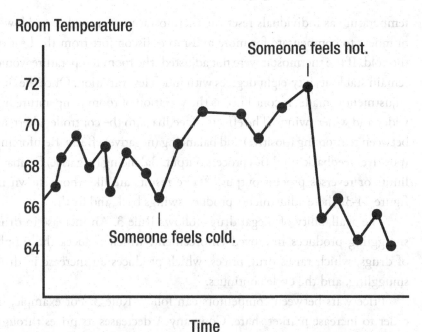

Figure 14-5. Variation from tampering with the thermostat

If the capability of the furnace to regulate the temperature according to Rule 2 is ignored and people in the room tamper with the thermostat, the controller can't produce a stable process. The control process is now similar to Rule 3. Figure 14-5 is a time-ordered graph illustrating the possible variation of room temperature when individuals adjust the thermostat when they feel hot or cold. Wherever it is set, that temperature will be achieved on average by the built-in feedback loop. There will be some variation, perhaps as much as two degrees above and below that value. If the thermostat initially is set for sixty-eight degrees, when the room temperature reaches sixty-six degrees, someone may feel cold and overadjust the thermostat to seventy degrees. Of course, there is an increase in room temperature, and eventually someone feels it is too hot and overcompensates by setting the thermostat all the way back to sixty-six degrees. Due to variation around an average temperature of sixty-six degrees, the room temperature may reach sixty-four degrees, and someone may overcompensate for feeling cold and adjust the thermostat to seventy-two degrees. Eventually the room could reach seventy-four degrees. This continues on and on with subsequent larger jumps and dips in room temperature as individuals reset the thermostat to even higher and lower numbers to compensate for more and more discomfort from the heat or the cold. If the thermostat were not adjusted, the room temperature would remain stable at sixty-eight degrees with much less variation. Once the first adjustment is made, it continues as the variation of room temperature has wider and wider swings. The effects of feedback to the controller alternate between reinforcing (positive) and balancing (negative) effects. Reinforcing (positive) feedback amplifies process output. Balancing (negative) feedback limits or reverses process output.[376] The results are like those shown in figure 14-3 where adjustments produce swings back and forth.

The availability of illegal drugs follows Rule 3. An increase in drug smuggling produces improved enforcement, which reduces the supply of drugs, which raises drug prices, which produces an increase in drug smuggling, and the cycle continues.

Price wars between competitors can follow Rule 3. For example, in order to increase market share, Company A decreases its prices through rebates. As its market share increases, a competitor will introduce a larger rebate. Company A's market share will decrease, Company B's market share will increase, and marketing costs of both companies increase. This cycle continues with ups and down for each company until both decide that losses are too large. They both are fighting over a fixed pie. Better to innovate and expand the market, as some technology companies have done very successfully.

The results of following Rule 4 are shown in figure 14-4. Rule 4 could be the last resort of a process manager, who has given up trying to accurately and repeatedly hit the target. Only consistency, where each shot is like the previous one, is the goal. A process manager who tries to make each shot like the previous one by adjusting the aim after each shot to hit the place where the previous shot or drop ended up is operating on wishes and hopes and without relevant theory.

Under Rule 4, positive, reinforcing feedback accelerates results to, in Deming's words, "the Milky Way." Price wars may also follow Rule 4, in a process of escalation and retaliation when eventually one of the competitors stops or goes out of business. The arms race of previous decades is described by Rule 4. Participants increased their numbers of missiles. Fortunately, a negative, balancing feedback of agreements between the United States and Russia limited and reversed the escalation before it exploded into unthinkable destruction.

Rule 4 describes the way rumors and gossip function when each person who is told something tells it to another person, but each new person that hears it changes it in the retelling. You can see this in action in the children's telephone game. The first child is told a short story and then tells it to the next child, and so on. The first and last child to hear the story each tells the group what they heard. Although the attempt was to repeat exactly what they heard, the story at the end of the process is quite different from what the first child was told.

Deming gives other examples of Rule 4: Cost of living adjustments increase wages to match the cost of living index, then the cost of living index is adjusted to the increased wages. A new batch of paint is matched to the last batch rather than to a standard, as batches move into other parts of the color spectrum. If you are building shelves and using the last board to cut the next board, see how much shorter is the last shelf than the first.[377]

The growth of social networks accelerates as more and more new members bring in more and more new members. Videos go viral on the Internet this way. Eventually growth slows down, reaches limits, and even reverses, as fewer people are available to participate or competitors appear.

The same dynamic occurs with Ponzi investment schemes that accelerate growth by bringing in new participants, but collapse is built in since eventually there will not be enough money from new investors to pay current investors. Before it collapses, the scheme may be interrupted by legal action.

Panic buying at the supermarket during threat of a severe storm is an example of Rule 4. When some people are seen hoarding goods, others rush in to do the same. This is limited by a finite supply of available goods. A cattle stampede operates the same way. A few start to run when faced with danger, and the others join in.

Many stock market investors can behave more with a kind of follower instinct than with rational thought and theory. When analysts predict that a stock will not perform well, whatever the basis for their prediction, people begin to sell. Others see this selling, and they sell. Then the media report decline of the stock, along with their own opinions, amplifying the emotions of fear and greed and accelerating selling. Eventually selling reaches a panic level, and the analysts are proven to be prescient. The expectation produces action, which amplifies, reinforcing the expectation, and so on—a reinforcing, positive feedback loop.

The effects of Rule 4 can be seen with the effects of compounding interest. Starting with one cent and doubling it every day will yield nearly $5.4 million after thirty days. The money not only grows, but the rate of growth accelerates. Figure 14-4 also could represent the opposite situation: the compounding of debt of an individual, organization, or a government like a series of chemical reactions that eventually explode. Compounding interest would end when the financial institution no longer has the funds to pay the interest. The lender and the debtor both could take actions to limit, ease, or erase the debt.

Peter Senge observed that a "state-controlled economy fails because it severs the multiple, self-correcting processes that operate in a free market system."[378] The same can be said of enterprises that engage in practices that constrain the freedom of the market.

Self-Fulfilling Prophecies

A self-fulfilling prophecy, also known as the Pygmalion effect, could produce results illustrated in figure 14-4. *Pygmalion* is a play by George Bernard Shaw, which was the basis for *My Fair Lady*. Performance is influenced by the expectations managers have of employees, teachers have of students, and parents have of children. The higher the expectations placed on them, the better people perform; the lower the expectations, the poorer they perform. Deming[379] cited the book *Pygmalion in the Classroom*, which describes research that found this result with students who initially had been matched in ability but differed only in the expectation created in the teacher. Teachers paid more attention to students whom they expected to do well, and less attention to others.[380]

The grade-school teacher described in an earlier chapter was tampering with the psyche of the young student when she sent her to remedial education because of two successive exams below average. The teacher had no evidence that the test results were due to anything but chance, yet she had an image of the student as one who needs help, who doesn't meet the specification of an A student. Will the teacher lower her expectations for the student and fall into a negative self-fulfilling prophecy?

The myth in enterprise that the cream will rise to the top can become a self-fulfilling prophecy. Individuals are identified as high potential—cream—and then their rise is helped by the system. They get the resources and assignments that prepare them to succeed and move upward. Those rated low do not have such opportunities. Expectations are established early in an employee's career, perhaps because a company recruiter evaluated the individual as high potential in a college interview. In this manner, beliefs and expectations become fulfilled predictions.

Inaction, while not a Western cultural value, often can be productive. One needs profound knowledge to know when and where to act and not to act. We try to do our best in order to improve results, but instead we can make them worse because we do not understand theory of variation, the dynamic behavior of systems, and the effects of extrinsic rewards on human behavior—all components of Deming's System of Profound Knowledge.

A recurring theme in this book is that we can't separate the world from the way we each think about it. We see the world and act upon it according to the theories, the viewpoints, and the mental maps that are the content of our consciousness. Each of us is a force in the world in which we live, and we help to shape it, whether intentionally or unintentionally. In return, it provides feedback; it rewards or punishes us, and therefore it shapes us. Profound knowledge allows us to better predict the consequences of our actions, act more sanely, and shape a better world for ourselves and others.

FOURTH MOVEMENT: KNOWLEDGE OF PSYCHOLOGY

Chapter 15

~

Psychology of the Individual in the System

One inherits a right to enjoy his work. Good management helps us
to nurture and preserve these positive, innate, attributes of people.
—W. Edwards Deming[381]

Psychological Effects of Management Systems

Dr. Deming was concerned about the psychological effects of management systems on people and their consequences for organizations. He used the red bead demonstration, including the letter from Ann, to illustrate his concern that the management of many different types of organizations still behaves as if employees are parts of a machine. Ann was the psychologically devastated willing worker he referred to in his discussion on variation (see chapter 13). He also expressed his concern through his criticisms of rating, ranking, grading, and management's overreliance on extrinsic motivation.

Deming included knowledge of psychology in his System of Profound Knowledge because he saw that such knowledge was not evident in management practices, nor in many human relationships within enterprise. He believed that management's primary role was the leadership of people, and that requires some knowledge of psychology. He said that psychology helps us to understand people, their differences, and their interactions, such as the everyday interactions between manager and employees, coworkers, customers and suppliers, teacher and student, the individual and the system.[382] Deming did not refer to or rely on any specific theory of psychology. Rather, his insights were based on years of experience seen through his knowledge of variation and systems and his appreciation for the talents of human beings, which often are suppressed by the various institutions of society, especially business and education. Knowledge of psychology interacts with the other components of Deming's System of Profound Knowledge. He explained, for example, that knowledge of psychology for management is incomplete without knowledge of variation and that a psychologist with some knowledge of variation, as he taught in the red bead demonstration, could not participate in the development and application of methods for ranking people.[383]

Destruction of Minds and Hearts by Scientific Management

During the summers of 1924 and 1925, Deming worked on transmitters in the AT&T Western Electric Hawthorne manufacturing plant in Chicago. He was dismayed at the employee work environment that he saw. Employees couldn't wait for the work shift to end to leave their monotonous jobs in a hot and dirty plant. He said that when he started there, he was warned not to be caught on a stairway when the whistle blew. Employees, most of them women, would trample him to death with their high heels, and there would be no trace of him.[384] Deming was not aware at that time of the now-famous experiments on working conditions that began to be conducted by behavioral scientists while he was at the Hawthorne plant. The studies investigated sources of job satisfaction beyond those of economic incentives, such as the social climate and satisfaction from the work itself. This was in contrast to the *scientific management* methods of Frederick Taylor and other efficiency experts that were being applied to increase worker productivity. "Taylorism" was based on the view that workers, as well as foremen, did not have the education or mental capacity to decide how work should be done. That responsibility was given to engineers who planned the work methods and established work standards. In order to do this, jobs were fragmented into simple motions that were timed to determine the fastest and best way to do the job. The foreman and the workers only had to execute the plans. They had no discretion regarding how the work was done. Piecework incentives were established based on the work standards. It was believed that this incentive system, along with wage penalties and disciplinary measures, would control worker variation and produce desired performance.

People endured the situation for their wages. The Taylor method dehumanized and fragmented workers. Mind was separated from body, and body was separated into parts, necessary for the discrete and standardized motions and tasks determined by the engineers. *Division of labor* is an appropriate description for what has been called Taylorism. The new series of motions that could be done quickest and best replaced the many "inferior" series of motions that, it was thought, would naturally be practiced by workers. The best method became the standard until a better method was found. Piece-rate payment was promoted as a means to motivate workers, as if motivation were the only problem once the "best method" was identified. Rather than understanding why workers "malingered," "goldbricked," and "loafed," Taylor put the onus on the "unmotivated" worker who, it was assumed, would try to get away with what they could without losing pay. Cooperation meant that every worker followed the standard. The decoupling of human beings at work from their wholeness as human beings was institutionalized by Taylor's management methods. In order to maximize the speed and efficiency of production, work was broken into simple, repetitive tasks. Parts of people produced parts of products. People did not understand how they fit into the larger picture. Some people who screwed parts together all day long may have gotten the idea that the company was in the screw-tightening business. Being able to see the big picture could have helped them see the value of what they were doing.[385]

An advancement of sorts in the Taylor approach to scientific management was made by Lillian and Frank Gilbreth. They developed their own approach to scientific management, which is described in Lillian's book, *The Psychology of Management*, published in 1914. The approach included an early form of ergonomics, industrial psychology, and industrial engineering. An aim was not only efficiency and reduction of waste but also reduction of worker fatigue, which improved both efficiency and motivation. Gilbreth wrote that the equipment, materials, and methods must be adapted to the worker and not vice versa.

A review of Gilbreth's form of scientific management helps to see the origin of some of today's management methods.[386] Her scientific management model is similar in some ways to the machine-age mental model held by physical scientists. The subject of science is that which is observable and measurable, and external forces can be used to manipulate physical objects once the cause-and-effect relationship is understood. This view was applied to the management of people. Extrinsic incentives were used to motivate or move workers to maintain and improve their performance. The output of each worker was kept on separate records, which other workers could see. This would make it possible for the worker to relate his compensation to his output and motivate him to improve over his past performance, give supervisors a basis to praise and positively reinforce workers, and motivate workers to improve their performance over other workers through "friendly competition." Competition was encouraged as if work was an "athletic contest." Gilbreth compared the work environment to a baseball team where each man has his separate place and his separate work and where his work shows up separately with separate records, such as "batting average" and "fielding average." She believed that competition could be managed to be friendly. She was concerned how workers thought about the work and wrote that workers should "not be grouped according to any distinction that would cause hatred or ill feeling, that the results shall be ultimately beneficial to the workers themselves, and that *all* high scores will win high prizes." She sought to avoid having competition "which speeds up the men uselessly," breeds "ill feeling" between workers or a feeling that the weaker ones don't have a fair chance. She wrote that no one can do his best work continually if he thinks that he will not be treated fairly, or that "someone stronger than he will be allowed to cheat or to domineer over him, or that he will be speeded up to such an extent that while his work will increase for one day, the next day his work will fall down because of the effect of the fatigue of the day before."

Although we can see that Gilbreth acknowledged that the employee had a mind and that there were psychological factors affecting worker behavior, her approach to scientific management was a form of behaviorism that relied heavily on the use of extrinsic reward and punishment to shape, manipulate, and control individual employee behavior. She acknowledged, as did behaviorist psychologists, that extrinsic incentives such as pay and praise could bring about the desired behavior of employees by affecting internal states, such as self-confidence, initiative, pride, desire for personal recognition, and interest in one's work. However, these internal states could not be directly seen or manipulated; therefore, the specific effects of the incentive system on employees' internal states could not be examined for their effect on their behavior. It was sufficient to manage employee behavior and produce the desired actions by the manipulation of behavior through what now is called *extrinsic motivation*. That was the way to reach the worker's mind, which, it was acknowledged, ultimately controls his efficiency.

Gilbreth and Taylor theorized that the greatest outputs could be achieved when the work was divided, with management doing the planning and workers performing. A planning department relieved the worker of determining things such as what work is to be done, the method by which it is to be done, the time needed, and the quality of output. The men were given standard tasks to do, with teachers to help them. Management's assumption, one that still exists today in many organizations, was that after being trained, employees were in complete control of their performance. Therefore they were rewarded with a wage according to their performance. However, such expectations were unreasonable since, for example, quality depends on others such as suppliers and machine maintenance, and speed of production depends on availability and quality of materials. Yet each worker's reward and punishment depended on their individual output records.

Gilbreth's reliance on extrinsic incentives appears similar to the methods of behaviorism used to train animals. The idea was that when a worker knows for sure that a reward immediately will follow success, the reward will help him concentrate his attention and maintain his interest. The intent was to stimulate interest in the work, but it is more likely it only stimulated interest in the reward; the work became a means to the reward and not interesting in itself. Gilbreth cited a dictionary definition of incentive as "a stimulus that stirs passions and spurs the individual to action." She also noted that an incentive can be used as a goal. Incentives, she said, play an enormous role in the doing of the work, both mental and manual. Attending a baseball game would be an incentive for the businessman to finish his work early, implying that the work itself was not rewarding. The student, in order to avoid the punishment of staying after school, would rush through her arithmetic, implying that the child did not want to learn or that the teacher had no responsibility to interest her in the subject matter. The piece-worker would have the incentive to produce as much quality output as she could in order to be paid.

Gilbreth acknowledged that there were incentives that aroused the "natural instinct" of workers, which would move them to do certain things even if there were no material rewards. For example, the natural desire to beat out other workers in a competition to accomplish the most in the shortest time. She called these instincts "direct incentives," while extrinsic rewards and punishment were seen as "indirect incentives" since they worked through internal states to produce behavior. A direct incentive can motivate the worker by appealing to, what can be interpreted as, his innate desires to compete and win, to play, to seek personal recognition, and other intrinsic motives that she assumed were naturally present in men. Extrinsic rewards and punishments worked through what she called "native reaction." Yet, believing this, workers were still managed by making reward and punishment dependent on output, as if they had complete control of the speed and quality of production. Rewards were seen as *anything* that could be given to the worker—promotion, wages, bonuses, shorter hours—to increase his *desire* to continue doing the work. Punishments could consist of anything that could be done to the worker to show him that he had not performed as expected and should lead him to do better. This might be withholding reward, giving fines, firing, or reassignment to work that is less desirable with lower pay.

Incentives were geared to each individual. She said that a man who has what she called an "elementary type of mind" would require immediate reward after completing the work since he did not have the intellect to look very far into the future. A man with high intellectual development would understand that a reward would come, so prompt rewarding was not as necessary. She didn't seem to account for the fact that workers, even those who were believed to be intelligent, were able to pay their bills.[387]

In Gilbreth's management system, forms of which are practiced today, managers must spend the time to administer rewards and punishments as well as to monitor people and inspect results to assure that they are following the prescribed methods.

Extrinsic Motivation by KITA

Frederick Herzberg wrote a classic article for the *Harvard Business Review*, "One More Time: How Do You Motivate Employees?" Herzberg would get a group of managers together and ask them, "If I have six-week-old puppy, and I want it to move, how do I get it to move?" He usually would hear the reply, "Kick him in the a—!" Then Herzberg would ask, "Is that motivation?" Managers would agree that it is. Herzberg therefore referred to rewards and punishments as positive and negative KITAs, a manager's process of *causing* someone to do something.[388]

If management thinks performance is good, it will praise the individual and perhaps provide other incentives to encourage the employee to keep up the good work. When performance is considered to be poor, the employee may be warned to improve or else be penalized or disciplined. If management applied theory of variation, they would be able to consider whether performance was from the system or from local special causes that might or might not be due to the individual. A supervisor who tries to *get* employees to do better by threats or praise may be disappointed if the process is stable. In a stable process, performance typically has its ups and downs within a range of the normal variation. It is more likely that rewarding and punishing the employee for the ups and downs will force them to tamper in order to please the boss. This will increase process variation.

Extrinsic motivation of human beings doesn't seem much different from offering animals the promise of a cracker to *get them* to do what their masters want, not what they want. (Deming said that people like animal crackers, and animals like people crackers.) In contrast, Deming thought that leaders understand that human motivation mainly comes from within and is self-sustaining without external pushes and pulls. He did acknowledge that some extrinsic motivation can have positive results; praise may help to build self-esteem. However, he thought that total reliance on extrinsic motivation may destroy the individual. Joy in work, joy in learning become secondary to achieving the high scores necessary to please the boss, teacher, or parent. A person who does or would do something for the intrinsic pleasure and satisfaction of doing it will most likely be insulted, even humiliated, by an offer of money or some other reward. Deming used the term *over-justification* to characterize the use of a reward such as money or a prize for an act that initially was intrinsically motivated, done for its own sake, done because it is valued as the right thing to do and therefore gives pleasure and satisfaction to the doer. The reward demeans the act and the person. People become conditioned to expect rewards and awards for good performance, whether in school, at home, or at work. Desire for tangible rewards governs their action. They value extrinsic rewards to make them feel good. Extrinsic rewards put a person in the control of others who dole out the rewards.[389]

The reliance on extrinsic reward is a systemic, cultural phenomenon. It starts very early in a child's life when the inherent inclination to be curious, to learn, to socialize and cooperate is replaced by extrinsic forces as the child encounters the various institutions of society. Joy is suppressed and is replaced by fear.[390] Individuals and the enterprise lose when people do not share information or help each other.

Alfie Kohn, in his book *Punished by Rewards*, describes the use of incentives, especially in schools, as bribery.[391] When the management system relies on bribes and punishments, it encourages individuals, or "teams," to behave within the enterprise in competitive, self-protective ways. When people are focused on achieving rewards and avoiding losses, they are being denied the opportunity to develop a sense of responsibility to others and to the organization and its purposes.

Extrinsic incentives distort the system and motivate individuals to focus on their own rewards, particularly annual bonuses, for appearing to meet management's objectives, even when the system is not capable. This was made public by revelations in 2014 of dishonesty in the Veterans Administration health care reporting system. The system rewards and punishes employees, especially managers, with bonuses for meeting the goal of giving a veteran an appointment within fourteen days of the request. Bonuses encouraged false reporting and other manipulation of waiting lists that showed the target was being met, even as veterans suffered while not being seen. This was a systemic (common cause) problem within the VA since it was occurring at many of the hospitals across the system. Management was motivated to make the system look good rather than be good for veterans. Records were falsified, books were cooked, reporting was dishonest to make it seem as if hospitals were meeting administrative goals of seeing patients within the fourteen-day target.

The Psychology of Behaviorism

The model of behaviorist psychologists, such as J. B. Watson and B. F. Skinner, looks only at the relationship between the behavior of an individual and whether its consequences are rewarding or punishing for that individual. Since mind doesn't matter, rats can be studied instead of human beings, which makes experimentation a lot easier. It is as if the contributions of people over the millennia to engineering, the arts, and other aspects of civilization are not much different from the behavior of rats in a cage pressing a bar for food. Therefore, a person can be managed without regard to what that person thinks or feels. The only thing that matters is that the employee behaves as management wants. Management can shape, condition, and control an employee's behavior by strengthening or weakening the connection between the behavior that management wants and its consequences for the employee. Behaviorism has its own language, its own operational definitions to discuss this in precise terms, but we can simply say that employee actions are controlled by management's use of extrinsic incentives that reward and punish employees. Behaviorism does acknowledge that events occur within the individual, but since those internal states can't be observed, all discussion of them is pure inference. Therefore, the invisible world of human consciousness, motives, purpose, desires—what makes human beings human—is ignored. Behaviorism is aligned with a model of the physical world that is deterministic and mechanistic. Behavior, whether of physical objects or people, can be understood and then controlled by cause-and-effect relationships between external manipulations and results. This model of so-called scientific psychology was the model applied by scientific management, which began in the early twentieth century, and which, in my opinion, continues to be the underlying model applied by managers who rely heavily on extrinsic incentives in an attempt to produce the results they want.

The Deming-based model maintains that internal states within the individual explain and produce the person's behavior. This is the main difference between the Deming model and behaviorism, which refuses to make inferences about things that can't be observed or measured. Deming tried to understand the effects of the environment—the system—on people by the mediation of internal events, which have names such as pride, jealousy, purpose, self-esteem, and all of those other words we use to describe an individual's psychology. People, unlike machines or animals, can tell you what they are thinking and how they are feeling. Deming gained his knowledge of psychology in the manner of a clinician, by speaking with people. Over the years, he heard many reports by employees, from the shop floor to management, about the system and the effects on them, both negative and positive. Thus, even though Deming was trained as a physicist, his approach to psychology appears to be aligned with the origin of the word *psychology*, which comes from the Greek word *psyche*, which refers to the invisible world of spirit and soul. Deming's aim was to transform the visible world of commerce, business, and education, but this had to be preceded by a transformation of the invisible aspects of being human—intellect, theories, beliefs, and assumptions, purpose, motives, and feelings. He had a great respect for the potential capacity of human beings and was dismayed by its destruction by forces of ignorance.

Human psychology can be understood as embedded in an ecology of relationships. People give feedback to each other by what they say and do. Feedback, discussed in chapter 14, is a key characteristic of a system. The individual's actions can modify the environment, which in turn affects the individual. This is a joint, reciprocal relationship, not one of linear cause and effect. The individual and the environment are one system. Even in systems of autocratic management, whether in enterprise, school, or by parents, there are mutually reinforcing effects. Skinner validated much of his behaviorist theory by studying laboratory rats. While I was taking a graduate course in behaviorism, I often wondered who was controlling whom. The experimenter thought that he was controlling the rat's behavior by rewarding it with food, water, or the chance to exercise on a wheel when it did what the experimenter wanted it to do. The rat may have been thinking, *Wow, I can make this guy give me what I want by eating, drinking, and running when I feel like it. I just need to keep reinforcing his behavior.* The rats were, in the language of behaviorism, on schedules of reinforcement. But so were the experimenters who had to visit the laboratory at specific times to look at the data, see how the rats were behaving, and replenish the cage with food pellets and water to keep reinforcing their behavior.

Joseph Wood Krutch summed it up this way: "If you study man by the method suited to chemistry, or even if you study him in the light of what you have discovered about rats and dogs, it is certainly to be expected that what you discover will be what chemistry and animal behavior have to teach. But it is also not surprising or even significant if by such methods you fail to discover anything else."[392]

Management without KITA

Deming wrote that a job description is not to prescribe motions, not to tell the person "do this or do that." Rather, management should help the employee to understand the intent of the process—what the work will be used for and how it contributes to the aim of the system. People must understand where they fit in and why they are doing what they do. Deming observed that if the job is to wash the table, the employee can't do a good job without knowing how the table will be used. Cleaning a dining table is a different process than cleaning an operating table.[393]

What makes a job boring or inherently interesting is how you think about it. Any job could be boring unless you understand why it is important; then you can take interest in the work and be intrinsically motivated to do a good job. It isn't necessarily the repetitive nature of the work. Artisans working on a handloom weaving cloth can repeat the operation thousands of times. They can take pride in their work because they control the operation and know how it will be used. The same is true for knitting.

Larry Miller, in his book *Barbarians to Bureaucrats*, wrote that what may appear to an observer as punishment won't be seen that way to those doing the work if they believe they are doing it for a worthy cause or a noble purpose. Motivation is derived from high self-esteem, and that follows from understanding one's purpose. Miller reinforced his point with this quote from Jack London: "God's own mad lover should die for the kiss, but not for thirty thousand dollars a year."[394]

While at a meeting at General Motors, some employees told Dr. Deming that more pay would not make a difference in their performance, although if management was going to study the effects of doubling their pay, they would like to participate.[395] Generally, though, certain basic needs must be satisfied by work. Frederick Hertzberg, a psychologist noted for introducing job enrichment and Motivator-Hygiene theory, wrote that work can be intrinsically motivating when, for example, it is challenging, allows for growth and learning, and gives the employee responsibility for planning. However, these will not stimulate employees unless the work provides "hygiene factors," such as adequate working conditions and wages.[396] This aligns with psychologist Abraham Maslow's Hierarchy of Needs. He postulated that people will work to satisfy needs but in a hierarchical order of importance. Lower-level needs such as food, shelter, and safety must be satisfied, at least partially, for higher-level needs such as self-respect, respect from others, and self-expression to be satisfied.[397] Douglas McGregor described the set of management assumptions under what he called Theory X and Theory Y. Theory X managers hold beliefs similar to those of the Taylor system of management: work is inherently distasteful to most people and will be avoided if possible; what people do at work is less important than what they get paid for doing; workers must be stimulated to perform in the desired manner with monetary incentives for meeting standards and with penalties for failure; employees must be closely supervised and controlled with reward and punishment. Theory Y contains assumptions aligned with the power of intrinsic motivation: the work is a potential source of satisfaction if it provides opportunities for successful accomplishment; most employees are willing and able to exercise self-control and self-direction; employees have an internal drive for accomplishment and derive satisfaction from producing quality results.[398]

It is not the specific nature of the work as much as how it is managed. Deming wrote that when management replaces work standards with knowledgeable and intelligent leadership, quality and productivity increase, and people are happier on the job. The job of a leader is not to find and record people's failures but to remove the causes of failure and to help people do a better job with less effort, which will bring pride of workmanship to people. It is a continuing responsibility of leadership to improve the system in order to make it possible for everybody to do a better job with greater satisfaction.[399]

Intrinsically Rewarding Activities

When are activities considered play, fun, and enjoyable, and when do they feel like work? Why do people enjoy activities outside of the job that are not so different from those that they experience on the job as boring, unsatisfying, and energy draining? Why do we voluntarily do things under conditions that we would dislike in the context of our jobs? Why do golfers get up early on the weekend to play, even in the kind of bad weather that if it occurred during the week would make them wish that they didn't have to go to work that day? Why does an automotive assembly line worker who dislikes his job look forward to the end of the shift so he can go home and work on his classic car? Why do people who feel tired at the end of the workday find energy that evening to play a few games of racquetball or to practice with other musicians or volunteer for civic activities?

When we enjoy doing things, we don't call them work. We refer to them as hobbies, games, and interests. What makes an activity intrinsically joyful and satisfying? What do we value in play that may be absent on the job? What makes work "work" and play "fun?" Or more to the point, what would make work fun? An activity that is enjoyed in the context of a leisure activity can feel like punishment on the job. Would a round of golf be as much fun if your boss decided to manage your golf play and told you that you had to shoot eighty or else you would receive a poor performance evaluation? Golf would become an instrument, a means to achieve someone else's objective, someone else's ends. Golf would lose its intrinsic value and feel like work. How will golfers perform if they feel intimidated and worried about their golfing performance appraisal? What if the boss continually pressures the golfer to improve? Will the golfer tamper (i.e., make spontaneous adjustments to their swing) in an attempt to respond to the pressure to do better? Will they become even more erratic, less consistent, and further off target? Will they adjust their swing even more until they are so exasperated that they throw their club into the pond?

Management can reap the benefits that accompany employees' joy and pride in work, but it cannot do it in an environment where employees value the work primarily for its financial benefits. Praise, rather than fostering pride in work, may serve only to signal the possibility of a pay raise, bonus, or promotion. Pay raises can give a temporary high, but this still has little to do with enjoyment of the work itself.

The energy, enthusiasm, joy, and pride we experience in our leisure activities derive from the intrinsic value of the experience itself. A person feels involved in accomplishing an outcome that is personally meaningful. During our hobbies and recreational activities, we are system and process managers. We know where we fit in, what we are trying to accomplish, and why. We feel an ownership of the results and can be proud of our contributions. In a hobby, means and ends are integrated. An activity has value in itself.

Chapter 16

Performance Evaluation by Grading, Rating, Ranking, and Labeling

Branding irons are to be used in the suture
of our commutable contusions.
—Mark Van Aken Williams[400]

We carry over the practice of numerical scoring that is used in professional sports and other competitive games to the rest of life. In business, schools, government, and other organizations, managers keep score of performance with numbers in a way that can separate individuals and units from each other. Feedback on their performance often is based on a misinterpretation of the numbers—as we have seen in the discussion of variation—and can destroy a person's spirit. Grading, rating, and ranking are wounds, contusions that are made visible when individuals are labeled as poor performers, but the effects on their psyche are invisible when they see themselves as a person of low worth. The wounds are commutable because they are shared with others who are so labeled. Leaders, however, score a whole-in-one by orchestrating a system of cooperation where everyone can gain. They energize people rather than enervate them.

Rating and Ranking in Organizations

A requirement in most organizations is the formal performance appraisal. Often dreaded by both the supervisor-rater and the employee-ratee, appraisals usually are given annually. The results are used to award merit salary increases and to promote, reassign, and take other personnel actions. It is also a time when supervisors try to motivate employees to perform well. The appraisal process is a general review of results attributed to each individual employee, usually by evaluating accomplishment of objectives. Rating and ranking the employee is an integral part of the review process. There are eager customers for the data in the hungry computers of management, and the human resources department is also anxious to dine on the results and to force a distribution of rankings.

The mental map of management in organizations that grade, rate, and rank employees contains beliefs, assumptions, values, and models that make the practice seem correct. They are still living in the ancient mythology of scientific management. Beliefs have been reinforced by the continual use of these methods over the years by many organizations. The practice, on the face of it, seems logical and intuitively appropriate and is culturally accepted. The use of rating and ranking pervades people's lives, starting with grading in school and continuing into the workplace. It seems the right thing to do because so many people in leadership positions do it. Managers often attribute some of their own success to the annual rating that enabled their bosses to see their accomplishments and potential. Profound knowledge should help us to understand that the thinking behind these management practices is wrong in logic and theory and is harmful in application. They do not produce the kinds of behavior that will serve the long-term health and well-being of individuals, organizations, and society as a whole.

The psychological effects of traditional methods of evaluation and the attachment of numbers to people in the form of grades, ratings, and rankings will vary among individuals, but Deming didn't hold back when he listed the devastating effects of the practice to the individual psyche and to the organization. He said that people feel afraid, bitter, crushed, bruised, battered, desolate, despondent, inferior, perhaps even depressed. Some people may be too dejected to work after the rating.[401] Deming's comments may seem harsh, but some people tend to view themselves as losers when they are not ranked on top. People view the person as the rank, the label, "You *are* a loser," and people then think of themselves, "I *am* a loser." Deming asked why a business would want its employees to be losers.[402] I knew a member of the clergy who applied for a leadership position in a large church that he admired. The selection committee told him that he was "ranked number two" and would not get the position. At first, he felt as if he had lost a competition, and it hurt for a while. He had translated the selection committee decision into a generalized judgment about himself. Then, calling upon his training as pastor and counselor, he reflected on the experience. He considered his own response to being ranked to learn something about himself and to evaluate his own needs, desires, ambitions, and his future direction.

The performance appraisal is based on the assumption that systems and processes are designed to enable employees to do their job; therefore, the performance of each employee or unit can be evaluated separately from the system. Failure to accomplish objectives, to make mistakes, and other judgments of unacceptable performance are attributed to individual employees or units who are held responsible for their results. The idea of individual-in-environment does not apply.

Performance appraisal deflects responsibility for improvement away from management—who is responsible for the system—to the individual employee. I heard a manager say that the rating and ranking process was intended to *inspire* individuals to give their *best* performance, as if extrinsic reward and punishment could be a source of inspiration. The suboptimizing effects of managing from this view were not obvious to this person.

A Fair Rating Is Impossible, and Ranking Is a Farce

These conclusions of Dr. Deming were obvious to him from his System of Profound Knowledge. Performance, he said, results from the combination of many forces in addition to the person being evaluated and includes the processes and management and supervision. What actually is being evaluated? Dr. Deming expressed the contribution to performance of the individual and the system as Performance $= x + yx$, where x is the individual's contribution to performance and yx is the interaction of the system, y, with the individual, x.[403]

The system is not in the equation by itself since its effect on performance occurs only through the yx interaction. How much of this performance model does the rater take into account? Is performance attributed only to the individual, ignoring the *yx* interaction?

Leadership, said Deming, requires investigation into possible causes of performance. Management must know what the numbers tell them about the meaning of differences and their implications for management action. Apparent differences at any given time, even huge differences, could be due only to chance produced by the same system of common causes. In order to attribute superior performance to an individual, that person over a number of years continually would demonstrate superior performance according to measures related to the job. If it is determined that the person just can't learn the job, the company has a moral obligation to put that person into the right job since the company hired them.[404]

The performance appraisal is built around fear and discomfort. It discourages honest and open communication between supervisor and employee; both may not be comfortable with the process. The supervisor is placed in the role of judge who, in a forced rating and ranking system, has to tell half of the employees why they are below average and tell the bottom 10 percent why they may have no future with the organization. Employees continually are worried about the consequences of a poor evaluation and make decisions based on the expected payoff, to themselves as well as the organization.

Employees who receive high ratings and are given labels such as Employee of the Month or Teacher of the Year may feel good about it. However, they may be embarrassed in front of other employees who can't understand why that person was selected, especially if the selection process is no more than a lottery. This practice can disturb relationships between employees who may feel unappreciated and no longer want to work with those who have received special recognition. The title "associate" has replaced "employee" in many organizations, as has "team member." This latter characterization may not be accurate where rating and ranking is used since it can destroy teamwork by putting individuals into a competitive relationship to gain a limited number of good ratings.

Forced ranking creates arbitrary, artificial distinctions in the performance of a system. The differences in the figures produced by processes in a common cause system are due to chance. Rating and ranking people according to those differences is equivalent to finding a cause for the outcomes of a lottery or a casino game of chance. Deming did not see any harm in awarding prizes or merit raises as long as the selection process was advertised as a lottery.[405] When people are placed into rating categories based on the chance variation of outcomes produced by a common cause system, in effect they have won or lost a lottery.

Over the years, senior managers of some other companies benchmarked the methods of General Electric's CEO Jack Welch, whom they admired for producing substantial profitability for GE. Welch used "rank and yank," as others called it, [406] a process of "differentiation," as Welch called it, to distinguish between top-, middle-, and bottom-performing employees within GE's businesses. This was intended to continually improve the performance of the salaried workforce. Each employee was graded as A, B, or C. Welch believed in meritocracy and was against quotas based on characteristics other than an employee's performance. Yet there was a different kind of quota, one based on performance ratings, that allocated a preestablished percentage of employees to each one of the three rating categories. Employees who received a C grade were among the 10 percent who eventually would be culled from the company, much in the way parts are culled from production after they have been inspected and found faulty. One could infer from this approach that eventually all employees would be above average, and there would be no bottom 10 percent. However, this is not possible since ranking always forces a percentage of employees into the lowest grade. It is as if a company has an unending supply of defective employees, even though there are processes to select capable people, train them, and assign and develop them. GE was financially successful under Welch, but the losses from artificially differentiating employees cannot be known.[407]

Organizations have argued that they use rating and ranking to avoid unfairly discriminating against employees by appearing to favor some and not others based on factors other than performance. However, the reverse has occurred. A number of companies have been sued by their employees for unfair discrimination for using rating and ranking to reduce the size of the workforce. Some suits claimed discrimination was based on ethnicity, some on gender, and others on age. There were class action suits, and lawyers had ammunition when they were able to show that older employees who had a history of favorable ratings suddenly began to receive low ratings. Early in the 2000s, many companies began to end the practice of forced ranking, both from the exposure to lawsuits and from an uproar of discontent from employees. Microsoft ended "stacked ranking" in November 2013 to encourage employees to work together rather than to compete. Yahoo Inc. in 2016 continued to rate and rank, has fired hundreds of employees, and was facing at least one lawsuit for alleged violations of Title VII of the Civil Rights Act of 1964. The complaint claims that managers were required to rank their employees so that a sufficient percentage of employees were assigned to each of five performance "buckets" or rankings, ranging from Greatly Exceeds to Misses, even if all the employees were performing well or at the same level. The managers were each given a targeted mean employee score for all of their reports. They then entered their employee scores into the company computer system. Then the scores were modified up or down by higher-level management, who often had no actual contact with the employees. Sometimes an employee ranked as Occasionally Misses for one or two quarters during the year was terminated. Sometimes the scores were averaged over several quarters, and the bottom 5 percent were terminated. The complaint claims that the measurement used to identify "bottom" performers was changed in order to achieve a headcount reduction goal.[408]

The performance review process also is known as an appraisal. Appraisal is a term usually reserved for valuing material objects, such as steel or jewelry, in order to establish a price for them in an economic transaction. This could imply that employees are viewed solely as an economic entity, to be valued by the accountants only for their worth as commodities or equipment, to be consumed or worn down and then discarded. What is the thinking when some managers say that the aim of the review is to remove the "deadwood"? When do human beings become deadwood, floating on the surface of the water, no longer able to be moved by the push and pull of extrinsic forces? When do they have to be "culled out," as if they were defective product, or "weeded out" of what would otherwise be a pristine garden? What do the rating numbers and rankings mean? What do the differences between rating numbers mean? More importantly, what is the meaning of human beings to managers, school administrators, and teachers who reduce individuals to a number or a label? In one of his arguments against performance appraisal, Douglas

McGregor, former professor at MIT Sloan Kettering and president of Antioch College, wrote, "The needs of the organization are obviously important, but when they come into conflict with our convictions about the worth and dignity of the human personality, one or the other must give."[409]

Blast It Out

People often asked Dr. Deming how they might improve their performance appraisal system. He answered with, "Why improve it? You could not find a better way to beat people." When then asked, "How should I do away with performance appraisal?" he sometimes responded with, "Just blast it out," or, "Just stop it; stop it now." Management was puzzled and often angered by Deming's admonition to end the annual performance review and related practices such as merit raises. He contended that the annual review should be replaced by frequent conversations between employee and supervisor. In *Out of the Crisis*, chapter 3, Deming allocated many pages in his discussion of diseases and obstacles to explain his objections to performance reviews. He commented that ranking of people who belong to the system violates scientific logic and is ruinous as a policy. It is meaningless as a predictor of performance. Joy and innovation become secondary to a good rating. Intrinsic motivation is crushed. Neither children nor adults can enjoy learning if they are constantly worried about grading and gold stars for their performance. No one can enjoy their work if they are ranked against others. When people have joy in work, they likely will not move to another organization just for higher pay.[410]

Dr. Deming continually made his case during his meetings with a client company's senior executives. He wanted management to abandon the annual performance review and manage from what he said were "modern principles of leadership." Responding to his urging, a management level committee was formed to review the performance appraisal system. Committee members represented the major functions in the company. He told the committee to eliminate the nine-category rating scale and develop a three-category method, one based on his theory of variation. Employees would be identified either as performing within the system of common causes or as a special cause on the low or high side. The intent would be to continually improve the performance capability of the system as a whole. The process would provide opportunity for frequent conversations between supervisor and employee. The supervisor was to take on the role of coach. Feedback would be in both directions, and appropriate personnel decisions would become clearer. After a year of discussion, the committee agreed to replace the performance appraisal system with a new performance management process. A consensus solution was reached, which was a compromise between no ratings and a nine-category scale. The nine-category scale was reduced to four, bearing little resemblance in theory or practice to Deming's recommendation. Management was well intentioned, but people were arguing for their position from traditional models, especially since they were changing a system that they believed helped to put them in their current positions.

One lesson from this experience is that consensus decision making without the outside view provided by profound knowledge is not likely to produce desired results. Supervisors, using the revised rating format, continued to force employee ratings into a bell-shaped distribution. This constrained communication between supervisor and employee and interfered with the coaching process.

Grading and Ranking in Schools

Evaluation of student performance in schools has similarities to outmoded methods of quality control in mass production. Product quality is achieved by inspection through a detection process of find and then fix or discard. Deming raised management's awareness of the wastefulness of this process that he described as burning the toast and then scraping it. This process of inspection and detection of defective product has been replaced within much of industry with continual process improvement to prevent defective items from being produced in the first place. If inspection is needed, and if it is possible, it is done by operators during the production process. However, in the twenty-first century, we see schools using the mass production model of inspect and detect to sort students into categories that seem to imply "needs rework" and "scrap." It seems that it is typically the student as "product" that is being graded, not the systems and processes that produced the grade.

How many students look forward to school? Do parents value their children's learning and development of their ability to think, or do they value getting the right answers and high test scores? Do they even see that these two values may not be compatible? Why is it that teachers who chose the profession for love of teaching can reach a point where they no longer want to be in the classroom? Why do students who have a natural curiosity and an inclination to learn dislike school? Teaching and learning for its own sake is easily destroyed by a management system that relies on extrinsic incentives to produce results. The system can stamp out natural curiosity and, as Deming liked to say, "a yearning for learning."

Parents, of course, want their children to learn and develop, to be proud of them. The operative word is "better," and doing better often equates to being better. Doing better is defined by comparing the grades of one's children to those of other children. The measure of excellence and success, for the parents and perhaps the students as well, are A grades and placement on the honor roll. The outcome is what matters. The development of intellectual skills, such as critical thinking, and social skills, such as cooperation (known in some schools as cheating), is harder to show to others by numbers than are test scores and grades.

Has learning become overvalued for the economic gains it can bring? I saw a video of a high school class where students were taught some of the techniques being used in business to improve quality and productivity. The emphasis was on the general usefulness of the techniques to solve problems. The students were asked what they got out of the class. Some of the students said, "This is really great because I can now put it on my résumé, and it will help me get a better job." Certainly that is important, but where was the balance between the economic value of learning and acquiring knowledge to face life's problems? Both are needed to contribute to work life and to life in society, especially as a responsible citizen. All are part of the same whole.

One justification given for forced ranking of employees is that it is an objective and fair method to identify, reward, and develop A- and B-grade performers and downsize the company by firing C-grade performers. Schools have similar practices when they grade students on a curve. However, the lines drawn on a bell-shaped curve to divide the curve into rating or grading categories, such as A, B, and C, have no valid statistical basis. They are specifications from the mind of management, administrators, and teachers. Analytical thinking divides what is connected, what is naturally whole. It artificially divides a distribution of scores into grades or rating categories. People are allocated to those categories with most in the middle and smaller percentages at the top and bottom. Forced ranking is rarely questioned because it has always been done that way. There is a story of the daughter who asked her mother why she always cut off the ends of the ham before placing it in the oven. Mom said that she did it that way because her mother did. The girl then asked her grandmother why she did it. The answer was that her own mother did it. Then the girl, when she was visiting her ninety-eight-year-old great-grandmother, asked the same question. The answer was that she had to since the ham was too large for the pan. So much for tradition!

The Bell Curve Is on a Mental Map

Often the normal (bell-shaped) curve is cited as the rationale for forced ranking of employees and students. Numerical scores from tests and ratings are *imagined* to be distributed in the shape of a bell-shaped curve. Then the curve is divided, according to subjective criteria of a manager or teacher or administrator, into sections or categories or "buckets" ranging from a top rating, such as "Outstanding" or "A," on down. Individual employees or students are forced into one of these categories, with only a limited number allocated to the top categories. There is no justification from the statistical theory of the normal curve to assume that the performance of a group of people, as reflected in a distribution of grades, ratings, and rankings is bell shaped. There is no bell curve in nature, only a model in a mental map, an idealized, perfectly symmetrical abstraction that was created in the mind of a statistician, Carl Frederick Gauss, to describe the distribution of characteristics or events based on many observations. A frequency distribution—a histogram—of employee performance ratings or student test scores or grades may or may not take on the bell shape, and it may not be stable. It depends on the dynamics of the rating or grading process, including the rater's mental map.

The Rater's Map Is the Territory

A rating of a person can't be separated from the rater's mental map (e.g., the model the rater applies), personal values and preferences, desire to please their boss, general rating biases (e.g., hard or easy), specific biases (e.g., gender, ethnicity), human resource policies and pressures from management, especially to limit top grades or ratings, and expectations and memories about the rater from previous ratings. These factors influence the rater and have little to do with the individual being evaluated. The evaluator's map is the territory for that evaluator. The occurrence of rater subjective biases has been recognized by industrial psychologists, and statistical adjustments of rating data have been developed to minimize the rating biases—after the rating has been given.

Likewise, the rating that a person believes they should get is on their map. For example, a student may think that they received a low score on a test because "It was unfairly difficult" or "The teacher does not know the subject as well as I do." There is a report about a student who took a final examination in physics. The instructor handed him an altimeter and told him to use it to determine the height of the campus tower. The student got a piece of string, went up the tower, tied the altimeter to the string, lowered it to the base of the tower, and then measured the string. The instructor flunked the student. The student appealed to the administration, which decided to let him retake the examination. Again, the instructor handed the student an altimeter and asked him to use it to determine the height of the tower. The student got a goniometer, a device that measures angles. He went out some distance from the tower and used the device to triangulate the tower. Once more the instructor flunked the student, and the student petitioned the administration, which allowed him to take the test with the altimeter. The student saw that the tower had a spiral staircase in the shape of a flat screw. He went along each step with the altimeter, determined the path of the screw, and again came up with a number. The instructor thought that he failed the test because he didn't read the altimeter. The administration thought that the student had demonstrated knowledge beyond simply reading the altimeter to determine the height of the tower, so they passed him.[411]

The point is not whether we agree with the teacher or the administration but that people vary in the criteria they use to judge others. Some managers appreciate innovation and creativity; others require more conformity and the "right" answer, as if context and environment didn't matter. Dr. Deming suggested a different kind of test to eliminate the problem of correct answers. He would give students a multiple-choice exam with three or four alternative answers. The student would have to describe under what conditions each alternative would be correct. What are the criteria of knowing, of being correct? Dr. Deming's concept is closer to the world in which we live. Should an employee's rating or a student's grade, with their consequences for that person's future, depend on the mental map of one individual evaluator, what the evaluator thinks is correct? Is there room for discussion?

Prediction or Characterization

A rating, a grade, a ranking, can be used to characterize a person. A rating, which is a judgment by the rater, is projected *onto* the person being rated, and the person is viewed as the rating. The person is flattened, reduced to a number or letter or label (e.g., a grade-C person or a grade-A person or fifth-rate). The individual now *is* the rating. Grading obscures both the individuality and the range of talents that a person possesses. Once a person is labeled, it becomes harder for management to see the person past the label, and a self-fulfilling prophecy, either positive or negative, can begin. There is no awareness that the label originated with an evaluator in a point in time. It is as if the grade were stamped on the person's forehead: grade-C person, poor performer, now and forever. The person has been graded when perhaps the system should have been graded. Now the individual is a member of a category that exists only in concept. You can't see a grade C. In this case, the map has no territory. It is an abstraction that doesn't represent anything that can be pointed to.

Similarly, when a person, who is viewed as authority, says to another person, "You *are* lazy" or stupid or bad, the recipient of this judgment may get the idea that he or she *is* that kind of person, has that *within* them, and they will always *be* that way. This is especially true when a parent talks to a child and goes way beyond the judgment that the behavior was unacceptable _to them_. Whether positive or negative, statements about a person, especially a child, that contain the words _is_ or _are_ characterize a child's being. Whether the label or implied ranking is positive or negative, people who make judgments and who evaluate others should be aware that their words, which come from their own biases and interpretations, have the power to shape the identity and self-image of the child—the child's mental map of who and what "I am," the "me," the "self."

A child, and an adult, must be able to experience their own success and failures and learn from them and not simply accept another person's characterization of them as a fact, as anything more than that person's judgment. If someone reports that the sky _is_ pink, the more accurate statement is that the sky _appears_ pink to me. A person who judges another person or object should qualify the personal nature of the evaluation with "it appears to me," "I think," or some other similar clarification. In this way, the evaluator acknowledges that errors of judgment are possible and especially that future possibilities are not limited. Then, instead of a one-way evaluation, the opportunity for discussion is opened up.

An Artificial Scarcity of Grade-A People

Deming had no argument against competitive games or sporting events. He understood that they could be fun for participants. Games are designed to produce a scarcity of winners. Only one player or team can win. One of the criteria for grading materials, minerals, metals, and other physical objects is their rarity or scarcity. Those that are rare or scarce will be valued and graded higher than those that are more abundant. Deming asked why it is that in our institutions of enterprise and education, as well as in the home, human beings are managed as if we live in a world of artificial scarcity of top grades and ratings. There is no scarcity of good pupils or of good people. There is no reason why everyone in a class should not have a top grade, or a bottom grade, or any grade. The effect of grading and ranking is to humiliate those who do not receive top grade or rank. It demoralizes the individual. Deming taught for many years at the graduate schools of business of New York University and Columbia University. He used his exams to evaluate how he was doing, how he could improve his teaching, how he could better help students. He did not grade students. If they completed the requirements, they passed the course.[412]

Deming was concerned that artificial scarcity, as with real scarcity, promotes adversarial competition. In the zero-sum accounting of games, in order to win, to come out ahead, others must lose. Deming asked whether management of an enterprise would want their employees, suppliers, customers to be losers, whether anyone would want to be married to a loser, whether parents would pit one child against another and create losers in the family.[413] The evaluation process creates self-fulfilling prophecies. By implanting self-images of "I am" or "I am not" or "I can't," it limits possibilities for growth, development, joy in learning, and joy in work.

A Child Is Beyond Comparison

There is a grade school near my house that advertises in big letters on the outside wall that the school is an A++. Does this mean that every child received an A++? While a school administrator thinks about performance of the school as a whole, and may see a child as one of many, the parent should see the child as a whole human being, an individual beyond comparison. Yet parents do grade, rate, and rank their children. Telling John, "Why can't you be as good as your brother?" or comparing a daughter to other girls is ranking: "How come Jackie got an A grade and you only got a C?" What is the purpose of doing this? Is it to motivate, to punish? Does it diagnose the situation? Does it shed light on the source of the problem? Do the differences in scores even mean that there is a problem? Test grades can vary just by chance. Do such comparisons divert a child's energy from creativity and joy to envy and fear? What does it mean to be "best" or "worst"? Children should be in an environment, in school and at home, that facilitates their development, their ability to form cooperative relationships with others, their natural curiosity, and, as Deming put it, their "yearning for learning." Grading and forced ranking is part of a destructive pattern of management of children's development, intellectual, social, and spiritual. It ignores the fact that children develop at different speeds and learn in different ways and that any measurement will vary over time. Grading and ranking is part of a process that tends not to recognize the uniqueness of each child by converting a natural intrinsic motivation to dependence on extrinsic sources. These extrinsic sources can stifle creativity and produce an automaton that conforms to someone else's idea of "should be" long before natural inclinations can fully unfold. In this system, cooperation means conforming, which is reminiscent of Gilbreth's definition of cooperation as conformance to management's work standards.

Seeing Differences in People as Possibilities

Deming understood the importance of diversity where the meeting of different ideas, world views, and talents was necessary for new and better ideas to emerge. He appreciated that people are unique and diverse in their abilities and inclinations. Deming did not like to use the term "replacement" for an employee who moved into a job vacated by another employee, as if people were replaceable parts. Management of industry, education, and government operate as if people are alike, said Deming. He wrote: "A manager of people needs to understand that all people are different."[414] Recognizing that people are different from one another is not ranking them.[415]

Any ecology requires diversity to remain viable. Can a social system survive as an ecology when the management system encourages internal competition rather than cooperation and when risk-taking is discouraged by fear of failure and poor evaluations? The enterprise managed as a social ecosystem will have a greater capability to adapt to change and to shape its future through creativity and innovation. An interaction between diverse components of a system produces newness rather than sameness as new system properties can emerge from those interactions, as discussed in chapter 12. Therefore, an enterprise mapped as an ecosystem will have a management system that allows employees freedoms that obviously were absent in the extreme illustration of autocratic management that we saw in the red bead demonstration.

The Art of Possibility by Rosamund and Benjamin Zander is about transforming professional and personal life. In their book, the authors recall Michelangelo's creative vision that within every block of stone or marble dwells a beautiful statue. In our education system, instead of comparing one child to another with grades, the process could focus on chipping away at the stone, getting rid of whatever is in the way of each child's developing skills, mastery, and self-expression. Rather than comparing people to each other or to a standard that they are expected to live up to, it would be more valuable to view each person as a possibility to live into.

Since grades say little about the work done or a student's mastery of the material, the Zanders developed a number of practices to manage the education of Ben's music students. One practice that follows this model of creating possibility is an innovation in grading. Students are told at the start of the class that each one will get an A for the course. In order to earn the A, during the first two weeks of the course they must write a letter to Ben and date it as of the end of the course. They are to place themselves in the future, looking back, and to report on all the insights they acquired and milestones they attained during the year, written in the past tense as if they had already occurred. The students must describe what happened to them to earn the A, including what they did to become what they wanted to be. Some students wrote that they stopped blaming themselves for mistakes and learned from them. Others wrote more profound insights: "I used to play just notes, but, now, I found out the real meaning of every piece and could play with more imagination." "I got my A because I examined my fears and I realized that they have no place in my life."

Zander is not denying that there are differences between people's individual accomplishments. No one wants to listen to a violinist who cannot play the notes or to be treated by an incompetent doctor. He doesn't give the A as a measure or performance against a standard. Rather it is intended to remove what he calls the "stranglehold of judgment" that grades have over consciousness. Zander's A grade is an invention that creates possibilities for both mentor and student, manager and employee, or for any human interaction. It allows teachers to align themselves with their students as they work to produce the outcome rather than aligning with the standards *against* the students. This makes possible teamwork of instructor and student or manager and employee. It removes the disparity in power that can be a distraction and an inhibitor to productivity and development, innovation and creativity. Freely granting an A, says Zander, creates a wholeness through partnership, teamwork, and relationship. Instead of judging others *against* our standards and destroying their intrinsic interest and motivation, the practice of granting an ongoing A in all our relationships enables us to align ourselves with others.[416]

A Leader's Dilemma

It troubles some leaders to flatten a human being by rating or grading and then to have to put that symbol into some kind of ranking. Marine General Walter Boomer, assistant commandant of the US Marine Corps, presented his candid views on the subject when I met him in 1993 during a four-day seminar conducted for the Department of the Navy (DON) by Dr. Deming. Ron Moen and I participated with Dr. Deming. More than four hundred Navy and Marine Corps officers and DON senior civilians were present. One day of the seminar was dedicated to Navy and Marine Corps issues and included a panel of their senior officers. General Boomer's comments appeared later in a report of the event in the Navy Public Affairs Library. He made the following points:

- "All of you in uniform are being paid to take risks. Without risk-taking you will fail in combat."
- "I detest the Marine Corps fitness report. I am in a minority. Those who sit on a promotion board love 'em. You rank people 1, 2, 3, 4, 5. What do you think it does to the superb lieutenant colonel who's ranked 7 of 7? I'll tell you what it does. It crushes them and they never recover."
- "I say Deming is right, but I don't have the answer either. We must promote; we must have some kind of performance appraisal system, and I think all we can do is try to devise one that keeps in mind some of the basic fundamentals that Dr. Deming is talking to us about."
- Regarding Dr. Deming's Point No. 8 of his 14 points—Drive out fear: "Encourage your people to express ideas and ask questions ... our sailors and marines and civilian workers have the answers to every problem that we have, if you've got the guts to ask them."

General Boomer was asked, "What would you tell those marines who contend that Marine Corps leadership has been perfected over two hundred years and needs no changes?" He replied, "I'd tell them that with that attitude, like the dinosaur, the Corps will eventually disappear. While it's true that some things have been perfected over two hundred years that are still working very well, everything isn't. What we need to do is hang on to those things that we know are good. Hang on to them, and build on them, and work changes from that foundation."

Employee Compensation and Promotion

Deming said that reward for good performance may be the same as reward to a meteorologist for good weather. However, there are principles that follow from Deming's System of Profound Knowledge that management can apply to develop compensation and promotion plans that will foster intrinsic motivation and minimize the use of extrinsic incentives. When Dr. Brian Joiner was the CEO of his consulting firm, Joiner Associates, he applied those principles to the compensation of his staff. He said that even though you would want every employee to be happy with a compensation plan, that won't always happen. People have different histories, expectations, and criteria of comparison. The Joiner Associates compensation plan followed this process: Salaries were established by market rates for new hires. Annual salary increases were the same percentage for everyone in order to keep the salaries of most associates in line with the market. Prosperity sharing for those with the firm at least two years was the same number of weeks of pay and prorated for those with less than two years. Some years there was nothing to share; some years there was more to share. Special adjustments upward were given to those with new responsibilities. When pay reached the ceiling for a position, a partial increase was given. The principle is that pay is not a motivator but can be a de-motivator. The work itself is the source of motivation.[417]

Dr. Deming viewed promotion as movement from a current job to a different job. A model on how to promote may be suggested by the way one chooses a physician, lawyer, or other professional. One relies on a recommendation from a person who has known the candidate very well over a long time and is on their honor. Isn't trusting the person who recommends better than deceiving ourselves that we have a valid prediction system? Besides, when it comes right down to it, when a selection committee, or a single executive, decides on a candidate, doesn't it come down to who knows the candidate?[418]

Chapter 17

∼∾∼

Whole-in-One:
A Social Ecology Performing in Concert

We can succeed only by concert. It is not "can any of us
imagine better?" but, "can we all do better?" The dogmas
of the quiet past are inadequate to the stormy present ... As
our case is new, so we must think anew, and act anew.
—President Abraham Lincoln[419]

Fritjof Capra, in *Belonging to the Universe*, said that a living system is an integrated whole with its own individuality, and it has the tendency to assert itself and to preserve that individuality. However, it has to integrate itself into the larger whole of which it is a part. These are opposite and contradictory tendencies. We need a dynamic balance between them, and that's essential for physical and mental health. In order to have a healthy life, individuals need both to assert themselves and to integrate themselves.[420] Peter Vaill made a similar point in his book *Managing as a Performing Art*: "Somehow, a curious union of opposites has to occur where performers have to find creative freedom in the closely interconnected workings of the system."[421] The novelist Aldous Huxley wondered if it is possible to make the best of both worlds—the world of individual freedom and the world of the organization. He said that perhaps more realistic conceptions of the nature of authority might enable us to do this.[422] Deming put it this way: "We must restore the individual, and do so in the complexities of interaction with the rest of the world."[423]

Deming represented the relationship between each individual and the systems with which they interact with this model, also discussed in the previous chapter:[424]

$$Performance = x + yx.$$

This model also can be expressed as:

$$Performance = I + (I \times S).$$

$(I \times S)$ is the interaction of the individual, I, with the system S. I contributes to performance with the attributes that makes that person a unique human being. S represents the organization's systems (i.e., the larger environment in which the individual performs). S is not in the equation by itself since its effect on performance occurs only through the activities of people in the $(I \times S)$ interaction. Deming maintained that the contributions of the system are not explicitly considered when most organizations evaluate an individual's performance. He tried to help management to understand that the influence of the system could be as high as 94 percent in some organizations.

When systems are managed as a social ecology, the components—the people and their systems—are in a mutually beneficial, positive relationship. The $(I \times S)$ interaction could be expressed as individual-in-the-system or as individual-in-the-environment. The interaction also means that the system is in the individual since management can either limit or free individuals to use their talents and knowledge and their intrinsic motivation and intelligence. Where the system greatly restricts the unique contributions of people, it can't function as an ecology. The people are not in a healthy relationship with each other and with the system. Many of the interactions are negative because, without knowing it, people harm each other. The long-term viability of the organization is far from assured. The repressive management system, illustrated in the red bead demonstration, is a system but not an ecological system.

Reflecting on his time as a prisoner in a concentration camp, Viktor Frankl considered human liberty and whether the individual can be psychologically and spiritually free from the influence of his surroundings. Frankl's observations and experiences of camp life proved to him that human beings can have "independence of mind, even in such terrible conditions of psychic and physical stress."[425] Frankl, who survived imprisonment in a Nazi concentration camp, wrote in his book *Man's Search for Meaning*, "It is not freedom from conditions, but it is freedom to take a stand toward the conditions."[426] Deming said that a leader should be able to express disagreement with management, even in the military. Deming began chapter 6, "The Management of People" in *The New Economics* with a quote from Captain Leslie E. Simon, who eventually rose to the rank of lieutenant general, "If you cannot argue with your boss, he is not worth working for." [427]

Restore the Individual as a Living System within a Larger Whole

The psychologist Alfred Adler founded what is known as individual psychology, yet Adler stressed that the effects of the environment, the effects of society, must be considered in understanding that person and their relationships. David Bohm pointed out that individuality seems to be the case because people have separate bodies; however, individuality of whole human beings must also consider the invisible world of mental processes. A common language could not exist, and we couldn't communicate unless we were shaped by a common cultural and societal conditioning.[428]

All important problems, including problems of general human relations, are social. John Donne, about four hundred years ago, put into poetry the thought that "No man is an island entire of itself."[429] We may see our bodies as separate, not realizing the interdependence with the physical, biological, and social environment. Others have commented about an individual's perceptions of their relationship to the containing environment. Albert Einstein wrote, "A human being is part of a whole, called by us the Universe, a part limited in time and space. He experiences himself, his thoughts and feelings, as something separated from the rest—a kind of optical delusion of his consciousness."[430] Wayne Dyer expressed it this way: "Though you have been conditioned to believe that you are an individual, you are actually part of the grand universal nature that is infinite in its possibilities."[431]

Deming, as we have seen, throughout the book, was worried about the destructive forces of governance that could exist in all of the institutions of society. He firmly believed that enterprise systems of extrinsic control fragment the individual psychologically and separate people from each other and from identification with the enterprise. These systems have destroyed the individual by replacing human intrinsic motivation with heavy reliance on forces of extrinsic control. They have humiliated people, destroyed self-esteem and natural curiosity, and squeezed out intrinsic motivation from the individual over a lifetime, replacing it with fear and self-defensiveness and an attitude of win-lose. They have smothered people. Matthew Fox, paraphrasing Studs Terkel, wrote that work needs to be part of a whole. We should not have to disassemble ourselves and send a piece of us to work every day.[432]

It was Deming's prediction, vision, and hope that a transformation would occur that preserved or restored the power of curiosity, joy in learning, and joy in accomplishment that people are born with. He wrote that the individual must be restored to release the power of human beings that is possible with intrinsic motivation. Instead of competing for high grades and ratings, people will cooperate on common problems. This will lead to greater innovation, expansion of market, greater service, and greater material reward for everyone. Then everyone will win.[433]

Free Individuals and the Common Good

Leaders learn to make a commitment to the common good ...
When you think ethically about this, individual freedom becomes
difficult to justify unless it results ultimately in the common good.
—Max DePree[434]

The motives, standards, and behaviors found in communities of professionals may provide a model for management of how a system of cooperation might work within an enterprise. It already exists when people from different companies work together in industry and professional associations for everyone's benefit. Michael Polanyi wrote that a free society works best when individuals are able to choose to cooperate with other individuals in order to pursue ends that all deem worthy. This is especially evident in the behavior of professionals such as scientists, judges, clergy, artists, writers, journalists, philosophers, historians, and economists. They associate with others in their field in order to achieve personal aims, yet each is part of the same whole because everyone accepts the same professional and ethical standards and recognizes the same precedent and tradition.

There is no central control, yet a "spontaneous ordered whole" emerges from the continual interactions of people. There is a system of control; it is one of "mutual adjustments" and "mutual authority." Science, for example, has made tremendous progress operating in this manner. Scientists influence each other through their sharing of information and research findings. Authority arises from respect, and respect is for knowledge and contribution. One's authority comes from the respect one is given by colleagues for his or her knowledge. Scientists tend to work with others in closely related fields, but science as a whole is a system of "overlapping neighborhoods."

According to Polanyi, the inner, private motives of individuals prod them into these systems of spontaneous social order, but the motive that moves them into the appropriate relationships with one another comes from the common understanding within the profession of their duties and obligations. Therefore, regardless of the private motives that move a person to be, for example, a judge—ambition for status, power, respect, money— one is not a judge unless one performs according to the activities and obligations that constitute being a judge. Judges are therefore motivated to find the relevant law and the relevant facts and to make a decision that either follows the precedents or creates a new precedent on grounds that one's colleagues can, or ought to, find reasonable.[435]

Polanyi criticized any political system and governments that constrained the natural variation produced by differences between individuals—differences in talents, inclinations, and interests that made possible a functioning economy. In this sense, he was echoing the moral and economic sentiments of Adam Smith.[436]

Transformation

Deming wrote that transformation comes from an understanding of the System of Profound Knowledge. It is the individual that must first be transformed. This doesn't happen all at once; it is discontinuous. It will enable the individual to perceive new meaning to their life, to events, to numbers, to interactions between people.[437] When people understand the System of Profound Knowledge, they will apply its principles in their relationships with other people and have a basis to judge their own decisions.[438]

Transformation requires a change in a person's knowledge and values. It is a change in the way of thinking, but it is more than intellectual. In the first edition of *The New Economics*, Dr. Deming characterized the transformation he sought as *metanoia*.[439] The word comes from the Greek *meta* (beyond, after, outside) and *noia* from *nous* (mind, perception, understanding). The word has been used in various contexts, including psychological and religious ones. Essentially it means a deep change of mind and heart, a spiritual conversion or awakening, a different way of thinking, a broadening of viewpoint, a basic change of character. It implies a new ability to see possibilities not seen before. Although Deming didn't use the words *transformation of consciousness*, it has to be a quality of the transformation he was seeking.

CODA

～

In one of their frequent meetings, the general manager of one of Ford's major businesses asked Dr. Deming how he was able to persist in his efforts when it seemed that the odds were against his bringing about the transformation he envisioned. Where did he find the strength for such an undertaking, and why, in his late eighties, did he keep going? Deming didn't really explain other than to say that he enjoyed his work. He had a bit more to say about this when, toward the end of a seminar, a participant asked, "Will I see this in my lifetime?" Dr. Deming answered in his usual succinct and witty way, "Well, you don't have much longer than that."

Coda is a word used in music to indicate that a passage, movement, or piece is coming to an end. As these pages come to an end, I leave their contents with you. I hope that your curiosity, learning, and knowledge will not end but instead that they will have been seeded and nourished. My heartfelt wish is that you are inspired to carry the message and the meaning in these pages into your life and your leadership to help your business enterprise and other organizations in your field of influence to develop and become sustainable entities that thrive and evolve, making our communities—our society—strong, vibrant, and joyful. When we have mapped the four movements as one whole, then we can open our eyes and the eyes of others wider so that together we see the many different aspects of our lives as part of a larger context ... a whole. With this shift in our thinking, systems of all kinds—businesses, schools, and governing bodies—can become life-affirming, healthier, innovative places to work and create value.

By acknowledging that our differences are assets, we open the door to more possibilities. We experience the harmony and rhythm of individuals cooperating, sharing knowledge and expertise to create something together that never could have been created separately. Joy and pride in our work come from knowing that we are working together in meaningful relationship to the whole in which we participate.

Will I see Deming's vision for transformation realized in my lifetime? Will you? Perhaps not everywhere we look. But there are enterprises making inroads. Change is taking place. It is happening through organizations like Aileron, who have been influenced by Deming and his System of Profound Knowledge. The vision and the possibilities are alive. Imagine a critical mass of organizations with leaders unafraid of change, bold enough to try another way. In these enterprises, individuals will come together as described by Deming with joy, self-respect, and a willingness to contribute to the purpose of the enterprise. Imagine yourself and others working together as if playing in concert, living all the aspects of your lives—family, work, social, and spiritual—thriving as part of a whole.

This book is a way for me to honor W. Edwards Deming and to invest in the next generation of leaders through the content and relevance of his body of work. These words from Hannah Senesh struck me as a way we might think of Dr. Deming:

"There are stars whose radiance is visible on earth though they have long been extinct. There are people whose brilliance continues to light the world though they are no longer among the living. These lights are particularly bright when the night is dark. They light the way for mankind."[440]

APPENDIX:
DEMING'S 14 POINTS

❦

As presented by Deming in *Out of the Crisis*, chapter 2, and the W. Edwards Deming Institute website, www.deming.org:

1. Create constancy of purpose toward improvement of product and service, with the aim to become competitive and to stay in business, and to provide jobs.

2. Adopt the new philosophy. We are in a new economic age. Western management must awaken to the challenge, must learn their responsibilities, and take on leadership for change.

3. Cease dependence on inspection to achieve quality. Eliminate the need for inspection on a mass basis by building quality into the product in the first place.

4. End the practice of awarding business on the basis of price tag. Instead, minimize total cost. Move toward a single supplier for any one item, on a long-term relationship of loyalty and trust.

5. Improve constantly and forever the system of production and service, to improve quality and productivity, and thus constantly decrease costs.

6. Institute training on the job.

7. Institute leadership (see Point 12 and chapter 8). The aim of supervision should be to help people and machines and gadgets to do a better job.

Supervision of management is in need of overhaul, as well as supervision of production workers.

8. Drive out fear, so that everyone may work effectively for the company (see chapter 3).

9. Break down barriers between departments. People in research, design, sales, and production must work as a team, to foresee problems of production and in use that may be encountered with the product or service.

10. Eliminate slogans, exhortations, and targets for the work force asking for zero defects and new levels of productivity. Such exhortations only create adversarial relationships, as the bulk of the causes of low quality and low productivity belong to the system and thus lie beyond the power of the work force.

- Eliminate work standards (quotas) on the factory floor. Substitute leadership.
- Eliminate management by objective. Eliminate management by numbers, numerical goals. Substitute leadership.

11. Remove barriers that rob the hourly workers of their rights to pride of workmanship. The responsibility of supervisors must be changed from sheer numbers to quality.

12. Remove barriers that rob people in management and in engineering of their right to pride of workmanship. This means, inter alia, abolishment of the annual or merit rating and of management by objective (see chapter 3).

13. Institute a vigorous program of education and self-improvement.

14. Put everybody in the company to work to accomplish the transformation. The transformation is everybody's job.

ACKNOWLEDGMENTS

W. Edwards Deming changed my life, as he changed the lives of others who were fortunate to learn from him. He was a modern renaissance man with a broad range of intellectual, scientific, and artistic interests and accomplishments. His being revealed the profound knowledge and wisdom that can transform human relationships.

Years ago, the editor of a major publisher contacted me and asked if I had a book they could consider. I explained the concept I had in mind for this book. I wanted to present my view of the deeper meaning of Deming's message—the moral and spiritual impact of his ideas that transcended the technical knowledge. Deming taught in the tradition of the great and profound thinkers of history. I wanted to write a book that offered his ideas on leadership and living as a whole, not just in terms of management of organizations. He listened patiently, but I don't think he heard me. He asked if I did not have something like total quality management, six-sigma, some new hook, a new program to get people to buy another book on quality. I told him that I would write a book that presented Deming's teaching as profound knowledge and that would help leaders to escape the limitations and constraints of our current thinking by opening our minds to new ones. He was not interested, but Clay Mathile, founder and chairman of Aileron, was. Clay has recognized the potential of Deming's teaching to individuals, to enterprise, and to society.

Clay's aim is to develop entrepreneurs and professional managers who can provide leadership to their organizations. This book is for them and for all others who aspire to be leaders of enterprises and of their own lives. Clay believes that Dr. Deming's principles and philosophy align with Aileron's vision to be a catalyst for raising the quality of life through professionally managed enterprises.

I owe much to Clay Mathile, Joni Fedders, Aileron president, and to the Aileron staff, who have supported the writing and publishing of this book. Nicole Luisi, the product manager, and Jean Holloway, when she was with Aileron as strategic development manager, have helped us steer the course, keep all the parts connected and moving in partnership with iUniverse and its editorial staff. Nicole assumed full responsibility for managing the project in its final stages and guided it to completion. Kelly McCracken, when she was with Aileron, launched the project, developed the publishing plan, and brought Marjorie Adler, editor, on board. Margie worked tirelessly and skillfully to shape the manuscript so that it serves its content and my intention. It has been a great pleasure to work with her.

My friend Janice Phelps Williams was very kind to review the manuscript and to offer many helpful editorial suggestions.

My words do not fully express my immense gratitude to Dr. Gipsie Ranney, a colleague for more than thirty years. She reviewed, with great care, an early draft of the manuscript. Her close association with Dr. Deming, her critical eye, and her deep knowledge of statistical thinking enabled her to make an extremely valuable contribution to the text. She is not responsible for any errors I may have committed.

I thank Terry Balderson for more than two decades of friendship and interesting, stimulating conversation. Terry is the "Fifth Business" in the lives of his friends, an invisible manager of human interactions. He makes the links that make it possible for things to happen. He made this book possible by sending some of my previous writing about Dr. Deming to Clay.

I thank Don Gschwind for his suggestions on the rifle sighting process. His knowledge of target shooting helped to improve my aim in the chapter on tampering. Don is a marksman, skeet shooter, engineer, and retired senior executive of a major manufacturing business.

Two people have been major influences on the professional direction of my life. Dr. John R. Schuck Jr. was a mentor, doctoral adviser, and friend. He broadened my knowledge of psychology and appreciation for theory and its practical application. Dr. John D. Hromi managed the department where I first worked when joining Ford. John saw my interest in the disciplines of quality and encouraged me to join the American Society for Quality Control (ASQC, now ASQ) and contribute articles to its publications. He made it possible to satisfy my professional interests in ways that I could not at Ford, until Dr. Deming came on the scene.

Two senior executives, officers of the Ford Motor Company, provided the leadership that Deming required as a condition for his commitment to the company. Jim Bakken guided Deming's intervention in the company. Jim gave me the opportunity to be part of the Ford transformation during the 1980s, from the beginning of Deming's involvement with the company. Don Petersen, while CEO and then as chairman of Ford, demonstrated his support of Dr. Deming through his meetings with him, public statements, and other communications. He even sat through one of my presentations, which, I discovered from his questions, was knowledge he already had.

I was fortunate to learn from Dr. Russell Ackoff. He was a genius and a man whom I came to know in seminars and discussions at Ford and other venues. He was an astute observer of the human condition, of management folly, and he was generous in sharing his knowledge.

Professor David Chambers was Deming's friend and his alter ego while consulting to Ford. I learned much from him about statistical thinking and the teaching of statistics, as well as what David called the "melt-down" technique that Deming applied to those who refused to acknowledge what they didn't know.

I appreciate the work of Dr. Joseph F. Castellano, professor of accounting, the University of Dayton, Ohio. He has introduced Deming's teaching to his MBA students. Joe used some of my earlier writings for his classes and encouraged me to write this book. He said it was needed.

It has been a pleasure to know Dr. H. Thomas Johnson, professor of management and self-described recovering management accountant. Tom makes the case for revising financial management and accounting practice guided by systems theory and Deming's System of Profound Knowledge.

I thank Dr. Deming's secretary, the late Cecelia (Ceil) Kilian, for her contribution to his impressive ability to accomplish so much.

I worked for ten years with the Deming family on the board of the W. Edwards Deming Institute. In addition to my own experiences with Dr. Deming over thirteen years, I learned much from them about the person who was their father and grandfather. Thanks to Diana, Linda, Kevin, and Vincent for the heartwarming and often humorous stories of their father.

My wife, Shige, has given me love beyond measure. She makes my life whole.

NOTES

Prelude

1 W. Edwards Deming, *The New Economics for Industry, Government, Education*, 2nd ed. (Cambridge, MA: MIT Press, 1994), 96–97.

2 Max DePree, *Leadership Jazz* (New York: DoubleDay Currency, 1992), 44, 103.

3 "Transcending Jazz," Elizabeth Farnsworth interviews saxophonist Joshua Redman, *PBS Newshour*, April 26, 2000.

4 Deming described his professional relationship with Ford in his *Code of Professional Conduct*, a six-page document he submitted to the company, which outlined the mutual obligations of the consultant and the client. W. Edwards Deming, A Code of Professional Conduct, @ *International Statistical Review* 40, no. 2 (August 1972): 215–219.

5 Edward M. Baker, "Signal Detection Theory Analysis of Quality Control," *Journal of Quality Technology* 7, no. 2 (April 1975): 62–71. Edward M. Baker and John R. Schuck, "Use of Signal Detection Theory to Clarify Problems of Evaluating Performance in Industry," *Organizational Behavior and Human Performance* 13, no. 3 (June 1975): 307–317.

6 These included Ford's businesses in Argentina, Brazil, Mexico, Venezuela, South Africa, and Windsor Export Supply in Canada.

7 www.deming.org.

8 W. Edwards Deming, *The New Economics for Industry, Government, Education*, 2nd ed. (Cambridge, MA: MIT Press 1994); *Out of the Crisis* (Cambridge, MA: MIT Center for Advanced Engineering Study, 1986), chapter 2.

9 Russell L Ackoff, *Management in Small Doses* (New York: John Wiley & Sons, 1986), x.

10 W. Edwards Deming, "Foreword from the Editor," in Walter A. Shewhart, *Statistical Method from the Viewpoint of Quality Control*, The Graduate School, The Department of Agriculture, Washington, 1939, iv.

11 Rosamund Stone Zander and Benjamin Zander, *The Art of Possibility: Transforming Professional and Personal Life* (Boston: Harvard Business School Press, 2000), 3–4.

Chapter 1

12 Albert Einstein, "Religion and Science: Irreconcilable?" A response to a greeting sent by the Liberal Ministers' Club of New York City. Published in the *Christian Register*, June 1948. Published in *Ideas and Opinions* (New York: Crown Publishers, Inc.), 1954.

13 W. Edwards Deming, *Out of the Crisis* (Cambridge, MA: MIT Center for Advanced Engineering Study, 1986), chapter 3.

14 Henri Amiel, *Journal Intime of Henri-Frederic Amiel* 2 (22 Aug. 1873): 153, trans. by Mrs. Humphry Ward, 1889.

15 W. Edwards Deming, *Out of the Crisis* (Cambridge, MA: MIT Center for Advanced Engineering Study, 1986), chapter 3.

16 Robert Helibroner, *The Worldly Philosophers*, Simon & Schuster, 7th ed., 1999. Note: Although considered a socialist for most of his life, Heilbroner wrote that capitalism won and socialism failed. He complimented Milton Friedman, Friedrich Hayek, and Ludwig von Mises on their insistence of the free market's superiority. (Robert Heilbroner, Reflections, "The Triumph of Capitalism," the *New Yorker*, 64, January 23, 1989, 98–109.

17 Robert Heilbroner, *The Worldly Philosophers*, 5th ed., 282–283

18 Mark Skousen, "Who Deserved the Nobel Prize?" *The Freeman Ideas on Liberty* 46, no. 4 (April 1996), published by the Foundation for Economic Education, August 04, 2011.

19 Andrea Gabor, *The Man Who Discovered Quality* (New York: Random House Times Books, 1990), 53.

20 These lectures became Walter Shewhart's book, edited by Deming, *Statistical Method from the Viewpoint of Quality Control*.

21 W. Edwards Deming, *Out of the Crisis* (Cambridge, MA: MIT Center for Advanced Engineering Study, 1986), 25.

22 Daniel J. Boorstin, "History's Hidden Turning Points," *U.S. News & World Report*, April 22, 1991, 52–65.

23 Robertson Davies, *Fifth Business* (New York: Viking Press, 1970).

24 Ibid., 139.

25 Listed in Cecelia S. Kilian, *The World of W. Edwards Deming*, 2nd ed. (Knoxville, Tennessee: SPC Press, 1992).

26 David Halberstam, *The Reckoning* (New York: William Morrow and Company, Inc., 1966), 312.

27 Ibid., 312.

28 Sheet music can be found in the book by his secretary, Cecelia S. Kilian, *The World of W. Edwards Deming*, 2nd ed. (Knoxville, TN: SPC Press, 1992), chapter 19, and on the website of the W. Edwards Deming Institute, Deming.org.

29 W. Edwards Deming, *The New Economics for Industry, Government, Education*, 2nd ed., (Cambridge, MA: MIT Center for Advanced Engineering Study, 1994), 2.

30 W. Edwards Deming, *The New Economics for Industry, Government, Education*, 2nd ed., (Cambridge, MA: MIT Center for Advanced Engineering Study, 1994), 49.

31 Cecelia S. Kilian, *The World of W. Edwards Deming*, 2nd ed. (Knoxville, TN: SPC Press, 1992), 264. Ceil has in her book some heartwarming stories about and written by Deming and his incredible work ethic even in the face of personal adversity and health problems ... and hers too.

32 W. Edwards Deming, "My Seventh Trip to Japan," November 1965, reprinted in Cecelia S. Kilian, *The World of W. Edwards Deming*, 2nd ed. (Knoxville, TN: SPC Press, 1992), chapter 15.

33 Linda Deming Ratcliff, presentation at W. Edwards Deming Institute Annual Conference, October 15–16, 2011.

34 W. Edwards Deming, *Out of the Crisis* (Cambridge, MA: MIT Center for Advanced Engineering Study, 1986), 109.

Chapter 2

35 *The Essays of Arthur Schopenhauer*; Studies in Pessimism: Psychological Observations, translated by Thomas Bailey Saunders.

36 *Military Science and Technology* 1, no. 3: 3.

37 "Transformation for Betterment of Society," statement dated August 19, 1992 sent to Congressman Newt Gingrich.

38 W. Edwards Deming, *The New Economics for Industry, Government, Education*, 2nd ed., (Cambridge, MA: MIT Press, 1994), 22–23, 49.

39 W. Edwards Deming, *The New Economics for Industry, Government, Education*, 2nd ed., (Cambridge, MA: MIT Press, 1994), 22.

40 Ibid., 35.

41 Russell L. Ackoff, *The Democratic Corporation* (New York: Oxford University Press, 1994), 73–79.

42 See *Out of the Crisis*, chapter 11, 359, example 4.

43 See discussion in Nassim Nicholas Taleb, *Fooled by Randomness: The Hidden Role of Chance in Life and in the Markets*, 2nd ed. (New York: Random House, 2005), 152–153.

44 W. Edwards Deming, *Out of the Crisis* (Cambridge, MA: MIT Press, 1986), 167, 182.

45 Russell Ackoff, *Redesigning the Future: A Systems Approach to Societal Problems* (New York: John Wiley, 1974).

46 Jack Welch with Suzy Welch, *Winning* (New York: HarperCollins, 2005).

47 Deming, Memo to Dean of A Business School, December 18, 1972. See also *The New Economics for Industry, Government, Education* (Cambridge, MA: MIT Press, 1994), 143–144.

48 W. Edwards Deming, *Out of the Crisis* (Cambridge, MA: MIT Press, 1986), 59. See also, *The New Economics for Industry, Government, Education*, 2nd ed. (Cambridge, MA: MIT Press, 1994), 98.

49 Linda Deming Ratcliff, presentation at W. Edwards Deming Institute Annual Conference, October 15–16, 2011.

50 W. Edwards Deming, *Out of the Crisis* (Cambridge, MA: MIT Press, 1986), 173.

Chapter 3

51 Russell L. Ackoff, *Strategy & Leadership* 31, no. 3 (2003): 20.

52 Joseph Campbell, *Transformations of Myth Through Time* (New York: Perennial Library, Harper and Row Publishers, 1990), 1.

53 W. Edwards Deming, *The New Economics for Industry, Government, Education*, 2nd ed. (Cambridge, MA: MIT Press, 1994), 109–110.

54 Ibid., 60, 114.

55 Ibid., 123.

56 Ibid., 145–146.

57 Joseph Campbell with Bill Moyers, *The Power of Myth* (New York: Doubleday, 1988), 33.

58 Ibid., 13.

59 W. Edwards Deming, *The New Economics for Industry, Government, Education*, 2nd ed. (Cambridge, Massachusetts: MIT Press, 1994), 92.

60 Ibid., 123.

61 W. Edwards Deming, *The New Economics for Industry, Government, Education*, 2nd ed. (Cambridge, MA: MIT Press, 1994), 74–83; *Out of the Crisis* (Cambridge, MA: MIT Press, 1986), 152–153.

62 "Transformation for Betterment of Society," statement dated 19 August, 1992 sent to Congressman Newt Gingrich

63 From an idea of Joseph Campbell, Joseph Campbell with Bill Moyers, *The Power of Myth* (New York: Doubleday, 1988), 24.

64 W. Edwards Deming, *The New Economics for Industry, Government, Education*, 2nd ed. (Cambridge, MA: MIT Press, 1994), 23.

65 W. Edwards Deming, *Out of the Crisis* (Cambridge, MA: MIT Press, 1986), 54.

66 Ibid., 248–249.

67 Robert K. Greenleaf, *Servant Leadership: The Nature of Legitimate Power and Greatness* (New York: Paulist Press, 1977).

68 Plato, *The Republic,* translated by Benjamin Jowett, Book VII.

69 Warren Bennis, *On Becoming A Leader,* 3rd ed. (New York: Basic Books, 2009), 35, 26.

70 Joseph Campbell, *The Hero with a Thousand Faces* (Princeton, NJ: Princeton University Press, 1949).

71 Cyril Morong, "The Calling of the Entrepreneur," *The New Leaders: The Business Bulletin for Transformative Leadership*, November/December 1992.

72 Ibid.

73 W. Edwards Deming, *Out of the Crisis* (Cambridge, MA: MIT Press, 1986), 155.

74 Ibid., 150. See also "deadly diseases of management," chapters 2 and 3.

75 W. Edwards Deming, *The New Economics for Industry, Government, Education*, 2nd ed. (Cambridge, MA: MIT Press, 1994), 92.

76 Ibid., xv.

77 W. Edwards Deming, *The New Economics for Industry, Government, Education*, 2nd ed. (Cambridge, MA: MIT Press, 1994), 56–57.

78 Ibid., 123.

Chapter 4

79 "Transcending Jazz," April 26, 2000, PBS NewsHour, Elizabeth Farnsworth interviews saxophonist Joshua Redman.

80 W. Edwards Deming, *The New Economics for Industry, Government, Education*, 2nd ed. (Cambridge, MA: MIT Press, 1994), 92.

81 Conversation between Dr. Russell Ackoff and Dr. Deming, the Deming Library, vol. 21, 1993. CC-M Production. Dr. Ackoff, a friend and associate of Deming for decades, was an influential systems theorist, thinker, practitioner, and teacher. He observed that problems require a systems view to understand and solve them.

82 W. Edwards Deming, *The New Economics for Industry, Government, Education*, 1st ed. and 2nd ed. (Cambridge, MA: MIT Press, 1993 and 1994).

83 "No knowledge of statistical theory, however profound, provides by itself a basis for deciding whether a proposed frame would be satisfactory for a study," W. Edwards Deming, "Principles of Professional Statistical Practice," the *Annals of Mathematical Statistics* 36, no. 6 (December 1965): 1886–7.

84 Baruch Spinoza, *Reflections and Maxims*, Dagobert D. Runes, Ed. (New York: Philosophical Library, 1965), 89.

85 *The Catholic Encyclopedia*, section I.

86 Fred Rosner, "The Life of Moses Maimonides: a Prominent Medieval Physician," *Einstein Quarterly, J. Biol. Med.* (2002) 19:125–128, 125.

87 Thomas À Kempis, *The Imitation of Christ* (Penguin Books, 1952), 11. Translation and introduction by Leo Sherley-Price, who said this of the author.

88 *The True Nature of Things* by Ven. Buddhadasa Bhikkhu.

89 Anagarika. B. Govinda, *Why I Am a Buddhist*, 11.

90 An Introduction to Sakugawa Koshiki Shorinjiryu Karatedo by Thomas Cauley, Zen Tohoku Karatedo Kempo Kumiai, Kyoshi 8th Dan Karatedo.

91 W. Edwards Deming, *The New Economics for Industry, Government, Education* 2nd ed. (Cambridge, MA: MIT Press, 1994), 93.

92 A file of his sheet music is available on W. Edwards Deming Institute, deming.org.

93 C. I. Lewis. *An Analysis of Knowledge and Valuation* (LaSalle, IL: the Open Court Publishing Company, 1946), 496–497.

94 Violinist Hilary Hahn, January 29, 2014, *Tavis Smiley Show*, PBS.

95 See the W. Edwards Deming Institute website, deming.org, and the book written by Cecelia S. Kilian, his assistant for four decades, *The World of W. Edwards Deming*, 2nd ed. (Knoxville, TN: SPC Press, 1992).

Chapter 5

96 W. Edwards Deming, *Out of the Crisis* (Cambridge, MA: MIT Press, 1986), 286.

97 C. I. Lewis, *An Analysis of Knowledge and Valuation* (LaSalle, IL: the Open Court Publishing Company, 1950), 256.

98 C. I. Lewis, *An Analysis of Knowledge and Valuation* (LaSalle, IL: the Open Court Publishing Company, 1946), 4.

99 W. Edwards Deming, *The New Economics for Industry, Government, Education*, 2nd ed. (Cambridge, MA: MIT Press, 1994), 100–102.

100 Ibid., 102–106.

101 Ibid., 149.

102 C. I. Lewis, *Mind and the World Order: Outline of a Theory of Knowledge* (New York: Dover, 1956), chapter 2, "The Given in Experience."

103 Walter A. Shewhart, *Statistical Method from the Viewpoint of Quality Control* (New York: Dover Publications, 1986), 20.

104 W. Edwards Deming, *The New Economics for Industry, Government, Education*, 2nd ed. (Cambridge, MA: MIT Press, 1994), 101–103.

105 Roz Chast, "Diary Of A Cat," the *New Yorker*, Sep. 7, 1987.

Chapter 6

106 "Einstein's genius changed science's perception of gravity," *Science News*, October 17, 2015.

107 Walter A. Shewhart, *Statistical Method from the Viewpoint of Quality Control* (New York: Dover Publications, 1986), 85–86.

108 W. Edwards Deming, *Out of the Crisis* (Cambridge, MA: MIT Press, 1986), 278–279.

109 W. Edwards Deming, *The New Economics for Industry, Government, Education*, 2nd ed. (Cambridge, MA: MIT Press, 1994), 36

110 Jay W. Forrester, *Industrial Dynamics* (Cambridge, MA: Productivity Press, 1961), 2, 344–5.

111 W. Edwards Deming, *Out of the Crisis* (Cambridge, MA: MIT Press, 1986), 19.

112 Ibid., 317.

113 W. Edwards Deming, "On the Use of Theory," *Industrial Quality Control* 13, no. 1 (July 1956): 1.

114 W. Edwards Deming, *Out of the Crisis* (Cambridge, MA: MIT Press, 1986), 403–404.

115 Epictetus, *The Enchiridion*, number 46, in *All The Works of Epictetus, Which are Now Extant*, translated by Elizabeth Carter, p. 408. First published by Hulton Bradley, Dublin, 1759.

116 W. Edwards Deming, *The New Economics for Industry, Government, Education,* 2nd ed. (Cambridge, MA: MIT Press, 1994), 102.

117 W. Edwards Deming, *Sample Design in Business Research* (New York: John Wiley & Sons, 1960), 243.

118 Walter A. Shewhart, *Statistical Method from the Viewpoint of Quality Control* (New York: Dover Publications, 1986), 149.

119 Ibid., 45–46.

120 W. Edwards Deming, *The New Economics for Industry, Government, Education,* 2nd ed. (Cambridge, MA: MIT Press, 1994), 131–132.

121 Ibid., 131–133.

122 W. Edwards Deming, *The New Economics for Industry, Government, Education,* 2nd ed. (Cambridge, MA: MIT Press, 1994), 54.

123 W. Edwards Deming, "On the Use of Theory," *Industrial Quality Control* 13, no. 1 (July 1956): 2.

124 W. Edwards Deming, *Out of the Crisis* (Cambridge, MA: MIT Press, 1986), 88–92

125 C. I. Lewis, *An Analysis of Knowledge and Valuation* (LaSalle, IL: the Open Court Publishing Company, 1946), 4.

126 Deming's forward to Walter Shewhart's book, *Statistical Method from the Viewpoint of Quality Control* (Graduate School, US Dept. of Agriculture 1939. Reprinted 1986, Dover), iii–iv.

127 C. I. Lewis, *An Analysis of Knowledge and Valuation* (LaSalle, IL: the Open Court Publishing Company, 1946), 255.

128 Martin Luther King Jr., "The Three Dimensions of a Complete Life," a sermon delivered at the Unitarian Church of Germantown, Philadelphia, PA, 11 December 1960.

129 Benjamin Jowett, _The Republic of Plato_ (New York: Wiley, 1901).

130 W. Edwards Deming, _The New Economics for Industry, Government, Education_, 2nd ed. (Cambridge, MA: MIT Press, 1994), 23.

131 E. F. Schumacher, _A Guide for the Perplexed_ (New York: Harper & Row Perennial Library, 1977), 33–34. Schumacher cites Maurice Nicoll, _Living Time and the Integration of the Life_, (London: Vincent Stuart, 1952), chapter 1.

132 Alfred Korzybski, _Science and Sanity_, 4th ed. (Lakeville, CN: International Non-Aristotelian Library Publishing Company, 1958), first published in 1933.

133 Clarence Irving Lewis, _Mind and the World Order: Outline of a Theory of Knowledge_ (New York: Dover, 1956), 37–38.

134 Michael Polanyi, _Personal Knowledge: Towards a Post-critical Philosophy_, 1958, 4. Cited by David Turnbull, _Maps Are Territories: Science Is an Atlas_ (Chicago: University of Chicago Press, 1989).

135 Walter A. Shewhart, _Statistical Method from the Viewpoint of Quality Control_, Graduate School, Department of Agriculture (Washington, 1939; Dover, 1986), 154.

136 David Bohm, _Thought as a System_ (New York: Routledge, 1992), 129.

137 J. B. Harley, "Maps, Knowledge and Power," in D. Cosgrove and S. Daniels (eds.), _The Iconography of Landscape: Essays on the Symbolic Representation, Design and Use of Past Environments_ (Cambridge, UK: Cambridge University Press, 1988), 300.

138 Clarence Irving Lewis, _Mind and the World Order: Outline of a Theory of Knowledge_ (New York: Dover, 1956), 55.

139 David Turnbull, _Maps Are Territories: Science Is an Atlas_ (Chicago: University of Chicago Press, 1989), 2.

140 From a transcript of a conversation between Professor Bohm and William M. Angelos videotaped in Amsterdam, Holland, in September 1990, by TELEAC, the Dutch Public Television Network.

141 J. B. Harley & D. Woodward (eds.), _The History of Cartography_ 1 (1987): xvi.

142 Clarence Irving Lewis, _Mind and the World Order: Outline of a Theory of Knowledge_ (New York: Dover, 1956), 51–52, 140, 235.

143 Ibid., 118.

144 Ibid., 55.

145 J. Bronowski, *Science and Human Values* (New York: Harper & Row, 1965), 20.

146 Immanuel Kant, *Prolegomena to Any Future Metaphysics That Will Be Able to Come Forward as Science*, first published 1783, translated by James W. Ellington (Indianapolis: Hackett Publishing Company, 1977). He also discussed it in his book *Critique of Pure Reason*.

147 Deming mentioned this in his book *Sample Design in Business Research* (New York: John Wiley & Sons, 1960), 23.

148 From a transcript of a conversation between Professor Bohm and William M. Angelos videotaped in Amsterdam, Holland, in September 1990, by TELEAC, the Dutch Public Television Network.

149 Russell L. Ackoff, *Creating the Corporate Future* (New York: John Wiley & Sons, 1981), 20–21.

150 Harry Weinberg, *Levels of Knowing and Existence: Studies in General Semantics* (New York: Harper & Row, 1959), 59–60.

151 W. Edwards Deming, *The New Economics for Industry, Government, Education*, 2nd ed. (Cambridge, MA: MIT Press, 1994), 92.

152 Ibid., 103.

153 "10 Questions for Alan Greenspan," *Time*, Nov. 4, 2013, 72.

154 Gregory Bateson, *Mind and Nature: A Necessary Unity* (New York: Bantam Books, 1988), 30.

155 Alfred Korzybski, *Science and Sanity*, 4th ed. (Lakeville, CN: International Non-Aristotelian Library Publishing Company, 1958), 35.

156 Gregory Bateson and Mary Catherine Bateson, *Angels Fear: Towards an Epistemology of the Sacred* (New York: Bantam Books, 1988), 161.

157 Fritjof Capra, *The Web of Life* (New York: Anchor Books Doubleday, 1996), chapter 11.

158 Clarence Irving Lewis, *Mind and the World-Order: Outline of a Theory of Knowledge* (New York: Dover, 1956), 24–25.

159 Ibid., x, 14.

160 Paul Buckley and F. David Peat, eds., *Glimpsing Reality: Ideas in Physics and the Link to Biology* (Toronto: University of Toronto Press, 1996), 3–16.

161 Fritjof Capra, *Uncommon Wisdom* (New York: Bantam Books, 1988), 141–142.

162 Fritjof Capra, *The Tao of Physics*, 3rd ed. (Boston: Shambala, 1991), 140.

163 Milton Friedman, "Inflation and Unemployment," Nobel Lecture, *Journal of Political Economy* 85, no. 3 (June 1977): 452.

164 W. Edwards Deming, *The New Economics for Industry, Government, Education*, 2nd ed. (Cambridge, Massachusetts: MIT Press, 1994), 104.

165 W. Edwards Deming, *Out of the Crisis* (Cambridge, MA: MIT Press, 1986), 282.

166 W. Edwards Deming, *The New Economics for Industry, Government, Education*, 2nd ed., (Cambridge, MA: MIT Press, 1994), 105.

167 David Turnbull, *Maps Are Territories: Science Is an Atlas* (Chicago: University of Chicago Press, 1989), 10.

168 Clarence Irving Lewis, *Mind and the World Order: Outline of a Theory of Knowledge*, (New York: Dover, 1956), 10–12. Lewis, through his book *Mind and the World Order*, had a great influence on Dr. Deming's approach to theory of knowledge.

169 Stephen Hawking and Leonard Mlodinow, *The Grand Design*, 2010. Also Stephen Hawking during a debate with Roger Penrose in 1994 at the Isaac Newton Institute for Mathematical Sciences at the University of Cambridge, transcribed in *The Nature of Space and Time* (1996) by Stephen Hawking and Roger Penrose, 121.

170 Harry Prosch, *Michael Polanyi: A Critical Exposition* (State University of New York Press, 1986), 89. Also in Werner Heisenberg, *Physics and Beyond*, Arnold J. Pomerans, trans. (New York: Harper, 1971), 63.

171 Fritjof Capra, *The Tao of Physics*, 3rd ed. (Boston: Shambala, 1991), 140–141.

Chapter 7

172 Epictetus, *The Golden Sayings*, XCIII.

173 W. Edwards Deming, *Out of the Crisis* (Cambridge, MA: MIT Press, 1986), 309, from Chaucer, *The Tale of Melibeus*.

174 Ibid., 475, from Shakespeare's *Richard II*, III, iv.

175 W. Edwards Deming, *Out of the Crisis* (Cambridge, MA: MIT Press, 1986), 285.

176 Alfred Korzybski, *Science and Sanity* 4th ed. (Lakeville, CN: International Non-Aristotelian Library Publishing Company, 1958), first published in 1933, 66–69.

177 W. Edwards Deming, *Out of the Crisis* (Cambridge, MA: MIT Press, 1986), 279.

178 Deming's forward to Walter Shewhart's book, *Statistical Method from the Viewpoint of Quality Control*, Graduate School, US Dept. of Agriculture, 1939. Reprinted with a new foreword by W Edwards Deming: Dover 1986, pp. iii–iv.

179 W. Edwards Deming, dedication to 1980 reprint of Shewhart, *Economic Control of Quality of Manufactured Product* (Van Nostrand, 1931, republished American Society for Quality Control, 1980).

180 W. Edwards Deming, *Out of the Crisis* (Cambridge, MA: MIT Press, 1986), 285.

181 Clarence Irving Lewis, *Mind and the World Order: Outline of a Theory of Knowledge* (New York: Dover, 1956), 409.

182 C. I. Lewis, *An Analysis of Knowledge and Valuation* (LaSalle, IL: Open Court Publishing Company, 1946), 400.

183 Eric Ostermeier, "George H.W. Bush: Hater of Broccoli," July 9, 2013, *Smart Politics*, Humphrey School of Public Affairs, University of Minnesota; Susan Bowerman, "Hate broccoli? Spinach? Blame your Genes," What We Eat, *Los Angeles Times*, February 19, 2007.

184 W. Edwards Deming, *Out of the Crisis* (Cambridge, MA: MIT Press, 1986), 276–277

185 Ibid., 274.

186 W. Edwards Deming, *The New Economics for Industry, Government, Education*, 2nd ed. (Cambridge, MA: MIT Press, 1994), 105.

187 Dr. Gipsie Ranney, personal communication.

188 W. Edwards Deming, *Out of the Crisis* (Cambridge, MA: MIT Press, 1986), 293.

189 Ibid., 276–296.

190 W. Edwards Deming, *The New Economics for Industry, Government, Education*, 2nd ed. (Cambridge, MA: MIT Press, 1994), 106.

191 W. Edwards Deming, *Sample Design in Business Research* (New York: John Wiley & Sons, 1960), 6.

192 W. Edwards Deming, *Out of the Crisis* (Cambridge, MA: MIT Press, 1986), 104.

193 Harry L. M. Artinian and Edward M. Baker, "Improving Quality: The Critical Hidden Link," *ASQC Annual Quality Transactions*, May 1988.

194 Irving J. Lee, *Language Habits in Human Affairs* (New York: Harper & Row, 1941), 118, from Edwin R. Embree, "Can college graduates read?" in *Saturday Review of Literature*, July 16, 1938, 4.

195 Harry Weinberg, *Levels of Knowing and Existence: Studies in General Semantics* (New York: Harper & Row, 1959), 62–64.

196 S.I. Hayakawa, *Language in Thought and Action* (New York: Harcourt Brace Javanovich), 1978.

197 Chris Argyris, _Overcoming Organizational Defenses_ (Boston: Allyn and Bacon, 1990), 88–89.

198 Irving J. Lee, _Language Habits in Human Affairs_ (New York: Harper & Row, 1941), 192–193.

199 Ibid., 192–193.

Chapter 8

200 Epictetus, _The Enchiridion_, number 28, in _All The Works of Epictetus, Which Are Now Extant_, translated by Elizabeth Carter, p. 395, first published by Hulton Bradley, Dublin, 1759.

201 W. Edwards Deming, "On the Use of Theory," _Industrial Quality Control_ 13, no. 1 (July 1956): 2.

202 J. B. Harley, "Maps, Knowledge and Power," in D. Cosgrove and S. Daniels (eds.), _The Iconography of Landscape: Essays on the Symbolic Representation, Design and Use of Past Environments_ (Cambridge, UK: Cambridge University Press, 1988), 277–312; quote is from 278.

203 Thomas Sowell, _A Conflict of Visions_ (New York: William Morrow, 1987), 217–218.

204 Russell L. Ackoff, _Creating the Corporate Future_ (New York: John Wiley & Sons, 1981), 8–12.

205 Arthur Koestler, _Janus: A Summing Up_ (New York: Vintage Books, 1979), 24–26.

206 Michael Polanyi and Harry Prosch, _Meaning_ (Chicago: The University of Chicago Press, 1977), 164–173; Harry Prosch, _Michael Polanyi: A Critical Exposition_ (State University of New York Press, 1986), 124–134.

207 Russell L. Ackoff, _Creating the Corporate Future_ (New York: John Wiley & Sons, 1981), 16.

208 W. Edwards Deming, _The New Economics for Industry, Government, Education_, 2nd ed. (Cambridge, MA: MIT Press, 1994) 41.

209 Russell L. Ackoff, _Creating the Corporate Future_, (New York: John Wiley & Sons, 1981), 16.

210 Ibid., 36–37.

211 Ibid., 17–19.

212 Ibid., 8–21.

213 Ibid., 20–21; 189–193.

214 W. Edwards Deming, *The New Economics for Industry, Government, Education*, 2nd ed. (Cambridge, MA: MIT Press, 1994), 33, 36, 154.

215 Ibid., 107.

216 J. Bronowski, *Science and Human Values* (New York: Harper and Row, 1965), 55.

217 W. Edwards Deming, *Out of the Crisis* (Cambridge, MA: MIT Press, 1986), 297.

218 Sharon Danann, "Cracking the Electronic Whip," *Harper's* magazine, August 1990.

219 Sharman Apt Russell, *Kill the Cowboy* (New York: Addison-Wesley, 1993).

220 Eliza Gray, "The Original Genius Bar," *Time*, July 22, 2013, 38–43; Fareed Zakaria, "The Future of Innovation: Can America Keep Pace?" *Time*, June 13, 2011, 30–32.

221 James O'Toole, *The Executive's Compass: Business and the Good Society* (New York: Oxford University Press, 1993).

222 W. Edwards Deming, *The New Economics for Industry, Government, Education*, 2nd ed. (Cambridge, MA: MIT Press, 1994), 29; *Out of the Crisis* (Cambridge, MA: MIT Press, 1986), 149.

223 W. Edwards Deming, *The New Economics for Industry, Government, Education*, 2nd ed., (Cambridge, MA: MIT Press, 1994), 90.

224 Ibid., 52, 81.

225 Ibid., 50–52.

226 Ibid., 41.

227 W. Edwards Deming, *Out of the Crisis*, (Cambridge, MA: MIT Press, 1986), 24–26; W. Edwards Deming, *The New Economics for Industry, Government, Education*, 2nd ed., (Cambridge: MIT Press, 1994), 24.

228 J. Samuel Bois, *The Art of Awareness* (Dubuque, IA: Wm. C. Brown Company, 1966), 87–88.

229 W. Edwards Deming, *Out of the Crisis* (Cambridge, MA: MIT Press, 1986), 49–50; 139–141.

230 W. Edwards Deming, *The New Economics for Industry, Government, Education*, 2nd ed. (Cambridge, MA: MIT Press, 1994), 217–221.

231 Kosaku Yoshida, "Revisiting Deming's 14 Points in Light of Japanese Business Practices," *Quality Management Journal* 3, no. 1 (September 1995): 14–30.

232 Russell L. Ackoff, *Creating the Corporate Future* (New York: John Wiley & Sons, 1981), 42.

233 C. I. Lewis, *An Analysis of Knowledge and Valuation* (LaSalle, IL: Open Court Publishing Company, 1946), 371–372.

234 Ibid., 372–373.

235 Thomas S. Kuhn, *The Essential Tension: Selected Studies in the Scientific Tradition and Change* (Chicago: University of Chicago Press, 1977). George S. Howard, "The Role of Values in the Science of Psychology," *American Psychologist*, March 1985, 255–265; See also D. Allchin, "Values in Science and in Science Education," in B.J. Fraser and K. G. Tobin (eds.), *International Handbook of Science Education*, Kluwer Academic Publishers, Dordrecht, 1998 2:1083–1092.

236 W. Edwards Deming, *The New Economics for Industry, Government, Education*, 2nd ed. (Cambridge, MA: MIT Press, 1994), 93.

237 Russell L. Ackoff, *Creating the Corporate Future* (New York: John Wiley & Sons, 1981), 41.

238 Mortimer J. Adler, *The Great Ideas* (New York: Macmillan Publishing Company, 1992), 771.

239 W. Edwards Deming, "Principles of Professional Statistical Practice," the *Annals of Mathematical Statistics*, 36, no. 6 (December 1965): 1883–1900. A copy can be downloaded from the W. Edwards Deming Institute website, www.deming.org.

240 W. Edwards Deming, "Principles of Professional Statistical Practice," 1889.

Chapter 9

241 Donella, H. Meadows, "Whole Earth Models & Systems," *CoEvolution Quarterly*, Summer 1992.

242 Jay W. Forester, *Industrial Dynamics* (Cambridge, MA: Productivity Press, 1961), 1.

243 Ibid., 2–3.

244 Ibid., 1.

245 Ibid., 9.

246 Ibid., 2.

247 Russell L. Ackoff, "On Passing Through 80," Conference Proceedings, *Russell L. Ackoff and The Advent of Systems Thinking*, Villanova University March 4–6, 1999, 32–36; Interview with Russell L. Ackoff by Glenn Detrick, *Academy of Management Learning and Education* 1, no. 1 (September 2002).

248 Russell L. Ackoff, *Creating the Corporate Future* (New York: John Wiley & Sons: 1981), 246.

249 Gregory Bateson, *Mind and Nature: A Necessary Unity* (New York: Bantam Books, 1979), 39.

250 Russell Ackoff has defined a system and its properties in much of his writings over the years, for example, in *Creating the Corporate Future* (New York: John Wiley & Sons, 1981), 15–18; *The Democratic Corporation* (New York: Oxford University Press, 1994), 18–32.

251 W. Edwards Deming, *Out of the Crisis* (Cambridge, MA: MIT Press, 1986), 177.

252 Stafford Beer, *Platform for Change* (New York: John Wiley & Sons, 1978), 122.

253 The 14 Points were published in Deming's 1982 book, *Quality, Productivity, and Competitive Position*, chapter 2, and his 1986 book, *Out of the Crisis*, chapter 2. They preceded the publication of Deming's System of Profound Knowledge, but, as he explained in *The New Economics* (2nd ed., 1994, 93), the 14 Points follow from profound knowledge. All books were published by MIT Press, Cambridge, Massachusetts.

254 Stafford Beer, *Management Science* (New York: Doubleday & Company, 1968), 111–115. Beer used the term "cones of resolution" to describe the movement from the global measurements (e.g., profit and loss) seen by top management to the detail of lower level systems that contributed to those numbers.

255 Russell L. Ackoff, *The Democratic Corporation* (New York: Oxford University Press, 1994), 32–33.

256 Peter M. Senge, *The Fifth Discipline: The Art and practice of the Learning Organization* (New York: Doubleday, 1990); *The Fifth Discipline Fieldbook* (New York: Currency/Doubleday, 1994).

257 W. Edwards Deming, *The New Economics for Industry, Government, Education* (Cambridge, MA: MIT Press, 1994), 50.

258 Stafford Beer, *Brain of the Firm*, 2nd ed. (New York: John Wiley & Sons, 1981); *The Heart of Enterprise* (New York: John Wiley & Sons, 1979).

259 Russell Ackoff, "Stafford Beer," *Systems Practice* 3, no. 3 (June 1990): 223.

260 W. Edwards Deming, *Out of the Crisis* (Cambridge, MA: MIT Press, 1986), 87.

261 Dr. Gipsie Ranney, personal communication.

262 W. Edwards Deming, *Out of the Crisis* (Cambridge, MA: MIT Press, 1986), 77.

263 Donella, H. Meadows, "Whole Earth Models & Systems," *CoEvolution Quarterly*, Summer 1992, 101–102.

264 W. Edwards Deming, *Quality, Productivity, and Competitive Position* (Cambridge, MA: MIT Press, 1982), 184. This is a compilation of Deming's seminar notes,

which became his book _Out of the Crisis_. Also stated at his seminar, September 22, 1989.

265 W. Edwards Deming, _The New Economics for Industry, Government, Education_, 2nd ed. (Cambridge, MA: MIT Press, 1994), 129–131.

266 Ibid., 64.

267 "Transcending Jazz," April 26, 2000, PBS NewsHour, Elizabeth Farnsworth interviews saxophonist Joshua Redman.

268 Kareem Abdul-Jabbar, _Tavis Smiley Show_, PBS, February 4, 2016.

269 Willis W. Harman, "Business as a Component of the Global Ecology," _Noetic Sciences Review_, Autumn 1991, 19.

270 Dr. Gipsie Ranney, personal communication.

271 W. Edwards Deming, _The New Economics for Industry, Government, Education_, 2nd ed. (Cambridge, MA: MIT Press, 1994), 44–45. _Out of the Crisis_ (Cambridge, MA: MIT Press, 1986), 123.

272 H. Thomas Johnson, "Manage a Living System, Not a Ledger," _Manufacturing Engineering_ 137, no. 6 (December 2006).

273 Willis W. Harman, "Business as a Component of the Global Ecology," _Noetic Sciences Review_ (Autumn 1991): 22.

274 W. Edwards Deming, _Out of the Crisis_ (Cambridge, MA: MIT Press, 1986), 121–127.

275 Based on table in W. Edwards Deming, _The New Economics for Industry, Government, Education_, 2nd ed. (Cambridge, MA: MIT Press, 1994), 67.

276 W. Edwards Deming, _The New Economics for Industry, Government, Education_, (Cambridge, MA: MIT Press, 1994), 30, 96.

277 W. Edwards Deming, _Out of the Crisis_ (Cambridge, MA: MIT Press, 1986), 123.

278 Motoko Rich, "Latest Cheating Scandal Reignites Debate Over Tests' Role," _New York Times_, April 3, 2013, A13 New York edition.

279 W. Edwards Deming, _Out of the Crisis_ (Cambridge, MA: MIT Press, 1986), 76.

280 H.T. Johnson, and R.S. Kaplan, _Relevance Lost: The Rise and Fall of Management Accounting_ (Boston: Harvard Business School Press, 1992).

281 H.T. Johnson, _Relevance Regained: From Top-Down Control to Bottom-Up Empowerment_ (New York: The Free Press, 1992).

282 H. Thomas Johnson, "A Different Perspective on Quality: Bringing Management to Life," keynote presentation to the W. Edwards Deming Institute Fall Conference, October 1997.

283 H. Thomas Johnson and Anders Bröms, *Profit Beyond Measure: Extraordinary Results through Attention to Work and People* (New York: The Free Press, 2000). Also see Johnson's paper, "A Recovering Management Accountant Reflects on His Journey through the World of Cost Management," keynote presentation to the Second International Symposium on Accounting History, Osaka City University, Osaka, Japan, August 8, 2001. H. Thomas Johnson, "Manage a Living System, Not a Ledger," *Manufacturing Engineering* 137, no. 6 (December 2006). H. Thomas Johnson, "Lean Dilemma: Choose System Principles or Management Accounting Controls—not Both," chapter 1 in *Lean Accounting: Best Practices for Sustainable Integration*, edited by Joe Stenzel (Hoboken, NJ: John Wiley & Sons, Inc., 2007).

284 For example, Joseph F. Castellano, Saul Young, and Harper A. Roehm, "The Seven Fatal Flaws of Performance Measurement," *CPA Journal* LXXIV, no. 6 (June 2004): 32–35; Harper A. Roehm and Joseph F. Castellano, "The Danger of Relying on Accounting Numbers Alone," *Management Accounting Quarterly* 1, no. 1 (Fall 1999): 4–9; Joseph F. Castellano, Kenneth Rosenzweig, and Harper A. Roehm, "Unethical Distortion of Financial Numbers: The Role of Corporate Culture," *Management Accounting Quarterly Online*, Summer 2004.

285 W. Edwards Deming, *Out of the Crisis* (Cambridge, MA: MIT Press, 1986), 23–96.

286 H. Thomas Johnson and Anders Bröms, *Profit Beyond Measure: Extraordinary Results through Attention to Work and People* (New York: the Free Press, 2000), 142–151, 219–224.

287 Ibid., 145–148.

288 Stafford Beer, *Management Science* (New York: Doubleday & Company, 1968), 111–115.

289 H. Thomas Johnson and Anders Bröms, *Profit Beyond Measure: Extraordinary Results through Attention to Work and People* (New York: The Free Press, 2000), 142–151.

290 Lawrence M. Miller, *Barbarians to Bureaucrats: Corporate Life Cycle Strategies* (New York: Clarkson N. Potter, Inc., 1989).

291 H. Thomas Johnson, "Lean Dilemma: Choose System Principles or Management Accounting Controls—not Both," chapter 1 in *Lean Accounting: Best Practices for Sustainable Integration*, edited by Joe Stenzel (Hoboken, NJ: John Wiley & Sons, Inc., 2007).

292 H. Thomas Johnson, "How Toyota Ran Off the Road—and How It Can Get Back on Track," Systems Thinking in Action: Leverage Points Blog, posted by

Janice Molloy, Feb 09, 2010; "Tom Johnson on Toyota crisis," The Lean Edge, February 18, 2010, http://theleanedge.org, 462.

293 W. Edwards Deming, *Out of the Crisis* (Cambridge, MA: MIT Press, 1986), 123.

294 H. Thomas Johnson, "Management by Financial Targets Isn't Lean," *Manufacturing Engineering* magazine, December 2007.

295 Edward M. Baker, "Springing Ourselves from the Measurement Trap," in Peter Senge, Charlotte Roberts, Richard B. Ross, Bryan J. Smith, and Art Kleiner, *The Fifth Discipline Fieldbook*, (New York: Doubleday Currency, 1994), 454–457.

Chapter 11

296 Russell L. Ackoff, *The Democratic Corporation* (New York: Oxford University Press, 1994), 22.

297 Margaret J. Wheatley, "De-engineering The Corporation," *Industry Week*, April 18, 1994, 18.

298 Margaret J. Wheatley, *Leadership and the New Science* (San Francisco: Berrett-Koehler, 2006).

299 Russell L. Ackoff, *The Democratic Corporation* (New York: Oxford University Press, 1994), 32–33.

300 See the following discussions of performance and compensation: W. Edwards Deming, *Out of the Crisis* (Cambridge, MA: MIT Press, 1986), 101–126; Brian L. Joiner, *Fourth Generation Management* (New York: McGraw-Hill, 1994), 235–249; Joyce Orsini, "Bonuses: What is the Impact?" *National Productivity Review*, Spring 1987, 180–184; Peter R. Scholtes, *The Leader's Handbook* (New York: McGraw-Hill, 1998), 293–368.

301 Gregory Bateson, *Mind and Nature: A Necessary Unity* (New York: Bantam Books, 1988).

302 Michael Rothschild, *Bionomics: Economy as Ecosystem* (New York: Henry Holt and Company, 1990).

303 Ibid., 39–40.

304 Gregory Bateson, *Steps to an Ecology of Mind* (New York: Ballantine Books, 1972), 450–451.

305 Fritjof Capra, *The Web of Life* (New York: Anchor Books Doubleday, 1996), 6–7.

306 Adam Smith, *An Inquiry Into The Nature and Causes of The Wealth of Nations* (New York: Modern Library, 1937), 423.

307 Fritjof Capra, *The Web of Life* (New York: Anchor Books Doubleday, 1996), 62.

308 Michael Rothschild, *Bionomics: Economy as Ecosystem* (New York: Henry Holt and Company, 1990), 336.

309 Alfie Kohn, *No Contest: The Case Against Competition* (Boston: Houghton Mifflin Company, 1986); Stephen Jay Gould, "The Wheel of Fortune and the Wedge of Progress," *Natural History*, March 1989, 14–21.

310 Stafford Beer, *Brain of the Firm*, 2nd ed. (New York: John Wiley & Sons, 1981), 162.

311 H. Thomas Johnson and Anders Bröms, *Profit Beyond Measure: Extraordinary Results through Attention to Work and People* (New York: Free Press, 2000), 142–151, 219–224.

312 Stafford Beer, *Management Science* (New York: Doubleday & Company, 1968), 117–131.

313 H. Thomas Johnson, "A Different Perspective on Quality: Bringing Management to Life," Keynote presentation to the W. Edwards Deming Institute Fall Conference, October 1997.

Chapter 12

314 General Robert T. Herres, former chairman and CEO of USAA, *Aide* magazine, December 1993, 8.

315 Daniel Puig, "Gregory Bateson's Criteria of Mental Process as a Tool for Musical Composition with Guided Improvisation," The Global Composition Conference on Sound, Media, and the Environment, Darmstadt-Dieburg, Germany, July 25–28, 2012.

316 Interview with Tavis Smiley, PBS, Oct. 23, 2013.

317 Harvey Seifter and Peter Economy, *Leadership Ensemble: Lessons in Collaborative Management from the World-Famous Conductorless Orchestra* (New York: Henry Holt and Company, 2001).

318 Gregory Bateson, *Mind and Nature: A Necessary Unity* (New York: Bantam Books, 1988), 13.

319 W. Edwards Deming, "Dedication, to reprint of Walter A. Shewhart," *Economic Control of Quality of Manufactured Product*, republished by American Society for Quality Control, 1980.

320 Interview with Dave Koz, Tavis Smiley, PBS, December 4, 2013.

321 Reported in *New York Post*, Apr. 23, 2011.

322 *The Focus*, Egon Zehnder International's online publication.

323 Max DePree, _Leadership Jazz_ (New York: DoubleDay Currency, 1992), 156–157.

324 Ibid., 44.

325 Ibid., 103.

326 Peter B. Vaill, _Managing as a Performing Art: New Ideas for a World of Chaotic Change_ (San Francisco: Josey-Bass, 1989), 124.

327 Dr. Jaime A. Hermann designed and facilitated the process.

328 This enterprise is identified by name because Mac has given many public talks about changes in the business. The author consulted to the company. According to _Furniture Today_ 37, no. 11 (Nov. 12, 2013), Gallery Furniture's annual revenue for 2012 is around $125 million. It now has two locations, 250 employees, and is number fifty of the one hundred top furniture stores in the United States.

329 The author.

330 The author was the consultant.

Chapter 13

331 W. Edwards Deming, "On the Use of Theory," _Industrial Quality Control_ 13, (July 1, 1956): 3.

332 W. Edwards Deming, _Out of the Crisis_ (Cambridge, MA: MIT Press, 1986), 465.

333 W. Edwards Deming, _The New Economics for Industry, Government, Education,_ 2nd ed. (Cambridge, MA: MIT Press, 1994), 33.

334 W. Edwards Deming, _Sample Design in Business Research_ (New York: John Wiley & Sons, 1960), v.

335 W. Edwards Deming, _The New Economics for Industry, Government, Education,_ 2nd ed. (Cambridge, MA: MIT Press, 1994), 208–210.

336 Plato, _The Republic._

337 W. Edwards Deming, "Some Principles of the Shewhart Methods of Quality Control," _Mechanical Engineering_ 66 (1944).

338 W. Edwards Deming, _The New Economics for Industry, Government, Education,_ 2nd ed. (Cambridge, MA: MIT Press, 1994), 177–178.

339 W. Edwards Deming, _Out of the Crisis_ (Cambridge, MA: MIT Press, 1986), 56–58.

340 W. Edwards Deming, "On The Use of Theory," _Industrial Quality Control_ 13, no. 1 (July 1956): 2. Readers interested in further discussion of this are referred to Walter A. Shewhart, "Some Comments on Symbols and Nomenclature," in

355 Walter A. Shewhart, *Statistical Method from the Viewpoint of Quality Control* (New York: Dover Publications, 1986), 47.

356 W. Edwards Deming, *The New Economics for Industry, Government, Education*, 2nd ed. (Cambridge, MA: MIT Press, 1994), 165.

357 W. Edwards Deming, *Out of the Crisis* (Cambridge, MA: MIT Press, 1986), 292.

358 W. Edwards Deming, *The New Economics for Industry, Government, Education*, 2nd ed. (Cambridge, MA: MIT Press, 1994), Chapter 7.

359 W. Edwards Deming, *The New Economics for Industry, Government, Education*, 2nd ed. (Cambridge, MA: MIT Press, 1994), 166–167.

360 W. Edwards Deming, *The New Economics for Industry, Government, Education*, 2nd ed. (Cambridge, MA: MIT Press, 1994), 176–177 and *Out of the Crisis* (Cambridge, MA: MIT Press, 1986), 334–335.

361 W. Edwards Deming, *Some Theory of Sampling* (New York: Dover Publications, 1966), chapter 7. Deming also discusses this subject in various papers, e.g. "On probability as a basis for action," *The American Statistician* 29, no. 4 (1975): 146–152; "On the distinction between enumerative and analytic surveys," *Journal of the American Statistical Association* 48 (1953): 244–255; "The Logic of Evaluation," *Handbook of Evaluation Research*, vol. 1 (London: Sage Publications LTD, 1975), 53–68.

362 Letter to Theodore D. Woolsey, director, National Center for Health Statistics, April 3, 1972.

363 Ronald D. Moen, Thomas W. Nolan, Lloyd P. Provost, *Improving Quality Through Planned Experimentation* (New York: McGraw-Hill, 1991), 19–22.

364 W. Edwards Deming, *Out of the Crisis* (Cambridge, MA: MIT Press, 1986), 255.

365 Ibid., 353.

366 W. Edwards Deming, *Sample Design in Business Research* (New York: John Wiley & Sons, 1960), 23.

Chapter 14

367 Brian Joiner, *Fourth Generation Management: The New Business Consciousness* (New York: McGraw-Hill, Inc., 1994), 127.

368 See for example: Georgantzas NC and Orsini JN. 2003. Tampering dynamics. In *Proceedings of the 21st International System, Dynamics Society Conference*, 20–24 July, New York, NY. Nancy Roberts, et al., *Introduction to Computer Simulation: A System Dynamics Modeling Approach* (Portland, OR: Productivity Press, 1983).

The "Beer Game" simulation in Peter M Senge, *The Fifth Discipline: The Art and Practice of the Learning Organization* (New York: Doubleday/Currency, 1990).

369 W. Edwards Deming, *The New Economics for Industry, Government, Education,* chapter 9, and *Out of the Crisis*, 327–332.

370 Nassim Nicholas Taleb, *Fooled by Randomness: The Hidden Role of Chance in Life and in the Markets*, 2nd ed. (New York: Random House Trade Paperbacks, 2005).

371 W. Edwards Deming, *The New Economics for Industry, Government, Education,* 2nd ed. (Cambridge, MA: MIT Press, 1994), 195.

372 B. F. Skinner, Pigeons in a Pelican, *American Psychologist* 15, no. 1 (January 1960): 28–37.

373 W. Edwards Deming, *Out of the Crisis* (Cambridge, MA: MIT Press, 1986), 318, 327.

374 Ibid., 141–142, 330.

375 The following reference is a highly technical book that discusses statistical and feedback systems of control: George E. P. Box, Alberto Luceño, Maria del Carmen Paniagua-Quinones, *Statistical Control by Monitoring and Adjustment* (New Jersey: Wiley, 2009), Series in Probability and Statistics.

376 See for example Nancy Roberts, et al., *Introduction to Computer Simulation: A System Dynamics Modeling Approach* (Portland, OR: Productivity Press, 1983); Peter M Senge, *The Fifth Discipline: The Art and Practice of the Learning Organization* (New York: Doubleday/Currency, 1990), 57–126; Donella Meadows, *Leverage Points: Places to Intervene in a System,* the Sustainability Institute, 1999.

377 W. Edwards Deming, *The New Economics for Industry, Government, Education,* 2nd ed. (Cambridge, MA: MIT Press, 1994) 200–201.

378 Peter M Senge, *The Fifth Discipline: The Art and Practice of the Learning Organization* (New York: Doubleday/Currency, 1990), 86–87.

379 W. Edwards Deming, *The New Economics for Industry, Government, Education,* 2nd ed. (Cambridge, MA: MIT Press, 1994), 26.

380 Robert Rosenthal and Lenore Jacobson, *Pygmalion in the Classroom* (New York: Holt, Rinehart, and Winston, 1968).

Chapter 15

381 W. Edwards Deming, *The New Economics for Industry, Government, Education,* 2nd ed. (Cambridge, MA: MIT Press, 1994), 108.

382 Ibid., 107–108.

383 Ibid., 93–94.

384 Ibid., 173–174.

385 Frederick Winslow Taylor, _The Principles of Scientific Management_ (New York: Harper & Brothers, 1911).

386 Lillian M. Gilbreth, _The Psychology of Management: The Function of the Mind in Determining, Teaching, and Installing Methods of Least Waste_ (New York: The Macmillan Company, 1914), especially chapter 2 on individuality.

387 Ibid., chapter 2.

388 Frederick Hertzberg, "One More Time: How Do You Motivate Employees?" _Harvard Business Review_, January-February 1968.

389 W. Edwards Deming, _The New Economics for Industry, Government, Education_, 2nd ed. (Cambridge, MA: MIT Press, 1994), 110–112.

390 Ibid., 108–115, 121–122.

391 Alfie Kohn, _Punished by Rewards_ (New York: Houghton Mifflin Company, 1993).

392 Joseph Wood Krutch, _The Measure of Man_ (New York: Grosset & Dunlap, 1954), 105.

393 W. Edwards Deming, _The New Economics for Industry, Government, Education_, 2nd ed. (Cambridge, MA: MIT Press, 1994), 64.

394 Lawrence M. Miller, _Barbarians to Bureaucrats: Corporate Life Cycle Strategies_ (New York: Clarkson N. Potter, Inc.), 175.

395 W. Edwards Deming, _The New Economics for Industry, Government, Education_, 2nd ed. (Cambridge, MA: MIT Press, 1994), 109.

396 Frederick Hertzberg, Bernard Mausner, Barbara Snyderman, _The Motivation to Work_, 2nd ed. (New York: John Wiley and Sons, 1959); "An Interview with Frederick Hertzberg," _The Management Review_, July 1971, 2–15.

397 Abraham H. Maslow, _Motivation and Personality_ (New York: Harper and Bros., 1954).

398 Douglas McGregor, _The Human Side of Enterprise_ (New York: McGraw-Hill, 1960).

399 W. Edwards Deming, _Out of the Crisis_ (Cambridge, MA: MIT Press, 1986), 75, 248–249.

Chapter 16

400 Mark Van Aken Williams, *The Burlesque of Graceless Acting* (Harbor Springs, Michigan: Tylers Field, 2013), 7.

401 W. Edwards Deming, *Out of the Crisis* (Cambridge, MA: MIT Press, 1986), 101–110.

402 W. Edwards Deming, *The New Economics for Industry, Government, Education,* 2nd ed. (Cambridge, MA: MIT Press, 1994), 73.

403 W. Edwards Deming, *Out of the Crisis* (Cambridge, MA: MIT Press, 1986), 109. *The New Economics for Industry, Government, Education,* 2nd ed. (Cambridge, MA: MIT Press, 1994), 25–26.

404 W. Edwards Deming, *Out of the Crisis* (Cambridge, MA: MIT Press, 1986), 115–116.

405 Ibid., 275.

406 John Greenwald, "Rank And Fire" *Time*, June 18, 2001.

407 Jack Welch, with Suzy Welch, *Winning* (New York: HarperCollins, 2005).

408 Elizabeth G. Olson, "Microsoft, GE, and the futility of ranking employees," *Fortune*, November 18, 2013; "Yahoo Accused of Bias in Use of Rating System," *New York Times*, February 2, 2016, page B3.

409 Douglas McGregor, "An Uneasy Look at Performance Appraisal," *Harvard Business Review* 35, no. 3 (May–June 1957): 91.

410 W. Edwards Deming, *The New Economics for Industry, Government, Education,* 2nd ed. (Cambridge, MA: MIT Press, 1994), 109–110, 114.

411 Adapted from Humberto Maturana, "Everything Is Said by an Observer," in *Gaia: A Way of Knowing* (Hudson, New York: Lindisfarne Press, 1987), 78–79.

412 W. Edwards Deming, *The New Economics for Industry, Government, Education,* 2nd ed. (Cambridge, MA: MIT Press, 1994), 145–148.

413 Ibid., 72–73.

414 W. Edwards Deming, *The New Economics for Industry, Government, Education,* 2nd ed. (Cambridge, MA: MIT Press, 1994), 94.

415 Ibid., 108.

416 Rosamund Stone Zander and Benjamin Zander, *The Art of Possibility: Transforming Professional and Personal Life* (Boston: Harvard Business School Press, 2000), 26.

417 Brian L. Joiner, *Fourth Generation Management: The New Business Consciousness* (New York: McGraw-Hill, Inc., 1994), 246–248.

418 W. Edwards Deming, *The New Economics for Industry, Government, Education,* 2nd ed. (Cambridge, MA: MIT Press, 1994), 143.

Chapter 17

419 From President Abraham Lincoln's message to Congress, December 1, 1862, detailing the State of the Union.

420 Fritjof Capra, et al., *Belonging to the Universe: Explorations of the Frontiers of Science and Spirituality* (New York: HarperCollins, 1992), 74.

421 Peter B. Vaill, *Managing as a Performing Art: New Ideas for a World of Chaotic Change* (San Francisco: Josey-Bass, 1989), 124.

422 Letter to Dr. Humphrey Osmond, January 11, 1958, Grover Smith, editor, *Letters of Aldous Huxley* (New York: Harper & Row, 1969), 842.

423 W. Edwards Deming, *The New Economics for Industry, Government, Education,* 2nd ed. (Cambridge, MA: MIT Press, 1994), 123.

424 W. Edwards Deming, *The New Economics for Industry, Government, Education,* 2nd ed. (Cambridge, MA: MIT Press, 1994), 25–26.

425 Viktor E. Frankl, *Man's Search for Meaning* (New York: Washington Square Press, 1964), 103–104.

426 Ibid., 205.

427 W. Edwards Deming, *The New Economics for Industry, Government, Education,* 2nd ed. (Cambridge, MA: MIT Press, 1994), 121.

428 David Bohm, *Thought as a System* (New York: Routledge, 1992), 209.

429 John Donne, *Devotions Upon Emergent Occasions,* "Meditations Upon Our Human Condition," Number 17, London: Thomas Jones, 1924.

430 Albert Einstein, letter to Robert Marcus, February 12, 1950, www.lettersofnote. com/2011/11/delusion.html.

431 Wayne W. Dyer, *Manifest Your Destiny* (New York: Harper Perennial, 1997), 132.

432 Matthew Fox, *The Reinvention of Work* (San Francisco: Harper SanFrancisco, 1994), 84, 23, 26, 34.

433 W. Edwards Deming, *The New Economics for Industry, Government, Education,* 2nd ed. (Cambridge, MA: MIT Press, 1994), 121–123.

434 Max DePree, *Leadership Jazz* (New York: DoubleDay Currency, 1992), 138.

435 Michael Polanyi and Harry Prosch, *Meaning* (Chicago: The University of Chicago Press, 1975), 182–216.

436 Adam Smith, *An Inquiry Into the Nature and Causes of the Wealth of Nations* (New York: Random House—the Modern Library, 1937). *The Theory of Moral Sentiments,* D.D. Raphael and A.L. Macfie, eds. (Indianapolis: Liberty Classics, 1982).

437 W. Edwards Deming, *The New Economics for Industry, Government, Education,* 2nd ed. (Cambridge, MA: MIT Press, 1994), 92.

438 Ibid., 92–93.

439 W. Edwards Deming, *The New Economics for Industry, Government, Education,* 1st ed. (Cambridge, MA: MIT Press, 1992), 95. The term originated with Cardinal Newman.

Coda

440 *Hannah Senesh, Her Life and Diary,* the first complete edition (Woodstock, VT: Jewish Lights Publishing, 2007), 1.

INDEX

Open Book Editions
A Berrett-Koehler Partner

Open Book Editions is a joint venture between Berrett-Koehler Publishers and Author Solutions, the market leader in self-publishing. There are many more aspiring authors who share Berrett-Koehler's mission than we can sustainably publish. To serve these authors, Open Book Editions offers a comprehensive self-publishing opportunity.

A Shared Mission

Open Book Editions welcomes authors who share the Berrett-Koehler mission—Creating a World That Works for All. We believe that to truly create a better world, action is needed at all levels—individual, organizational, and societal. At the individual level, our publications help people align their lives with their values and with their aspirations for a better world. At the organizational level, we promote progressive leadership and management practices, socially responsible approaches to business, and humane and effective organizations. At the societal level, we publish content that advances social and economic justice, shared prosperity, sustainability, and new solutions to national and global issues.

Open Book Editions represents a new way to further the BK mission and expand our community. We look forward to helping more authors challenge conventional thinking, introduce new ideas, and foster positive change.

For more information, see the Open Book Editions website: http://www.iuniverse.com/Packages/OpenBookEditions.aspx

Join the BK Community! See exclusive author videos, join discussion groups, find out about upcoming events, read author blogs, and much more! http://bkcommunity.com/

Printed in the United States
by Bookmasters